# RADICAL PHILOSOPHY

## 2.06
Series 2 / Winter 2019

The inorganic body in the early Marx
**Judith Butler** . . . . . . . . . . . . . . . . . . . . . 3
*Securitati perpetuae*
**Mark Neocleous** . . . . . . . . . . . . . . . . . . 19
The revival of Hegelian Marxism
**Nathan Brown** . . . . . . . . . . . . . . . . . . . 34
On the origins of Marx's general intellect
**Matteo Pasquinelli** . . . . . . . . . . . . . . . . 43
The racial regime of aesthetics
**Lucie Kim-Chi Mercier** . . . . . . . . . . . . . . 57
Critical theory and lived experience
**Detlev Claussen with Jordi Maiso** . . . . . . . . . 63
Reviews . . . . . . . . . . . . . . . . . . . . . . . 83
    Erich Hörl, *Sacred Channels*
    **Megan Wiessner** . . . . . . . . . . . . . . . . 83
    David Marriott, *Whither Fanon?*
    **Nicholas Anthony Eppert** . . . . . . . . . . . . 86
    Chris Moffat, *India's Revolutionary Inheritance*
    **Ammar Ali Jan** . . . . . . . . . . . . . . . . . 90
    Abdelkebir Khatibi, *Plural Maghreb*
    **Alina Sajed** . . . . . . . . . . . . . . . . . . 94
    Brigitta Kuster, *Grenze filmen*
    **Isabell Lorey** . . . . . . . . . . . . . . . . . . 98
    Chantal Mouffe, *For a Left Populism*
    **Cam Scott** . . . . . . . . . . . . . . . . . . . 102
    Franziska Dubgen and Stefan Skupien, *Paulin Hountondji:*
    *African Philosophy as Critical Universalism*
    **Sanya Osha** . . . . . . . . . . . . . . . . . . 105
    Aaron Bastani, *Fully Automated Luxury Communism*
    **Atus Mariqueo-Russell and Rupert Read** . . . . . 108
    Alexi Kukuljevic, *Liquidation World*
    **Ryan Crawford** . . . . . . . . . . . . . . . . . 111
Letter from Kashmir
**Anil Persaud** . . . . . . . . . . . . . . . . . . . 114

**Editorial collective**
Claudia Aradau
Brenna Bhandar
Victoria Browne
David Cunningham
Peter Hallward
Stewart Martin
Lucie Mercier
Daniel Nemenyi
Hannah Proctor
Rahul Rao
Martina Tazzioli
Chris Wilbert

**Engineers**
Daniel Nemenyi
Alex Sassmanshausen

Creative Commons BY-NC-ND
Radical Philosophy, Winter 2019

ISSN 0300-211X
ISBN 978-1-9999793-5-5

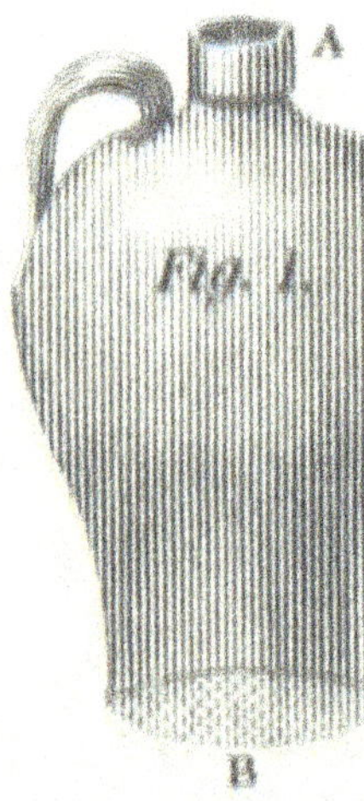
Fig. 1.
A
B

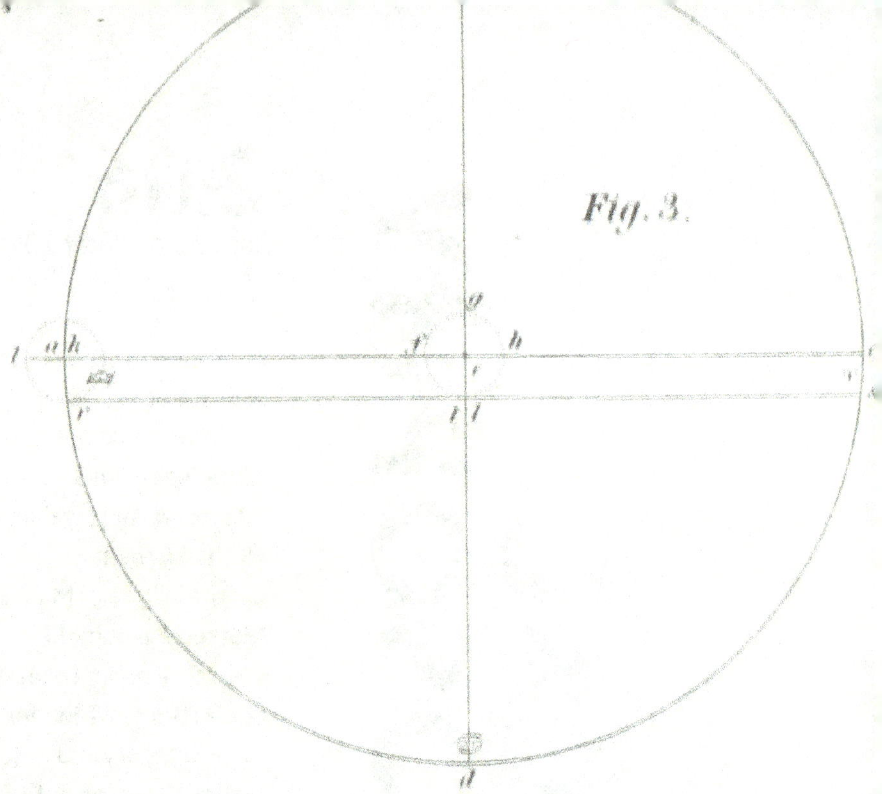
Fig. 3.

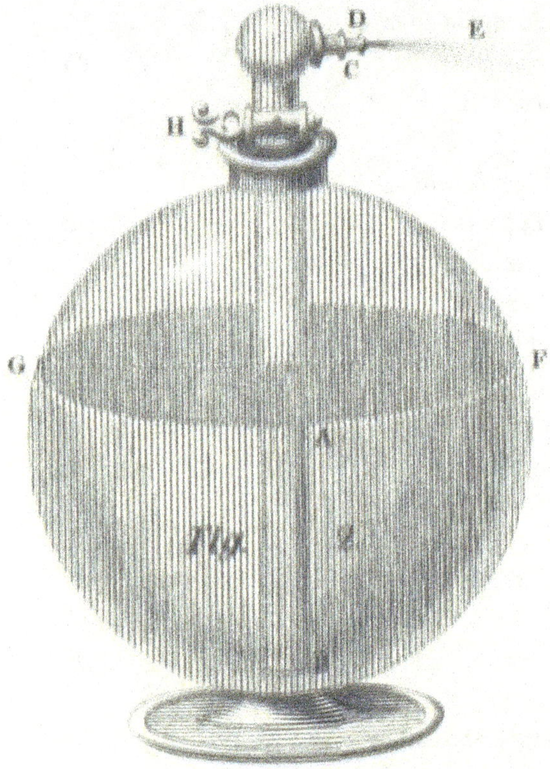
D
E
C
H
G
F
A
Fig. 2

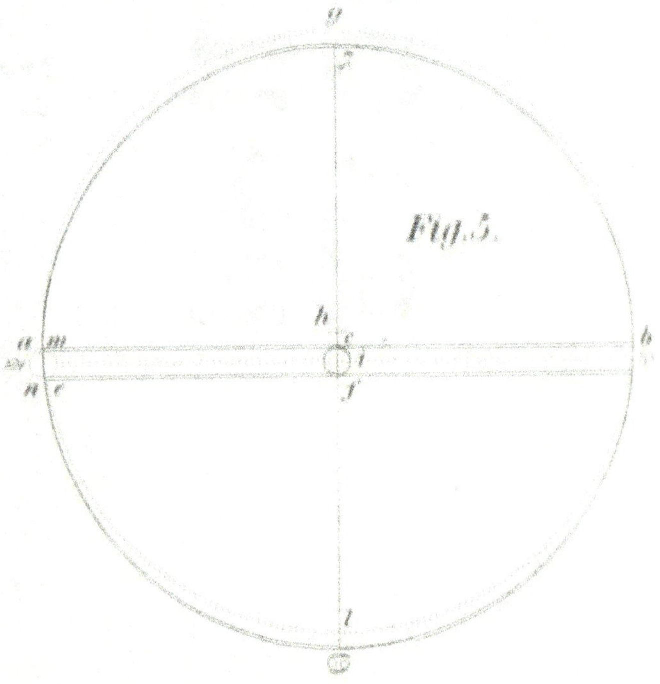
Fig. 5.

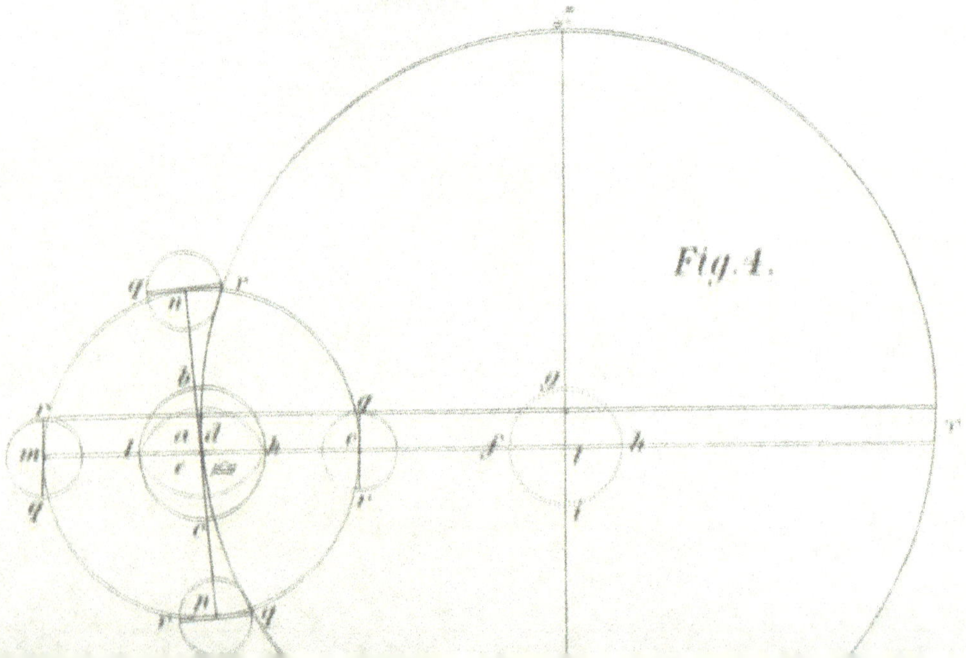
Fig. 4.

# The inorganic body in the early Marx
## A limit-concept of anthropocentrism
Judith Butler

The effort to revive and recover critical theory and its intellectual precedents has become more difficult at a time in which 'critique' is regularly denounced as negative, skeptical and anthropocentric. Bruno Latour, for instance, imagines that when we speak about what is 'critical', we have in mind a fully negative project, a practice of debunking and dismantling hegemonic presumptions about the world, and that critical theory only intensifies skepticism and lacks transformative power and commitment to emancipatory ideals.[1] The validity of his claim depends on a careful consideration of what 'negative' means, and a querying of whether 'the negative', in fact, deserves such a negative reputation. Even if a 'critical' approach is one that aims not to reproduce those forms of thought that ratify modes of social life that reproduce forms of domination or subjugation, that does not mean that critical theory refuses to reproduce all forms of thought or that it objects to all surface phenomena. To oppose a naturalised form of knowledge because oppression is taken for granted within its terms is not to oppose all nature, or to claim that nature ought to be replaced with expressions of a purely human expressive power. To make a naturalised mode of subjugation into an object of knowledge is not to destroy its reality, but only to form it as an object of knowledge, judgement and transformation. In this way, 'negation' – understood as 'suspending the taken for granted character of reality' – opens up a critical perspective on that form, and conditions the possibility of precisely those forms of intervention and aspiration that Latour denies to the critical project. One does not take leave of the world of facts, but, in recognising that it is a world, finds modes of dynamic engagement with them.

One problem with Latour's criticism of 'critique' is that he relies on an account of critical theory which positions it as the contemporary manifestation of the history of a consequential error inaugurated by Kant. Latour writes:

> The mistake we made, the mistake I made, was to believe that there was no efficient way to criticise matters of fact except by moving away from them and directing one's attention toward the conditions that made them possible. But this meant accepting much too uncritically what matters of fact were. This was remaining too faithful to the unfortunate solution inherited from the philosophy of Immanuel Kant.[2]

Latour seems to understand positivism here as the object of critique, and goes on to claim that matters of fact have to be re-approached in a way that affirms their own potential and agentic powers. That may well be the case. But why would such a project be antithetical to critique? Further, is Latour right to imagine that critical theorists have all been ensnared by a view that fails to attend to matters of fact (and recasts them as matters of concern) in order to discern their own critical potential? Latour seems to be asking whether it is not time to stop acting on the world, but in making this claim – if it is his claim – he seems to imagine action as an anthropocentric activity, even though there is a significant tradition of critical theory that contests such an assumption.

For Latour, critique is undertaken by a subject whose main aim is to distance itself from, and so to negate, the realm of what is (considered as what *simply* is). Negation, for Latour, cannot account for the shared agency at work between subjective and objective fields. This misunderstanding, in his view, follows from Kantian epistemology. Moreover, it fails to understand properly that the realm of 'facts' and 'matters of concern' offer critical possibilities themselves. Latour's argument could no doubt be easily refuted by a more nuanced consideration of the relation between subject and object, and between nature and life, in German Idealism that might prove to be not so very antithetical to his own views. Alternately, another criticism could show that Latour misunderstands negation, especially the Hegelian notion of determinate negation, as part of a philosophy of immanence, which has important considerations for a non-positivist account of nature. Critical theory, too, has offered an array of positions *against* skepticism, all of which are overlooked when Latour understands skepticism to be the signature characteristic of critical theory. Finally, the Kantian position he associates with a hyper-subjectivism that abandons the realm of objective reality is neither a fair and grounded characterisation of Kant nor of critical theory's concerns.

Yet, Latour's errant critique provides an opportunity to approach the 'critical' aspect of critical theory in contemporary terms, where we can see critique emerge from situations of crisis. If critical theory is sequestered from social engagement and activism, vacating the very domain from which the political problematic emerges, it deprives itself of the capacity to trace that very emergence. This important relation between working inside and outside of the academy is linked to the further problem of the border between the university and its world. Such a critical practice neither takes distance from facts nor negates their existence or importance; on the contrary, a constellation of such 'facts' impresses itself upon our thinking, and so the world acts on us and exercises a historical demand on thought. The demand for climate change intervention is but one case in point. An objection to how the environment has been toxified requires an intervention that would allow for its detoxification and renewal. This is not a form of mastery, but an acknowledgement that organic creatures require the continuation of their own organic life and organic life more broadly. So, yes, critical thought is immersed in matters of concern, responsive to the demand those matters make upon us, but it also challenges the notion that we are subjects who only make our worlds and are not formed and affected by a world we never made. We are thinking creatures who register damage and potential in the somatic lives in which we live, feel and think. Caught up in the temporal vector of past, present and future, we think within a mode of thought formed in, by, against – and even for – the impress of the world.

## 'Anthropocentric'?

It is in light of the above conception of critical theory, and of its critique, that I want then to ask a more specific question in what follows: how best to re-approach, today, Marx's 1844 Manuscripts in order to take up the question of whether the young Marx is, as is commonly assumed, and in the form that Latour has most recently implied, *anthropocentric*? What prompts me to ask this question is a famous, but very enigmatic paragraph in those manuscripts that refers to nature as man's 'inorganic body'. It is a surprising claim, and I will first attempt to locate it in the text and to offer my understanding of this idea within the context of Marx's general arguments in these early writings. Most importantly, I want to suggest that a consideration of this notion of the inorganic body in Marx has implications for the contemporary critique of critique, especially as it relates to the accusation of anthropocentrism.

This is a question that was posed in a different way in a set of debates conducted in the 1970s and 1980s by British scholars, especially John Clark, who sought to settle the question of whether Marx's views were compatible with an ecological perspective, and which in turn prompted a series of inquiries into how best to understand Marx's theory of nature.[3] The issues raised by this are important not only because the early manuscripts of 1844 are usually understood to be superseded by Marx's later work, especially by *Capital* and the *Grundrisse*, but because it is widely assumed that the early manuscripts rely on a theory of alienation and an account of the subject that is speculative at best and which deflects from the structure and aims of the theorisation of the structural or systemic character of capitalism developed in *Capital* and Marx's subsequent writings. Although a return to the early Marx does not necessarily aim to retrieve or rehabilitate his early account of labour, it does raise questions about how we understand labour and the labouring body, the human and its relation to nature and other living processes.[4]

We know that the labourer works on nature, and that he or she requires nature for the purposes of subsistence. We also know, I presume, that the body is sensuous, and that its work on natural objects implies a sensuous engagement with those objects. But if nature is in some sense the 'inorganic body' of the human, then another kind of relationship is posited, namely, one in which the body of the human is no longer exactly discrete. Indeed, its boundaries are neither exactly known nor knowable. If there is an inorganic body of the human, and it is all of nature, then the human body extends to all of nature, or, conversely, all of nature comprises the human body. The relation of the human body to all of nature proves essential to the human body, or the relation of nature to the human body proves essential to nature. How we conceive of this relation has implications for answering the question of just how anthropocentric are the early manuscripts, or whether there is a largely unexamined critique of anthropocentrism to be found within their pages? My suggestion is that we need to reconsider this speculative claim about nature as 'inorganic body' to answer that question.

To call nature an 'inorganic body' proves enigmatic in part because it is referred to as a singular body, suggesting that it is in some way a unity, even if internally differentiated. Moreover, there is an obvious question as to why nature would be called 'inorganic' rather than 'organic' – what is the difference, and how does the former turn into the latter? We might expect the organic to turn into the inorganic as a result of human labour, but in this case – and in relation to the problem of subsistence – the inverse is in fact the case. To understand what this means, we have first to understand the difference between the organic and the inorganic in Marx, and to see what it means when these become two modalities for describing the body or, rather, two modalities through which the body appears.

As I hope to show, we are left to infer that 'man' has both an organic and an inorganic body: 'his' organic body is the one that 'he' experiences as bounded and discrete, separate from the rest of nature, but nature – the whole of nature – constitutes his *in*organic body.[5] So, he is one body and distinguished from another, but the distinction is also one that he himself lives. Are we to presume that there are two bodies, or only one body which has an organic as well as an inorganic dimension or modality? It would seem that the organic body – what Marx calls the human *Leib* – is discrete, but the inorganic body – what he calls *Körper* – is not, and that therefore we ought not to assume an absolute distinction between these two dimensions. What becomes immediately clear, however, is that there is a living character to the organic body (*Leib*) that is distinct from the inorganic body. The problem is made more complex by the fact that usually *Leib* denotes the lived body, and *Körper* can mean a simple discrete density, alive or dead.[6] And yet, it would not be right to say that the inorganic body is simply dead. Nature is alive, but not quite in the same sense that the body is. So, organic is not to inorganic as life is to death. Organic and inorganic are potentials of one another, and the problem of life seems to cut across that distinction in a way that is yet to be clarified.

But first, we should ask: how does that distinction inform our interpretation of what is going on with this phrase, nature as 'inorganic body', and with the broader question of whether Marx in his early manuscripts proposes an anthropocentric account of nature? Nature is an object of work and an occasion for the labourer's self-reflection; it is the substance on which he works, as well as that which sustains his existence: sometimes the object on which the labourer works is food. Nature is of course one basis for one human's connection with other humans, but it is also that which constitutes his 'species being'. For the human creature may belong to his own species, but if that species is one among many such species, and if, as a living species, it is linked with other forms of life, then we have to understand the kind of link or relation that this is. This may well give us some insight into the sense of Marx's claim that 'nature is man's inorganic body'.

I will consider the paragraph in which Marx introduces this formulation in a moment, but first let me offer some background. In the 1970s and 80s, Marxist theorists in the UK and elsewhere became concerned with the question of whether Marx's views are compatible with ecological thinking. Some asked the question: is the claim that 'nature is man's inorganic body' an ecological claim? Is it the case that humans should act, or are naturally disposed to act, as if their own bodies were in some sense coextensive with nature? Is it the case that man acts in such a way that he participates organically in nature? Is the action that is proper to man at once a natural activity, overcoming, as it were, a radical distinction between human action and natural process? John Clark points out that Marx also describes locomotives and railways as 'organs of the human brain',[7] thereby suggesting that these human institutions develop from ideas emerging from human consciousness, but that they emerge from the organic dimension of the brain as well, since without the brain, those ideas would not exist at all.[8] The brain is not simply the condition of possibility for the mind, but seems in some sense to be generative of human inventions such as locomotives and railways. These latter are not simply produced by the brain/mind, if you will, but they are organs of the human brain. The organ is not in the brain, or not exclusively in the brain, but also in the expression or work itself. This is but one instance in which the expectation that organs are necessarily or entirely lodged inside the body turns out to be not quite right, since they are not only in the means of production (railways and locomotives), but they are ontologically bound up with one another. Note how the copula works: the locomotives are the organs of the brain; nature is the inorganic body of humans. How do we understand equations or ontological equivalences such as these?

Carolyn Merchant points out that *organic* in the seventeenth century referred to the bodily organs, structures and organisation of living beings.[9] *Inorganic* referred to the absence of bodily organs. The human would seem, then, to be organic, and external nature to be inorganic, if we follow that distinction. However, in the case of Marx, as Foster and Burkett argue, one sense of the 'inorganic' would refer specifically to the extension of the human body and its activities through the use of tools and instruments; hence, a technical augmentation of bodily powers. And yet, as Foster and Burkett also point out, none of these distinctions can quite capture the Hegelian background of Marx's distinction.[10] That understanding underscores the appropriation of nature for the purposes of amplifying human powers. As I will hope to show, the distinction between organic and inorganic body is thus a relative one, and one that shifts according to how we understand the relationship between work and the means to live. Indeed, in the midst of this discussion, Marx offers an alternative way of considering labour, one that is neither distinctively humanist nor modeled on domination.

In any case, the idea of a technical amplification of the body suggested by those railways considered as the organs of brains is far from the model of artisanal work that informs Marx's discussion of human alienation and the value of labour. Human consciousness is that which, through labour, seeks to externalise itself in a natural object for the purposes of gaining a reflection of its own value in the object that it transforms by labour. The entire theory of alienation is based upon this early and generalised labour theory of value. But the theory of alienation also tends to assume that there are essential human activities and that labour is chief among them. Labour provides what is needed to live; labour also expresses essential human potentials; and labour links us with other labouring beings, actualising our species-being.[11]

## 'Humanist'?

The efforts in the last several decades to move beyond the early Marx have been based on a number of arguments, chief among them the speculative and ungrounded character of the early theory of labour itself. Louis Althusser, in particular, provided a powerful criticism of the early Marx, claiming that he was still here under the influence of Feuerbach's humanism, and insisting that his description of essential human capacities and requirements constituted a philosophical anthropology that should be displaced by a structuralist account of ideology. In his early essay on 'Marxism and Humanism', Althusser quotes the key formulation by Marx in the 1844 Manuscripts: "'Communism ... [is] the real appropriation of the human essence through and for men ... this communism as a fully developed naturalism = Humanism".'[12] Althusser contrasts an ideological view of the human with a scientific, that is, structural account of how capitalism works to produce a subject. He criticises the Feuerbachian humanism of the early Marx for basing its critical project on the notion that social reality produced within the terms of political economy contradicts the essence of man. The problem with this view, of course, is that it must first assume what the essence of man is in order to show how present reality produces an alienated reality. On this model, alienation is to be understood as a contradiction that needs to be resolved. Althusser writes:

> History is the alienation and production of reason in unreason, of the true man in the alienated man. Without knowing it, man realises the essence of man in the alienated products of his labour (commodities, State, religion). The loss of man that produces history and man must pre-

suppose a definite pre-existing essence. At the end of history, this man, having become inhuman objectivity, has merely to re-grasp as subject his own essence alienated in property, religion and the State to become total man, true man.[13]

Althusser rightly remarks that this recourse to human nature as the foundation of political organisation and political theory required accepting a theoretical humanism that has no foundation. Who is this 'man' who anchors the social organisation of political economy? Althusser's great contribution was to insist that this man is himself *a product* of that economy, understandable only in relation to its constituting social structures. Over and against this early humanism, Althusser tells us, Marx came to accept a theoretical anti-humanism, one that relied on an analysis of human practice. In 'Marxism and Humanism', Althusser claims that Marx's turn away from anthropocentrism happened when he turned to 'the different specific *levels* of *human practice* (economic practice, political practice, ideological practice, scientific practice) in their characteristic articulations, based on the specific articulations of the unity of human society.'[14]

In every instance, a practice would be related to a social structure rather than an idea of human essences, or essential human activities. The conclusion was that if we take any human activity as definitive of the human, we obliterate the constitutive power of social structures. For Althusser, there can be no analysis of human action outside of the context of human structure. By following this imperative, the early Althusser argued, the transition from an ideological analysis to a scientific analysis becomes possible. Humanism, and all of its presuppositions, is an ideology. And ideologies are not themselves inventions of 'consciousness' but part of the very structure of societies.

Althusser's theory of interpellation will follow from this claim: subjects are produced by societies in ways that reproduce – or seek to reproduce – the structures of society. Ideologies, however, cannot be understood as purely instrumental. They represent the *imaginary* relation of individuals to the conditions of their existence. We could elaborate on this point for quite some time, especially with the assistance of the work of Étienne Balibar, but let us for the moment simply note that humanism, expressed symptomatically by the early Marx, is considered to be an ideology, that is, it represents an imaginary relation to the conditions of existence, and that it does not qualify as a science. It tells us nothing about the essence of man; indeed, to speak of an essence is to once again evade the social structures and their imaginary relation to the conditions of existence. As those conditions change historically, so too does the imaginary relation to those conditions. And since those conditions are transformed over time, and so by definition subject to transformation, so too is the imaginary relation to those conditions. The key question is thus displaced from *what is man?*, *or what is essential to man?* – a question that belongs to a theoretically humanist version of philosophical anthropology – to the question, *what is the imaginary relation to the conditions of life?* – which takes us to a specific and complex understanding of the subject in light of both psychoanalysis and history. This is a wonderful trajectory that I cannot continue here. But note that the preoccupation with alienation is replaced by a preoccupation with ideology. Indeed, to some extent, alienation became so tainted by its humanist conceits that most leftwing intellectuals did not return to the topic for several decades.

Those of us who have worked within the domains of structuralism and post-structuralism over the past decades are profoundly indebted to Althusser's revolutionary intellectual move. My own debt to this shift in perspective is enormous, regardless of whether or not I always knew it. But just as Étienne Balibar has recently sought to return to the idea of a philosophical anthropology to ask whether we have considered its possible meanings, so I am asking whether attributing an unequivocal humanism to the early Marx is fully justifiable. Althusser was, in my view, right to claim that we do not need to foreground a contradiction between the essence of human nature and the actual conditions of life to develop a criticism of capitalism. One problem is the reliance on contradiction to expose the problem; the other is a presumption about what constitute the essential activities of humans. If we proceed without reliance on contradiction or humanism, then what is left? The imaginary is not reducible to the human imagination; Althusser's deployment of Lacan seeks to establish how the human is constituted within the imaginary but not as its origin. This is another excellent topic, but not precisely my own in this essay.

The effort to move beyond the early Marx has been supported not only by Althusser's brilliant reading, but also by those who claim that Marx's relation to nature is primarily one of domination. Further, it is argued that Marx did not anticipate the destruction of nature that would follow from an unrestrained mode of production. If it is the human essence to work on nature, and this is so for all time, then, for the human essence to be perpetually realised, nature must remain a limitless resource. This last has been termed a 'productivist ideology' in Marx,[15] even though Marx explicitly condemns 'the drive toward unlimited extension of production'. In the 1844 manuscripts, at least, labour is understood as an appropriation of nature or, better formulated, an expropriation of nature. Whether these are necessarily forms of domination remains, however, a question.

Nature is not only that upon which humans act, but nature belongs properly to the labouring subject. This becomes most clear when the worker is reduced to a struggle for physical subsistence. The natural and the physical aspects of human work are not the same, but the reproduction of the physical person is required for work to continue. Nature can sometimes mean the physical, but it is also a relationship of one natural creature to others, or to life, or indeed to living processes. His essence is not his nature, but those two concepts overlap as well. Humans lose their essence when they work only for subsistence, that is, to reproduce themselves as living beings. Labour that creates value is different from subsistence labour. Deprived of a proper sense of work, the human would not be able to realise his consciousness in the object that he creates. He becomes increasingly concerned with his subsistence rather than with the realisation of his essential powers, at which point physical nature and consciousness diverge from one another.

In fact, one dimension of alienation consists in the worker's failure to recognise himself as a realised consciousness, since he becomes an object, an instrument, a form of labour whose profits are calculated and exploited by those who own the means of production. Through this process, he is deprived of human spiritual or conscious activity. So, nature, considered as external to the worker, is required for the life of the labourer, which is also nature, and it provides the object for labour, especially when labour is considered on an artisanal model.

Under conditions of capitalist political economy, where the worker's labour does not belong to himself, where his labour is valued according to its exchangeability, the more he works, the less he is paid and the more jeopardised is his own physical subsistence. Here we see one version of an operative contradiction in the account of alienation, but it is a conditioned contradiction, one that only becomes possible once work no longer secures subsistence. Even so, there is no way to separate the question of subsistence from realisation, even though the essence that is realised is one that has to persist in life for itself and with others – indeed, those last two purposes are part of the essence itself; the essence cannot be separated from the living character of the worker.

If we were to refer to 'human nature' in this sense there would emerge something of a tension, if not a contradiction, since the sense of what is natural – including the requirements of subsistence – are presupposed by the sense of what is 'human': the realisation of essential human potentialities. And yet, we may ask, is the natural only a condition of possibility for the realisation of the human, is it a proper part of the human? Does the human have its own part of nature, its own nature, and if so how is it related to other parts, other natures? This last question is raised by Marx's concept of the *species-being*, which raises in turn the question of whether the consideration of nature in Marx, or indeed in the Hegel upon which he draws, is distinctively human, or whether that distinction derives from a vital set of differences, and so posits the human in a de-centred way, as a proper part of a larger nature? In his discussion of estranged labour, Marx refers to nature as the material on which the labourer labours, but also the means of life of the labourer. Thus, nature becomes linked to notions of materiality, and to life and what is living, as well as the means to life. Marx writes the following:

> Let us now look more closely at the objectification, at the production of the worker; and in it at the estrangement [alienation], the loss of the object, of his product. The worker can create nothing without nature, without the sensuous external world. It is the material on which his labour is realised, in which it is active, from which, and by means of which it produces. But just as nature provides labour with [the] means of life in the sense that labour cannot live without objects on which to operate, on the other hand, it also provides the means of life in the more restricted sense, i.e., the means for the physical subsistence of the worker himself. Thus the more the worker by his labour appropriates the external world, sensuous nature, the more he deprives himself of means of life in two respects: first, in that the sensuous external world more and more ceases to be an object belonging to his labour – to be his labour's means of life; and, second, in that it more and more ceases to be means of life in the immediate sense, means for the physical subsistence of the worker. In both respects, therefore, the worker becomes a servant of his object, first, in that he receives an object of labour, i.e., in that he receives work, and, secondly, in that he receives means of subsistence. This enables him to exist, first as a worker; and second, as a physical subject.[16]

On this account, nature emerges first as the sensuous external world, the condition of the worker's labour. He must work on nature; he must have a sensuous object before him. Labour is realised through the work he performs on and through the object. Human labour *animates* the object, and its realisation requires that object for that purpose. In this first sense, then, human labour animates the object. The object is not itself animated nor does it animate anything other than itself. But why not? Why is the animated character of the object dependent on humans animating the object? Why does animation find its source in the human?

This formulation seems to confirm the anthropocentric understanding of Marx's view, one that is suggested by those object-oriented ontologies that emerge from the framework offered by Bruno Latour. The second claim, however, complicates the first. Nature provides humans with *the means of life*. And this is true for two separate, but related reasons. The first is that nature provides the object on which to labour, so there is no labour without nature (at least according to this model of labour), without its object. But labour is required for human life in the sense of subsistence. Under conditions of political economy, one must work in order to subsist as a physical subject, and so one's own continuing sensuous existence depends upon the ability to find and sustain work that will provide one with a wage that can secure the means of subsistence. The more one works on the sensuous object, the more exploited one's labour, the more value is extracted from labour for the purposes of accumulating profit. The result, Marx tells us, is that the labourer's own physical subsistence is imperilled. This is different from the non-realisation of his human express-

9

ive capacities, but related. Physical subsistence does not suffice to realise those expressive capacities, but the realisation of those expressive capacities cannot take place without physical subsistence.

The labourer cannot work on the object and derive from that labour the means to live. The more he works on the object, the less he possesses the means to live. In this sense, the labourer becomes a servant to the object. But this is only true to the extent that the object belongs to someone or to a system that seeks to keeps his life alive enough to continue to work. And this is only true to the extent that the object of labour is a condensation of that power, that system. But when labour is in great supply, even the labourer's subsistence is no longer required. The labour can be extracted from the living being and the living being can fall ill or die, and those who own the means of production will find another labourer from whom labour can be extracted until the physicality of the worker is exhausted or broken beyond repair. So the labourer works on nature in order to secure his own subsistence, but the organisation of labour is such that the more he works on the object, the more the value of his labour is separated from his subsistence, and his life is threatened. The more he works on the sensuous object, the more his own sensuous existence becomes imperiled. He risks the loss of his own physicality, his sensuous existence, his very life, by pursuing the means of life within a system of work that is willing and able to dispense with his life. Work does not sustain him or provide subsistence, but becomes the means through which subsistence is imperiled; in this way, work deviates from the goal of the realisation of essential powers or activities.

The means to live is called 'subsistence' within the language of political economy; it foregrounds the continuing physical life of the worker and demonstrates the condition of induced precarity imposed not only by a capitalist system of work (which will be given further elaboration in Marx's subsequent texts), but by conditions in which work is temporary, contingent, and where the radical substitutability and dispensability of the worker becomes the norm.

We might be tempted to say that Marx understood *the proletariat* as the name for the collective potential of the worker, and that, today, *the precariat* is the better name for the collective for whom work is elusive, temporary, and debt has become unpayable. But we can see even in the early Marx that an understanding of precarity is already at work, even if this is not his own term. Precarity is the constant threat to the worker's prospect of physical subsistence or, indeed, for those who cannot find work, for those who are regularly abandoned by a system of work that considers them to be exhaustible and replaceable and for whom little or no social protections exist, for whom the entire idea of social protection is fading.

Subsistence is not simply the condition for the realisation of labour; it is also the object of labour and the variable standard used by capitalist modes of production. Indeed, one argument Marx makes is that standards of subsistence are regulated by those who seek to exploit the worker. There is no one standard of subsistence; there is no agreed upon set of requirements. Those requirements are themselves established by those who seek to keep them to a minimum or who are indifferent to the prospect of the worker being injured, falling ill, becoming incapacitated, or even dying. Or, when it is assumed that workers will be replaced at will, subsistence as a standard does not exist as such, since it is hardly required for the purposes of production. And though, as we have seen, Marx does distinguish between the domain of physical need and the true domain of human freedom, he shows us at the same time that such a distinction is tenuous at best. To understand this, we have to understand what kind of animal the human is, which means that we have two more notions to consider in our reconsideration of the 1844 Manuscripts. The first is 'species-being' and the second is Marx's contention that 'nature is the inorganic body of man'.

## 'A Continuous Interchange'

Consider the paragraph from 'Estranged Labour' in which both these concepts are discussed together:

> Man is a species-being, not only because in practice and in theory he adopts the species (his own as well as those of other things) as his object, but – and this is only another way of expressing it – also *because he treats himself as the actual, living species* [my emphasis]; because he treats himself as a universal and therefore a free being. The life of the species, both in man and in animals, consists physically in the fact that man (like the animal) lives on organic nature; and the more universal man (or the animal) is, the more universal is the sphere of inorganic nature on which he lives. Just as plants, animals, stones,

air, light, etc., constitute theoretically a part of human consciousness, partly as objects of natural science, partly as objects of art = *his spiritual inorganic nature, spiritual nourishment which he must first prepare to make palatable and digestible* = so also *in the realm of practice* they constitute a part of human life and human activity. Physically man lives only on these products of nature, whether they appear in the form of food, heating, clothes, a dwelling, etc. *The universality of man appears in practice precisely in the universality which makes all nature his inorganic body* = both inasmuch as nature is (1) his direct means of life, and (2) the material, the object and the instrument of his life activity. *Nature is man's inorganic body* = nature, that is, insofar as it is not itself human body. Man lives on nature = means that nature is his body, with which he must remain in *continuous interchange* if he is not to die. That man's physical and spiritual life is linked to nature means simply that *nature is linked to itself,* for man is a part of nature. In estranging from man (1) nature, and (2) himself, his own active functions, his life activity, estranged labour estranges the species from man. It changes for him the life of the species into a means of individual life. First it estranges the life of the species and individual life, and secondly it makes individual life in its abstract form the purpose of the life of the species, likewise in its abstract and estranged form.[17]

We know that for Marx alienation can be from the object of labour, and from the activity of labouring, but also from one's species-being (*Gattungswesen*). In what sense, however, is the human supposed to be a species-being? First, Marx explains that the human is a species-being both in a practical and theoretical sense, but only insofar as he makes the species into his object, and regards himself as a species among species. He relates to himself as a contemporary and living species insofar as he relates to himself as a universal and, therefore, free being (*Wesen*). We might reasonably expect humans to be distinguished from animals on the grounds that humans achieve or evince freedom and universality as an aspect of their species-being and animals do not. Indeed, Marx gives us reasons for doing so, when he writes, for instance, that the 'generic character' of man is 'free conscious activity' and that this differentiates humans from animals. Further, the distinctive feature that distinguishes 'man' as a species-being is that he can cast his own life as an object not only for himself, but also 'the whole of nature'. In this respect, only 'man' produces universally, and not animals. At the same time, however, Marx approaches this distinction from another angle: we learn that humans are animals among animals, and that animality is never overcome as long as humans relate to themselves as a species-being. When we speak about the life of the species, *das Gattungsleben*, we refer to that which commonly characterised both humans and animals. Marx makes this more precise when he claims that the life of species consists in the fact that, physically, both humans and animals live on (*von*: or 'from') 'inorganic nature'. Contrary to expectation, it turns out that what is universal in humans turns out to be universal in animals as well, since this inorganic nature is the very field or domain of universality. Marx here describes a relation of dependency on nature without which neither humans nor animals can survive. They are joined in this dependency, this requirement to find and secure a means to live, to ready and make palatable an exterior nature for the purposes of subsistence. They do not have a life separate from the process by which they live on (or from) nature. Moreover, they must prepare this nature – he uses the word '*Zubearbeiten*' – and make it ready for consumption or for pleasure. One form of nature thus works over another form of nature.

This is not a form of labour that dominates nature, neither is it necessarily part of the system of exchange. This 'working over' and 'working with' material conceived as a form of preparation characterises the preparation of food as much as it describes readying the object of science or art (considered as theoretical domains) for consideration. Considered theoretically, those objects constitute the *spiritual* inorganic nature of man; but when they are considered practically, they constitute the *material* inorganic nature of man, that is, as part of the furtherance and reproduction of the living being and beings. The spiritual and the material are not differentiated in a timeless way; they transform into one another depending on how they are approached. Further, these dimensions of inorganic nature are not simply the external objects upon which the human works, but constitute part of what the human is. We know that the human changes the object through work, and that the work comes to reflect the human labourer. But it is also the case that the labourer is changed by his object, and the entire system of nature. These latter are a proper part of his activity; in fact, they constitute his body in a very specific sense in that the body has now an organic and inorganic dimension. The distinction between the two varies depending on whether the approach to nature is theoretical or practical. How, then, does this distinction work, and what does this dual kind of body imply for Marx and the putative anthropocentrism of his early writings?

From a contemporary perspective, we have grounds to ask why nature, or some part of nature, was ever described as 'inorganic'? We might reasonably expect that animals and humans depend upon organic nature, in the sense that they depend on food or natural materials used for shelter. In what sense is wood, for instance, inorganic; or under what conditions does wood become inorganic in Marx's sense? My understanding is that, first, organic nature is animated whereas inorganic nature remains inanimate or de-animated, and, second, a tree is understood as organic until it is transformed into usable wood and thereby becomes 'inorganic' in Marx's terms. It retains its material character, but its life now derives from the human activity that prepares it for use or consumption or enjoyment. As it is worked with and worked over, the object becomes inorganic and inanimate, but it also acquires an animate quality as a consequence of this form of labouring.

Does this passage unequivocally support the thesis that Marx affirms the human domination of nature for the expression of a properly or distinctly human universality? Or, is something else going on, a relation between humans, animals and nature that cannot be centred on the human? At one point, Marx describes this as an 'interchange' suggesting that what is universal in nature is this dependency of living creatures on nature in order to continue to live. We could use the word subsistence [*Subsistenz*] to describe this human requirement to live on nature, but subsistence is a variable standard derived from political economy, which is different from the sense of living dependency that Marx here brings into relief. Perhaps persistence is the better word to describe the activity and aim of seeking the means to live. In this key paragraph, where Marx discusses nature as the inorganic body of the human, he claims that, in a practical sense, the universality of humans appears practically in the course of making the entirety of nature into its inorganic body: *Die Universalität des Menschen erscheint praktisch eben in der Universalität, die die ganze Natur zu seinem unorganischen Leib macht*.[18] Inorganic nature does not exist as such but is achieved through a certain form of labouring. This establishment of inorganic nature takes place as nature becomes the immediate means of life [*Lebensmittel*]; nature is relieved of its own animate quality as it animates, brings alive, or keeps alive, the labourer: its matter, as it were, is made into the object and product [*Werkzeug*] of the life activity of the labourer.

Let us be clear: there is no life activity and no life without this Nature. And the universal, far from characterising a pure freedom or disembodied form of reason is, at least in one significant sense, precisely this dependency on life that is co-existent with all living beings, human or animal. So when Marx then claims that 'Nature is the inorganic body of the human', he is claiming that only as inorganic can nature keep the human alive.

This seems counter-intuitive. But Marx is working with a specific distinction between organic and inorganic that derives in part from Hegel's philosophy of nature. Marx first explains this phrase in the following way: 'the human lives from [or on] nature and this means that nature is his body, with which he must be in a continuous [ongoing] process [*bestandigem Prozeß*] in order not to die'.[19] His point is then clarified that the human creature is not separable from the life processes on which he/she depends, and that this continuous interchange, this ongoing process is precisely what is meant by universality. Nature 'hangs together' [*zusammenhängt*] with its own self, and this relation, this continuous process, is, or constitutes, the inorganic body of humans. Nature becomes *in*organic, but it remains a *Leib* rather than a *Körper* until nature enters into this exchange (although Marx himself shifts from a first reference to '*unorganischer Körper*' to a second, '*unorganisches Leib*', to mark the difference); indeed, the exchange with nature that characterises this form of labour transforms nature from an organic into an inorganic reality. This process holds for psychic and spiritual activities as well as eating and drinking.

The human, he then asserts, is a part of nature. As s/he eats, s/he is absorbed by nature. If the living human creature has both a *Körper* and a *Leib*, then it would appear to have two bodies or, rather, one body that appears under two distinct but related perspectives: one, animate and seeking to live, belongs properly to itself and that is *Leib*, and the other is the nature upon which it depends and with which it is in continuous interchange, and that is *Körper*. A living body, in other words, can only persist if there is a continuous exchange with nature, such that the conditions for persistence are provided for and prepared for the continuation of life. The continuation of the interchange is the continuation of life itself, human life, so there is no life without interchange, and no way of conceptualising life outside the framework of this interchange. No human body can live without the body of nature; it is and is not its own body, and its very survival depends upon this doubling. This interchange involves dependency, interchange (not exchange), and animation; it establishes the body of nature as essential to the body of man.

Marx asks us to imagine this unity at the same time that he has affirmed the human in its creaturely dependency on a natural world that is worked over in such a way to offer a means to live, and only in such a way, that it supports the continuation, the persistence, of the lives of every species being. What we end up with here is not a straightforward vision of humans dominating nature, but human creatures, dependent on nature, as well as on the activity by which nature becomes support and sustenance for living beings. The human does not in this form of labour seek to glean a reflection of itself in nature, but works with nature to secure the means to live. That form of work could become the domination or destruction of nature for human use, consumption and exchange (profit). But if it did, it would no longer be the form of labouring activity that has as its end the achievement of a means of life not so much for the individual, but for the species-being, that wider domain of sociality related to what Hegel called the system of needs. Let us remember that only under conditions in which individuals are separated off from modes of social labour do they find themselves seeking the means to live on their own. This is an effect of social and economic formations, not an ontological premise of their operation.

If I am right – and others have made this argument as well[20] – then perhaps we have to consider this very specific use of both the terms organic and inorganic in Marx's work. Foster and Burkett point out that a consideration of the Hegelian influence on Marx would show that there is no absolute distinction (or 'barrier') between organic and inorganic, but only 'a dialectical relation of interdependence'.[21] They thus call into question the presumption that Marx's theory of labour is an instrumentalist one, suggesting that this misunderstanding can be tracked to the particular ways in which the notions of the organic and inorganic emerge in his work. This perspective has been amplified by Jason Moore when he refers affirmatively to 'an open conception of life-making, one that views the boundaries of the organic and inorganic as ever-shifting',[22] and later calls for 'a language that comprehends the irreducibly dialectical relation between human and extra-human nature'.[23] The dialectic that unfolds at the site of the inorganic body, however, is one that requires a perspectival theory and a practice of perspectival variation. For it is only from the perspective of the human organism that nature appears as inorganic (and that this implies no refutation of the claim that nature is *in itself* organic); it means only that nature transforms from organic to inorganic as it enters into the process by which the living and organic human *Leib* seeks the means to live. Nature is organic, as it were, in itself, but considered from the human perspective, it starts to become inorganic once it starts to sustain the human at which point it is the human life that is sustained and animated by nature.

This last is surely a distinctly anthropocentric view, so it seems I have refuted my thesis that a non-anthropocentric trend can be found in the early Marx. There is, however, a countervailing process that is at work in this labouring for life that reverses the order of the transformative sequence we just traced, and is part of the dialectical unity that is being enacted. Marx is also arguing that humans are, and should be, understood as part of a larger organic nature. When human life ends, it becomes pure *Körper*, de-animated, but also co-extensive with a nature that is no longer approached to secure human sustenance. The body is no longer sustained by nature, and so becomes nature in a distinctly non-anthropocentric sense that was always a potentiality of its living version precisely because death is a potential in and of life (a potential in life, but one that is realised as necessity at a time that is for the most part unpredictable). So there are no two natures, and there are no two bodies, but there is a perpetual oscillation of perspectives (organic/inorganic) that depends on whether nature is approached theoretically or practically, facilitated by that practical mode of work that prepares nature as a means to live for the human. The same nature appears inorganic when it is external to human life, as something outside itself; this can happen through a theoretical perspective, but also one in which the problem of sustenance does not guide the human perspective and approach (with the implication that theory is a form of not being hungry).

To grasp the variable relation between the organic and inorganic body (and to make sure we do not accept these as two separate kinds of substances), it is important to return to Hegel whose influence on the early Marx can hardly be doubted. Indeed, it would appear that Marx draws on Hegel's discussion as he elaborates his own views on the inorganic body of man that is the entirety of nature, but also his notion of species-being. In the *Encyclopedia Logic*, Hegel remarks that the living being lives inside itself, as a 'constantly renewed inner process that the living being is.' But that its corporeity can become an object for itself, appear as something external, and in this moment, its own body appears as 'inorganic nature'.[24] Inorganic nature, interestingly enough, exists in the living being 'as a *want [als ein Mangel]*'.[25] Its organs are distinct; they are 'external' to one another, and the body appears not as a lived body, but as an external power: 'the living being confronts an inorganic nature to which it relates as the power over it, and which it assimilates.'[26] It wants what is external to itself in order to live, but also to 'overcome' that externality. Hegel writes,

> Inorganic nature, which is subdued by the living being, suffers this subjection because it is *in-itself* the same as what life is *for-itself*. So, in the other the living being only comes together with itself.[27]

With death, the 'species' proves to be more powerful than the individual living being. And the externality is overcome, not however by enhancing the living being, but by affirming the dialectical interdependency that is life itself. Hegel adds, 'For the animal, the process of the species [*die Gattung*] is the highest point of its living career.'[28] What the 'process of the species' does, however, is prove that this life, this immediate life, is mediated, that it belongs with others' lives and finds its means of living only in the social and economic organisation of life – or, at least, this would be the Marxist variant on Hegel's claim. The living being is not simply existing, immediate, but both mediated and generated; and just as it is generated from elsewhere it also passes away in its immediacy. It is a life that returns to itself in life, although the immediate life is not the same as the mediate one, and the inorganic cedes to the organic in death.

When Marx speaks about subsistence, he is not referring to the steady state of continuing as an organism, but about a renewed and ongoing activity, one that is required for the continuation of life, for persistence itself. As a living being is generated, it is animated, brought to life, and only then animates the external world in turn; becoming animated is a function of being generated, which means that the powers of animation are from the start outside of the human subject, as are the forms of interdependency that condition and define the organic social creature, the species-being, that no longer complies with conventional humanism. While it is beyond the scope of the current discussion, I would like to link this idea of persistence to *the desire to live*. The desire to live may or may not emerge from the human organism, but this relation to alterity is named as want, as lack, suggesting that persistence and the desire to persist may not be fully separable. The effort to overcome externality can take the form of domination or dissolution, but another process is delineated here, one that brings us close to forms of work related to maintenance, to what is sometimes called reproductive labour.

The human organism is bound up with inorganic nature for its own life, and can become inorganic for itself, living as a being both animated in some respects and de-animated in others. The body is in its natural world not as an ontologically separate entity, but a relational process between terms that can become separated or unified. The body is in and of nature to the degree that this ongoing process, if disrupted or destroyed, can expose the body to precarity, and is an ongoing interchange that requires renewal – and the conditions for renewal.

What we might learn from the early Marx is that there are conditions under which the desire to live becomes more possible, conditions of labour that sustain or fail to sustain, forms of labouring that sustain or fail to sustain, and that the desire to live is always a desire to live in this world, and in a specific way. When the world is no longer sustaining, and persistence is imperilled, what then happens to the desire to live? If living is an interchange between this living body and the body of an inorganic nature to which it is ineluctably tied, and the social and economic organisation of sustenance destroys – or threatens to destroy – that exchange, the desire to live may well be imperilled.

As mediated, as species, we are always more and less than this body, and this body extends to others and to the conditions of life itself. Neither persistence nor the desire to live can be taken for granted. They are less essential capacities or attributes than social possibilities for persistence that are enlivened or deadened depending on the conditions of life, including the presence or absence of work, forms of work that sustain or wreck bodies, economic formations that regularly abandon those they employ on a contingent basis, policies that imply the decimation of pensions, or the complete loss of social welfare and protection. And yet the avowal of this interdependency, and the decentring of the living subject it implies, gives us another way to think about interdependency and perhaps ultimately solidarity that refuses the strict distinction between the human condition and a sustained and sustainable environment. The human is not in nature and neither does it grasp nature simply as an object of knowledge, but its knowing is from the start vital without therefore exemplifying a form of vitalism.

The effort here to show the duality in Marx's early theory relates, of course, to the question of whether Marx can, and ought to be, mobilised for environmental politics; questions that are urgent but which are not possible to pursue here. If there is a duality to the distinctively human body, it is one that asserts and challenges that very distinctiveness, insisting on the living character of thought, and the necessity of life. The nature of work is not simply to remake nature as a reflection and expression of human powers, but to subdue human powers through modes of work that presume that the living human and the web of life are connected from the start. The dynamic activity that has as its aim the production of a livable life necessarily limits the powers of the human in relation to the living world. It avows a dependency without which neither life nor thought nor work is possible. One is this nature that one is not, and that paradox can give way to a dialectic that can hardly be grasped by following only one sequence in Marx's exposition at the expense of another. A practice of critique in and for this world must attend to, and intervene within, the accelerating destruction of various species and the threat of climate change to the continuation of the world as we have so far known it. Any project of social justice that is critical, that seeks to stop the acceleration of ecological destruction, has to begin with the presumption that the world in which all lives are valued equally, in which all are given their expressive freedom on grounds of equality, are bound to the living world at the level of need, desire and obligation. So, this body, though separate from the body of nature, is bound to that body, and that bind, that relation, is what we now mean by 'body'.

*Judith Butler is Maxine Elliot Professor in the Department of Comparative Literature and the Program of Critical Theory at the University of California, Berkeley. Her recent publications include* Senses of the Subject and Notes Toward a Performative Theory of Assembly *and the co-edited volume* Vulnerability in Resistance *(2015). Her new book,* The Force of Nonviolence, *will be published by Verso in 2020.*

**Notes**

1. Bruno Latour, 'Why Has Critique Run Out of Steam?: From Matters of Fact to Matters of Concern', *Critical Inquiry* 30 (2004), 231–2.
2. Ibid., 233.
3. John P. Clark, 'Marx's Inorganic Body', *Environmental Ethics* 11:3 (Fall 1989), 243–58.
4. See Antonio Negri and Michael Hardt's *Labour of Dionysus: Critique of the State-Form* (Minneapolis: University of Minnesota, 1994), and the reformulation of labour not only as a mode of production, but as the performative mode of producing the political.
5. Editors' note: In gendering 'man' and, specifically, the worker as male here, and throughout the article, the author follows Marx's own practice (and that of his translators) in the 1844 Manuscripts and elsewhere.
6. This distinction becomes more important in the twentieth century for Merleau-Ponty and then for Helmut Plessner. See Hans-Peter Krüger, 'Persons and their Bodies: the Körper/Leib Distinction and Helmuth Plessner's Theories of Ex-centric Positionality and Homo Absconditus', *Journal of Speculative Philosophy* 24:3 (2010), 256–74.
7. Clark, 'Marx's Inorganic Body', 243–58.
8. Karl Marx, *Grundrisse: Foundations of the Critique of Political Economy*, trans. M. Nicolaus (New York: Penguin, 1993), 706.
9. Carolyn Merchant, *The Death of Nature: Women, Ecology and the Scientific Revolution* (London: Bravo Ltd., 1990)
10. John Bellamy Foster and Paul Burkett, 'Marx and the Dialectic of Organic/Inorganic Relations', *Organisation & Environment* 14:4 (December 2001), 451–462; John Bellamy Foster and Paul Burkett, 'The Dialectic of Organic/Inorganic Relations: Marx and the Hegelian Philosophy of Nature', *Organisation and Environment* 13 (2000), 403–425. See also more recently, Jason W. Moore, *Capitalism in the Web of Life: Ecology and the Accumulation of Capital* (London: Verso, 2015).
11. Rahel Jaeggi, *Alienation*, trans. Frederick Neuhouser and Alan E. Smith (New York: Columbia University Press, 2016).
12. Louis Althusser, *For Marx*, trans. Ben Brewster (London: Verso, 2005), 222.
13. Ibid., 226.
14. Ibid., 219–20.
15. Jean Baudrillard, *The Mirror of Production*, trans. Mark Poster (New York: Telos Press, 1975).
16. The German is as follows: Betrachten wir nun näher die *Vergegenständlichung*, die Produktion des Arbeiters und in ihr die *Entfremdung*, den *Verlust* des Gegenstandes, seines Produkts.

Der Arbeiter kann nichts schaffen ohne die *Natur*, ohne die *sinnliche Außenwelt*. Sie ist der Stoff, an welchem sich seine Arbeit verwirklicht, in welchem sie tätig ist, aus welchem und mittelst welchem sie produziert.

Wie aber die Natur [die] *Lebensmittel* der Arbeit darbietet, in dem Sinn, daß die Arbeit nicht *leben* kann ohne Gegenstände, an denen sie ausgeübt wird, so bietet sie andrerseits auch d[ie] *Lebensmittel* in dem engern Sinn dar, nämlich die Mittel der physischen Subsistenz des *Arbeiters* selbst.

Je mehr also der Arbeiter die Außenwelt, die sinnliche Natur, durch seine Arbeit sich *aneignet*, um so mehr entzieht er sich *Lebensmittel* nach der doppelten Seite bin, erstens, daß immer mehr die sinnliche Außenwelt aufhört, ein seiner Arbeit angehöriger Gegenstand, ein *Lebensmittel* seiner Arbeit zu sein; zweitens, daß sie immer mehr aufhört, *Lebensmittel* im unmittelbaren Sinn, Mittel für die physische Subsistenz des Arbeiters zu sein.

Nach dieser doppelten Seite bin wird der Arbeiter also ein Knecht seines Gegenstandes, erstens, daß er einen *Gegenstand der Arbeit*, d.h., daß er Arbeit erhält, und zweitens, daß er *Subsistenzmittel* erhält. Erstens also, daß er als *Arbeiter*, und zweitens, daß er als *physisches Subjekt* existieren kann. Die Spitze dieser Knechtschaft ist, daß er nur mehr als *Arbeiter* sich als physisches Subjekt erhalten [kann] und nur mehr als *physisches Subjekt* Arbeiter ist.
17. In German the full passage reads as follows: Der Mensch ist ein Gattungswesen, nicht nur indem er praktisch und theoretisch die Gattung, sowohl seine eigne als die der übrigen Dinge, zu seinem Gegenstand macht, sondern – und dies ist nur ein andrer Ausdruck für dieselbe Sache – sondern auch indem er sich zu sich selbst als der gegenwärtigen, lebendigen Gattung verhält, indem er sich zu sich als einem *universellen*, darum freien Wesen verhält.

Das Gattungsleben, sowohl beim Menschen als beim Tier, besteht physisch einmal darin, daß der Mensch (wie das Tier) von der unorganischen Natur lebt, und um so universeller der Mensch als das Tier, um so universeller ist der Bereich der unorganischen Natur, von der er lebt. Wie Pflanzen, Tiere, Steine, Luft, Licht etc. theoretisch einen Teil des menschlichen Bewußtseins, teils als Gegenstände der Naturwissenschaft, teils als Gegenstände der Kunst bilden – seine geistige unorganische Natur, geistige Lebensmittel, die er erst zubereiten muß zum Genuß und zur Verdauung – so bilden sie auch praktisch einen Teil des menschlichen Lebens und der menschlichen Tätigkeit. Physisch lebt der Mensch nur von diesen Naturprodukten, mögen sie nun in der Form der Nahrung, Heizung, Kleidung, Wohnung etc. erscheinen. Die Universalität des Menschen erscheint praktisch eben in der Universalität, die die ganze Natur zu seinem *unorganischen* Körper macht, sowohl insofern sie 1. ein unmittelbares Lebensmittel, als inwiefern sie [2.] die Materie, der Gegenstand und das Werkzeug seiner Lebenstätigkeit ist. Die Natur ist der *unorganische Leib* des Menschen, nämlich die Natur, soweit sie nicht selbst menschlicher Körper ist. Der Mensch *lebt* von der Natur, heißt: Die Natur ist sein *Leib*, mit dem er in beständigem Prozeß bleiben muß, um nicht zu sterben. Daß das physische und geistige Leben des Menschen mit der Natur zusammenhängt, hat keinen andren Sinn, als daß die Natur mit sich selbst zusammenhängt, denn der Mensch ist ein Teil der Natur.

Indem die entfremdete Arbeit dem Menschen 1. die Natur entfremdet, 2. sich selbst, seine eigne tätige Funktion, seine Lebenstätigkeit, so entfremdet sie dem Menschen die *Gattung*; sie macht ihm das *Gattungsleben* zum Mittel des individuellen Lebens. Erstens entfremdet sie das Gattungsleben und das individuelle Leben, und zweitens macht sie das letztere in seiner Abstraktion zum Zweck des ersten, ebenfalls in seiner abstrakten und entfremdeten Form.

18. Karl Marx, *Ökonomisch-philosophische Manuskripte aus dem Jahre 1844* (Stuttgart: Reclam, 2008), 36; 'Economic and Philosophic Manuscripts of 1844' in *Marx Engels Reader*, trans. Robert C. Tucker (New York: Norton, 1978), 75.
19. Ibid.
20. Foster and Burkett, 'Marx and the Dialectic of Organic/Inorganic Relations', 451–62.
21. Ibid., 452.
22. Jason W. Moore, *Capitalism in the Web of Life: Ecology and the Accumulation of Capital*, 7.
23. Ibid., 9. I note that some forms of human labour, including chattel slavery, are also considered to be 'inorganic' – that is, not living in themselves, but only instrumental for the purposes of continuing the lives of those who are considered to be 'truly' living subjects. The distinction has thus been used for specific purposes within racial capitalism. See Angela Y. Davis, 'Women and Capitalism: Dialectics of Liberation and Oppression', in *The Angela Y. Davis Reader*, ed. Joy James and Angela Yvonne Davis (Oxford: Wiley-Blackwell, 1998), 161–209.
24. G.W.F. Hegel, *The Encyclopedia Logic*, trans. T. F. Geraets, W.A. Suchting and H.S. Harris (Indianapolis: Hackett, 1991), 292.
25. Ibid., 293.
26. Ibid.
27. Ibid.
28. Ibid., 294.

# independent thinking from polity

## Future Metaphysics
Armen Avanessian

Translated by James Wagner

The triumph of technological rationality and of the sciences as a whole has by no means provided answers to humanity's great questions. Instead, it has raised new questions and problems. To orient ourselves in the twenty-first century, this book takes a new look at the central categories of philosophy that, often unbeknownst to us, continue to shape our everyday thinking.

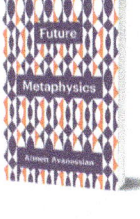

November 2019 / PB 978-1-5095-3797-6 / £9.99

## Twenty-First Century Socialism
Jeremy Gilbert

"This is essential reading. A provocative, accessible, and compelling argument for the necessity of socialism – and a common sense series of steps to start us on the path there."
**Nick Srnicek, Kings College London**

February 2020 / PB 978-1-5095-3656-6 / £9.99

## Habitus and Field
*General Sociology, Volume 2*
Pierre Bourdieu

An ideal introduction to some of Bourdieu's most important ideas, this volume will be of great interest to readers who want to know more about the work of one of the most important sociologists and social thinkers of the 20th century.

November 2019 / HB 978-1-5095-2669-7 / £30.00

## Resolutely Black
*Conversations with Francoise Verges*
Aimé Césaire

Translated by Matthew Smith

"The interviews … further underscore the unnerving prescience of Césaire when it comes to racial politics while also providing much-needed context, depth and texture. A 'must' for all students and scholars who study power, diaspora, culture, identity and belonging in the modern world."
**Michelle Wright, Emory University**

November 2019 / PB 978-1-5095-3715-0 / £14.99

Order your copy now:
free phone 0800 243407 | politybooks.com

 @politybooks    facebook.com/politybooks

ESSAYS FROM THE
**radical philosophy archive**  rpa

# CRITIQUE & BETRAYAL  1

| | |
|---|---|
| ROBERT BERNASCONI | ÉRIC ALLIEZ |
| BRENNA BHANDAR | ARIELLA AZOULAY |
| FRANÇOISE COLLIN | ÉTIENNE BALIBAR |
| SIMON CRITCHLEY | BORIS BUDEN |
| PENELOPE DEUTSCHER | HOWARD CAYGILL |
| MEENA DHANDA | SIMON CRITCHLEY |
| HARRY HAROOTUNIAN | PHILIP DERBYSHIRE |
| PAULINE JOHNSON | ANNA-SABINE ERNST |
| CHRISTIAN KERSLAKE | PETER HALLWARD |
| PHILIPPE LACOUE-LABARTHE | AXEL HONNETH |
| KOLJA LINDNER | GERWIN KLINGER |
| JOSEPH McCARNEY | LYNDA NEAD |
| ANDREW McGETTIGAN | OMEDI OCHIENG |
| PETER OSBORNE | PETER OSBORNE |
| ROSA & CHARLEY PARKIN | ANSON RABINBACH |
| STELLA SANDFORD | JONATHAN RÉE |
| LYNNE SEGAL | BILL SCHWARZ |
| ALBERTO TOSCANO | JOHN SELLARS |
| | CORNELIA SORABJI |

# PHILOSOPHY & NATIONS  2

**EDITED BY AUSTIN GROSS, MATT HARE & MARIE LOUISE KROGH**

The first two volumes in a new series of books from the archive of *Radical Philosophy* series 1 (1972–2016) offering thematic selections of articles on topics that continue to innervate theoretical and political debates on the Left

**PAPERBACKS**  UK£14.99/US$22.00  **ISBN** 978-1-9162292-0-4 | 978-1-9162292-2-8
**FREE DOWNLOAD**  www.radicalphilosophyarchive.com

# *Securitati perpetuae*
## Death, fear and the history of insecurity
Mark Neocleous

If we knocked on the graves and asked the dead whether they would like to rise again, they would shake their heads. ... With true instinct the ancients put on their tombstones: *Securitati perpetuae*.
Arthur Schopenhauer, *The World as Will and Representation*, Vol. II (1859).

It's not clear whether in making this statement Schopenhauer had in mind the satirical inscription to which Kant refers at the beginning of his 1795 essay on peace. The inscription in question, 'The Perpetual Peace', is said by Kant to have been seen on a Dutch innkeeper's signboard along with the image of a graveyard. In an essay known for its argument for a global community of lawful states and the implicit idea that such a community will lead to 'peace', Kant begins by hinting that *perpetual* peace really comes only with death: you will get peace when you finally 'rest in peace', but in the meantime you should commit to law. We might also observe that Kant's title *Zum ewigen Frieden* could easily be translated as 'Towards Eternal Peace' rather than the standard 'On Perpetual Peace', an alternative that has very different connotations indeed, especially given that just a year previously Kant had written an essay called 'The End of All Things' (1794) which begins with the image of a dying person passing from historical time into eternity.

The politics of *perpetual peace* in Kant's essay, then, perhaps really requires us to think about death rather than law. In that sense, Schopenhauer's twist with perpetual *security* might simply be a cheeky nod towards Kant. But Schopenhauer was not known for his cheekiness, and although, philosophically speaking, his suggestion that the ancients might have got it right in putting *Securitati perpetuae* on their tombstones is unremarkable, *politically* the idea is completely antithetical to security's status as the supreme concept of bourgeois society, to the extent that the claim might appear as nothing less than scandalous.

Borrowing Marx's astute formulation that security is the supreme concept of bourgeois society, I have for some time been arguing that a *critique of security* needs to be central to critical theory, not least because of the role security plays in the fabrication of social order and the pacification of political subjects.[1] The extent to which the security industry constantly bombards us with its double-sided message – 'more security with the next security measure', the interminable message from the state; 'better security with the next security product', the interminable message from capital – is obvious. Equally obvious is the way that obedient subjects are created through these products and measures. In this regard, *security is pacification*.[2] But what does this have to do with death?

Towards the end of his short book *The Loneliness of the Dying* (1982), Norbert Elias connects some of his earlier arguments about the civilising process as a process of pacification to the question of death, and makes the following comment:

> The greater pacification of developed industrial states and the marked advance of the embarrassment threshold in the face of violence gives rise in these societies to a usually tacit but noticeable antipathy of the living towards the dying ... Thus, a higher level of internal pacification also contributes to the aversion towards death, or more precisely towards the dying. So does a higher level of civilising restraint.[3]

Where pacification in his earlier work was examined through the shift in practices and behaviours, turning once dangerous territories into spaces of security, Elias here makes a clever move, suggesting that pacification in bourgeois modernity has also involved a shift in our relationship to death.

If security is pacification, and if pacification involves a certain kind of elision of death, then we need to consider the relationship between security and death. I want to use this relationship in order to extend a little the critique of security. And I want to do so through the lens of *insecurity*.*

One of the questions heard many times in response to the critique of security is whether this implies being somehow *for insecurity*. The backdrop to such a question lies in a common refrain concerning the 'insecurity' generated by capitalism. A remarkable feature of Kate Pickett and Richard Wilson's *The Spirit Level: Why Equality is Better for Everyone* (2009), for example, a widely-read and much-cited book that has frequently been described as ground-breaking and influential, is the extent to which the argument about 'inequality' veers into an argument about 'insecurity'. This becomes even more pronounced in their follow-up book *The Inner Level: How More Equal Societies Reduce Stress, Restore Sanity and Improve Everyone's Well-Being* (2019). That the ten-year period between their two books has seen an increase in their stress on insecurity should not surprise, for the rhetoric of insecurity has risen across the board in general. According to the catalogue of the British Library, there have been 330 books published since 2001 with 'insecurity' in the title, almost twice as many as had been published in the previous 400 years. The language of precarity has reinforced this growth, being largely a kind of left field thinking about insecurity: Isobel Lorey's *State of Insecurity* (2015), for example, has far more to say about 'precarity' than 'insecurity'; the original 2012 German text was *Die Regierung der Prekären*, its translated title presumably a result of the publisher's desire to benefit from the growth of interest in 'insecurity'.

There is no doubt, then, that we are living in an 'Age of Insecurity', as several books with that exact phrase as their title suggest. Yet is this not also the 'Age of Security'? Certainly the number of books with this as their title would suggest as much, as would the 21,000 books (and counting) published in English since 2001 with 'security' in the title. The more we talk about security, the more insecure we seem to be becoming. In one sense, this might not appear too much of a surprise. 'We can never think security without insecurity, and *vice versa*', observes Mick Dillon, pointing to the 'unified agonal relationship of mutual definition' between the two words. 'Modern usage proposes that there is a state of affairs – insecurity – and the negation of that state of affairs – security'. To this end, Dillon relies heavily on the idea of '(in)security'.[4] The radical ambivalence of this term '(in)security' has led to it becoming central to what is called 'Critical Security Studies', a body of thought which is critical of mainstream approaches to security, not least by placing a heavy emphasis on the possibility of 'emancipation'. For this reason Critical Security Studies has highlighted the role of 'insecurity' in thinking about 'security', to the extent that it has become, in effect, a kind of '(In)Security Studies', the *sine quo non* of which is that 'society is no longer focused on achieving perfect security' but, rather, on managing the fact that 'insecurity pervades all'.[5]

Yet there is a problem here: much as it might seem obvious that we can never think security without insecurity, the truth is that 'security' existed for a long time before 'insecurity' was ever invented. In other words, people were for centuries *more than capable of thinking security without thinking insecurity*. Thomas Hobbes, for example, is taken by Critical Security Studies and many other fields as 'the classic source of modern wisdom about security'.[6] But as we shall see, Hobbes has *absolutely nothing to say about insecurity*; in retrospect, my own *Critique of Security* (2008) elides this very point, along with most commentaries on Hobbes. To think of 'insecurity' as always already unified with security, then, and hence to imagine one single idea of '(in)security', is at the very least a poor engagement with historical sources, reading them a little too anachronistically.

The more telling point, however, is that insecurity does eventually emerge and become conjoined with security, but it does so *in the condition of bourgeois modernity*. To put one part of my argument in a nutshell: much as 'security' can be traced back to the Romans, 'insecurity' was invented as an ideological category under capitalism. In this regard, bourgeois thought could eventually develop a jargon of 'insecurity' in order to reinforce political acts carried out in the name of 'security'. Rather than

---

* This is a much-revised version of a paper first developed for the conference 'Insecurity' at the University of Wisconsin-Milwaukee, 4-6 May, 2019.

being understood as an unalterable truth intrinsic to the human condition, 'insecurity' needs to be understood as the product of very specific historical circumstances. In that sense, I am doubtful about the power of 'insecurity' as a critical concept.

The second part of my argument is that the politically-telling divergent and then convergent histories of security and insecurity requires us to address them in relation to *death*. Dillon suggests that 'the truth of security is the radical ambiguity of human freedom'.[7] I want to suggest that the truth of security is in fact death. If so, then perhaps what is at stake in security is not so much the insecurity of life and freedom, but of the nature of death in a condition of unfreedom. What is at stake is dying in a society in which the radical ambiguity of human freedom is, in part, our knowledge that we are unfree. Perhaps what is at stake in security and insecurity, then, is nothing less than the two things from which we appear unable to escape: capital and death.

## 'Security some men call the suburbs of hell'

The English word 'security' comes from the Latin *securitas*, a complex word derived from *sine*, meaning 'without', and *cura*, meaning 'troubling; solicitude; carefulness', giving us *securitas*: to be without care and untroubled. As can be seen, there is an immediate ambivalence here, something *untranslatable*, in that *cura* can express something troubling – such as anxiety or fear – but it can also express something beneficial, such as attentiveness or loving diligence. So *securitas* as the removal of *cura* can be either beneficial or harmful.[8]

The idea that *securitas* is beneficial is found in the Roman Republic and the work of writers such as Cicero and Seneca, the former being the most likely candidate to have invented the term. For Cicero, the *cura* that is cancelled in *securitas* means that *securitas* itself tends to be associated with the *beata vita* (blessed life) and *tranquillitas animi* (peace of mind). 'How can anyone be in possession of that desirable and much-coveted security, who has a multitude of evils attending him?', Cicero asks (*Tusculan Disputations*, Bk. 5.XIV). The peace of mind that Cicero calls *securitas* refers to an internal stability and feeling of peace. 'We must keep ourselves free from every disturbing emotion ... so that we may enjoy that calmness of soul and security [*tranquillitas animi et securitas*] which bring both moral stability and dignity of character' (Cicero, *De Officiis*, Bk. I, Para 69).[9] Note that this beneficial aspect of *securitas* makes it a highly personal thing, a question more of moral psychology rather than political order, which is itself quite remarkable for a deeply political thinker such as Cicero. For Cicero, the notion of *securitas* tends to apply to the 'private' realm, as distinct from *salus*, with its connotations of safety or protection within the city: hence the expression made famous by Cicero, *Salus populi suprema lex*, refers to the *safety* of the people as the supreme law. Hamilton expresses the distinction well: 'self-therapy produced *securitas*; state therapy engendered *salus*'.[10]

With the collapse of the Roman Republic, however, the earlier republican distinction between *salus* as public 'safety' and *securitas* as personal 'peace of mind' begins to break down – although in some languages it never really develops anyway, with Spanish (*seguridad*), German (*sicherheit*) and Italian (*sicurezza*) all combining safety and security – and *securitas* is increasingly employed in a decidedly public fashion.[11] Some authors increasingly connect the idea of an inner security with the idea of the security that is provided by the state (Seneca, *Epistulae morales*, I.73.2 and 73.4). 'What is a happy life?', asks Seneca. '*Securitas et perpetua tranquillitas*' (*Epistles Lucilium*, 92, 3). Tacitus makes a similar point in his book on Julius Agricola, the Governor of Britain in the second half of the first century (*Agricola*, III). During the first century AD, *securitas* and *securitati perpetuae* begin to appear on coins and medallions, hinting at an increasingly public and political dimension to the concept, not least in its connotations of imperial propaganda.[12]

All of this might be taken to suggest that *securitas* becomes political with the Romans and then stays with us, which would make for a nice and even story. Unfortunately, this is not the story. For the fact that *securitas* could imply the removal of a careful attention meant that it could also be seen as something negative, connoting a freedom from concern and danger and thus a state of *carelessness*. This is what we get with the rise of Christianity, for which *securitas* remains a personal peace but – and this is a huge but, for reasons we shall see – it is a personal peace that comes through union with God.

For Augustine, for example, security is a blessed state, but its blessedness points to the fact that security – and we need to perhaps qualify the word and say 'true security' – is only possible posthumously. 'There is no security except through God', Augustine claims in *The Confessions* (II.6.13). In *The City of God* he is even more explicit, suggesting that in 'situations of weakness and these times of evil, even anxiety if not without its use in leading them [worshippers] to seek, with more fervent longing, that state of security where peace is utterly complete and assured' (*City of God*, XIX).[13] Security, like peace, ultimately comes with eternal life (*City of God*, XIX.11). Herein lies the basis of Schopenhauer's observation about the inscription on ancient tombstones: *Securitati perpetuae*.

The implication of this, however, is that because security is a blessed state in the eternal realm of peace in which we are freed from the troubled nature of earthly existence, to claim security in this world is nothing less than an insult to God. One of the dangers on earth is that 'one should sin with deadly security [*mortiferas securitas*]' (Augustine, *Of Holy Virginity*, para. 50). Hence to think of oneself as *secure in this world* – or as we might now say, to aim for a *freedom from insecurity* – undermines the ideal of and desire for real security, which comes only with the peace of death; no person can or should be deemed 'secure' until after death. 'When people say "there is peace and security" then sudden destruction will come upon them' (*I Thess.* 5: 2-3); a passage which Hobbes will put to good use, as we shall shortly see. Hence, a figure such as Pope Gregory I (Saint Gregory, or Gregory the Great) comments in his *Exposition on the Book of Blessed Job* (578–595) that 'security is often the parent of negligence', adding that 'to keep security from generating carelessness, one must come to the service of God and stand in fear' (Vol. III, Pt. V, Bk. XXIV, 27). The last of Martin Luther's Ninety-Five Theses (1517) likewise exhorts us to 'be confident of entering into heaven through many tribulations rather than through the security of peace'. For Luther, people who think of themselves as secure are those who no longer put their faith in God, a condition which renders them unable to either work or pray; *fiducia*, like *certitudo*, is better than *securitas*. Robert Burton, in *The Anatomy of Melancholy*, published in various editions between 1621 and 1651, suggests two pieces of advice for warding off a melancholy despair: first, rely on God's word, and second, reject 'perverse security' (Vol. 3, Pt. 3, Sect. 4, Mem. 2, Subs. 6).

All of this goes some way to explaining why it is that the early references to security in the *Oxford English Dictionary* are to a *negative* state: 'our vayne glory, our viciousness, avarice, ydleness, security' (1564); 'they … were drowned in sinfull securitie' (1575). Shakespeare in *Macbeth* (1606) has Hecate declare that 'security is mortal's chiefest enemie', while John Webster in *The Duchess of Malfi* (1612-13) has the tomb-maker Bosola say that 'security some men call the suburbs of hell'. Security here is a careless, dangerous and, in most cases, sinful confidence. This is captured in the wider literature of the sixteenth and seventeenth centuries. For example, a 1585 sermon by Edwin Sandys, Archbishop of York, has him commenting that 'we sleep as well in security as in sin'. Because the world is one of perpetual warfare against God's adversaries, 'there is no place of security left for a Christian soldier' and 'there is nowhere any place wherein it is safe to be secure'. People have in the past sought peace, but 'their peace bred plenty; their plenty, their security; their security, their destruction'. Hence the message: 'watch, therefore, and sleep not in security'.[14] We find a similar message in John Stockwood's *A Very fruitfull and necessarye sermon of the moste lamentable destruction of Jerusalem* (1584), where the author invokes us from being 'lulled a sleepe in the cradle of securitie or carelesnesse'; Johann Habermann's *The Enimie of Securitie; or, A Daily Exercise of Godlie Meditations* (originally published in German and Latin in 1579, quickly translated into English and going through several editions) and William Est's *The Scourge of Securitie; or, The Expulsion and Returne of the Uncleane Spirit* (1609). Likewise, John Downame's *Guide to Godlynesse* (1622), the long subtitle of which includes a claim that it is a *Treatise on Carnal Security*, with that same section being published as a separate shorter book called *A Treatise of Security*, exhorts readers to rise out of the 'lethargy of carnal security', and lists security's various causes, including ignorance of God, customable sinning, the impunity of sinners and the neglect or contempt of the means of grace. Security, for Downame, is 'the mother and nurse of all other wickedness' and 'deprives us of eternal happiness'. In another text, *The Christian Warfare*, written between 1604 and 1618, Downame writes of 'their carnal security which so lulleth them asleep in the cradle of worldly vanities'.[15] The theme continues into late in the century: a sermon published in 1672 called *Security Surprized, or, The Destruction of the Careless* denounces those who go about in sin and 'horrible security'. 'Consider the evil of this security you are in ... when you cry peace, peace to your selves in the midst of God's displeasure. It is an evil disease, a spiritual lethargy'. And the Sermon makes clear that this applies to people, nations and kingdoms, all 'drowned in drunken security' and a 'spiritual Lethargy that leadeth to death'. Death was brought upon Sodom and Gomorrah precisely because of their security.[16]

Throughout much of Christianity, then, *securitas* is largely a pejorative term describing a sinful condition, a lethargy, an ignorance of God; security is wickedness. One might *seem* secure, but this is highly deceptive, being a false security and thus undesirable. Rather than *securitas*, the Christians were interested in *certitudo*, certainty of faith. To fail to recognise, accept and live with what we would now call 'insecurity' – although this term will only emerge gradually and much later, as we shall see – is to suffer from the *carelessness* of a security that leaves one more even more 'insecure' than ever. The Christianisation of the empire therefore meant that the positive connotations of *securitas* found in authors such as Cicero more or less vanished from political and religious usage, making it difficult to find any positive connotations of *securitas* in the Christian tradition. Although some such connotations can be found in a few legal contexts, Hamilton notes that the term *securitas* is, in general, 'not explicitly employed as a political or philosophical concept in any sustained manner before the fourteenth century'. What we find instead is a range of other words closer to what we understand as 'safety' (*salus*), 'certitude' (*certitudo*) and 'peace' (*pax*). In that sense, the concept of security only really enters European *political* thought when institutions that had historically claimed to offer stability and cohesion, most obviously the church, begin to weaken.[17] When it does so, the meaning of *securitas* will oscillate between an inner subjective sense of composure and an external objective sense of a public safety, with the two dimensions circulating around each other, generating many of the problems we now face.

## 'Let every man go about without fear'

With that in mind, we might benefit by pausing for a moment on Ambrogio Lorenzetti's so-called 'Good Government' and 'Bad Government' frescoes from the early fourteenth century. Since this series of three large paintings have been described as offering 'the most famous artistic political allegory of the fourteenth century',[18] and have been a major point of political discussion in the history of ideas, art history and political theory, it is worth considering what they have to say about security, as Hamilton and others have. At the same time, however, I want to use them to consider what they manifestly *do not* say about *insecurity*. This will allow me to segue into a discussion of security and the absence of insecurity in the work of Thomas Hobbes and Adam Smith, in order to draw out the point I want to make about death.

Lorenzetti's paintings occupy three complete walls of the Sala dei Nove in the Palazzo Pubblico in Siena. This room was the main Chamber of the Council of Nine, the ruling officials of the increasingly dominant merchant oligarchy that governed Siena between 1287 and 1355. The frescoes were commissioned by the Council and produced between 1337 and 1339. There are three walls. On the northern wall, in the middle and hence centre stage, is Peace, the central figure of the central image. Alongside peace we have virtues such as faith, charity, fortitude, temperance, justice and concord. The figure in the middle appears to be a King but since Siena was a republic the figure is seen by some as representing the 'Common Good', and by others as a kind of representative of the type of *signore* or *signoria* that a city needs to elect if the dictates of justice are to achieved.[19] On the western wall is what is taken to be *Bad Government* – dominated by a figure called *Tyrammides*, who sits enthroned like a King but carrying a dagger rather than any of the standard instruments of kingly authority. At his feet lies *Justice*, tied up and looking forlorn and unkempt, in contrast to the image of justice in the Good Government fresco where she is serene and beautiful. Surrounding *Tyrammides* are a black satanic goat and a black hybrid man-beast called *Furor*, and figures such as *Avarice*, *Superbia*, *Vainglory*, *Discordia* and *Guerra*. Over the city hovers *Timor*. In the city itself, the only activity appears to be people going off to war, on the left, and a man being murdered, at the bottom right. On the eastern wall is *Good Government*. On one side of the city wall is the hustle and bustle of the city: people working, shopping, talking, dancing. On the other side of the wall is the land just outside the city, where we see a lady going off to hunt with servants and dogs, people tending their cattle and tilling the land, which is itself very fertile, unlike the countryside in bad government. There is no apparent danger. People are at peace and at work on both sides of the city wall.[20] Some commentators have noted that if one follows the line of sight of Peace in the middle fresco, then one discovers that she is looking directly at this image. In other words, this is *literally* the 'vision of Peace'.

Overlooking the whole scene of Good Government is *Securitas*, hovering in the sky, overseeing town and country and thus establishing the good order of the city. She holds in her right hand a banner with the words:

> Let every man go about without fear
> And let every man sow
> While this lady rules the land
> For she has taken the power from all the guilty.

The city is under the rule of *Securitas*. *Securitas* enables work and leisure. *Securitas* oversees the peaceful and commercial city. *Securitas* ensures good order. *Securitas* appears as both the desire and product of the rising merchant class whose ruling oligarchy would meet in this very room to discuss, under the sign of security, how best to manage the commercial order of the city.

In one sense, what we see represented is an image of a social order founded on an institutional imposition of security. It is thus worth noting in passing that Siena is also at this moment a key stage in the history of police power, for by this stage in its history the city had become an experiment in policing, with a number of different forces in operation: the *quattrini*, charged with daytime custody of the city and numbering around 100; the captain of the people, with a small force of between 10 and 20; the force of the *Podesta*, the town's chief magistrate, of around 40 established by the constitution of 1337; the war captain's force, of between 50 and 100; the force of the Nine, also around 100 strong. William Bowsky calculates that, all told, by the mid-1330s there was one 'policeman' per 145 inhabitants of Siena, a proportion of police to populace far higher than places such as medieval Florence but higher too than modern states.[21] This tells us what we now know: the free circulation of goods and people requires a heavily policed city; a heavily policed city is policed under the sign of security. 'Security' and 'police' are beginning to come together as the supreme concepts of bourgeois society.

Lorenzetti's images go some way to capturing what was happening to *Securitas* in the early modern West. Whatever theological trappings remain in the images, *Securitas* has developed in three important and overlapping ways: it has started to take on decidedly positive connotations, despite the Christian context; it has started to connect the inner tranquillity of the soul with the public tranquillity of the city, as the self-therapy of 'secure subjects' begins to combine with the political therapy of 'secure cities'; and it has become increasingly secular and political. All of which is to say that security has started to become the sign of modernity, a policy objective as well as a personal goal.

Yet there is something fundamentally odd about the images: *insecurity is not represented*. The frescos possess a range of opposites between Good and Bad Government: peace versus war; charity versus avarice; concord versus discord; and so on. Yet despite the formidable presence of 'security' in Good Government, 'insecurity' does not yet exist in Bad Government. This tells us something important: insecurity does not yet exist as security's opposite. Indeed, 'insecurity' does not yet exist at all. Insecurity may well be talked into existence through 'discourses of danger',[22] but at this point in history, whatever dangers existed, and there were plenty of them, 'insecurity' has clearly not been talked into existence. What does exist, however, being talked into existence time and again as security's opposite, is fear. The banner of *Securitas* proclaims loudly: every man should go about the city *without fear*, not *without insecurity*.

This dominating presence of fear and complete absence of insecurity must be read in the light of both the final line on the banner held by *Securitas* ('she has taken the power from all the guilty') and what she holds in her other hand: a figure executed on the gallows. This somewhat complicates the message that *Securitas* will allow us to go without fear, for that message now appears to have two dimensions. On the one hand is the obvious: people can go about without fear because *Securitas* will punish those who commit crimes in the city; in contrast to Bad Government where killing takes place on the street in the absence of security, in Good Government killing takes place on the gallows in the hands of security. On the other hand, the image is also very much a message that one's fears might now need to be directed towards *Securitas* herself. The gallows reminds us that it *Securitas* who now holds power over life and death. *Securitas* removes fear of one kind of violent death, then, only to replace it with another, offering us a permanent reminder that we should *fear security itself*. *Securitas* appears as an apparatus in which the *death penalty is necessarily inscribed*, to use Derrida's formulation about sovereignty.[23] For Good Government to persist, *Securitas must hold death in her hands*. Or to use the wry formulation of Georg Christoph Lichtenberg, responding to the inscription with which Kant begins 'Perpetual Peace': walking past a graveyard one can at least say that its residents 'can now be sure they aren't going to be hanged, which is more than we can'.[24]

Now, one way to read Lorenzetti's paintings is through the lens of what has become a commonplace in the history of political thought, namely that the image shows us the gradual placement of security at the heart of the conceptions of state and social order. This is of course the very story we are told when we are introduced to modern political theory, in which we are taught that security comes to form the underpinning dynamic of modern ideas about sovereignty and that it does so because of the *insecurity* experienced by human beings: the insecurity of the state of nature leads us to create the social contract and the state, we are told, and it is insecurity that remains even after the creation of the sovereign that leads us to accept the ongoing authority of the state. Yet there's a problem with that story. It is a complex problem that has a number of overlapping dimensions upon which we have already touched and which are pertinent to my argument here: first, insecurity is not yet in the picture; second, what is very much in the picture is fear; and third, the key fear appears to be of death. I want to now unravel this a little through a discussion of Hobbes, because he is widely regarded as the philosopher of security par excellence, but I also want to use the work of Adam Smith in order to push home my point about capital.

## 'Acknowledge your darkness'

The idea for which Hobbes has become best known is that we need a sovereign power because without it 'we can neither expect from others, nor promise to our selves the least security' (*De Cive*, I.3). The extent to which security is central to Hobbes's thought is evident from the fact that he oscillates but often combines *securitas* and *salus*, along with other terms such as the New Testament Greek *asphaleia*, which refers to a firmness or stability, often in the literal sense of a 'security' against falling but also sometimes in the civic sense of the stability of institutions. Thus, when in 1628 Hobbes translates Thucydides' *History of the Peloponnesian War*, he frequently translates *asphaleia* as 'security', extending it to include military practice rather than just personal security (Thucydides, *History*, III.37). So he is certainly keen on pushing the point of security for which his work has become well known. At the same time, he also rejects Cicero's position on tranquillity, since there can be no such thing in a world in constant motion: 'there is no such thing as perpetual Tranquillity of mind, while we live here; because life it selfe is but Motion, and can never be without Desire, nor without Fear' (*Lev.*, VI).

Yet what Hobbes does *not* have is the concept of 'insecurity'. The frequently quoted passages on the generation of the Leviathan often describe this as a response to the insecurity of the state of nature and our insecurity as regards to others. Yet 'insecurity' is at this point not a common term. The *OED* gives the first use of 'insecurity' from 1646, in Sir Thomas Browne's *Pseudodoxia Epidemica*, where it is used to describe 'the insecurity of truth' with no political connotations whatsoever. So Hobbes might have been in a position to use 'insecurity', or even perhaps to develop the word himself, given how often he led the way in developing the English language. But he does not do so. What he does say a lot about, however, is *metus*, a Latin word which for him is the closest we might find as the opposite of *securitas* but which is usually translated as 'fear'. More to the point, it is *metus mortis violentae* = the fear of violent death =

that is key. We do not need to delve too deeply into his personal experiences here. (He liked to claim that his mother went into labour upon hearing the news of the Spanish Armada and that he was therefore born twinned with fear, and as an adult he was always fully aware that those like himself who were on the side of the king were liable to be executed.) For Hobbes, fear is the basis for the right of self-preservation – 'life it selfe is ... fear' – and is the very reason we cannot expect security from others. In the passage just cited from *De Cive*, the reason why we cannot expect security from others is explained as being due to 'mutual fear' which stems in turn from our 'mutual will of hurting'. In *De Homine*, 'security of future time' is set against fear of death as 'the greatest of all evils' (XI.6). The point is that a condition lacking in security, in which there is no industry, no cultivation, no navigation, no building, no transport, no knowledge, no arts and no society, is a condition not of 'insecurity' but, rather, of 'continual feare and danger of violent death' (*Lev.*, XIII). We create and choose to live with a sovereign 'for fear of one another' (*Lev.*, XX). Fear, not insecurity, drives Hobbes's philosophy.

Hobbes's whole work is organised around this fundamental fear of violent death, as Leo Strauss stresses in his book *The Political Philosophy of Thomas Hobbes* (1936) which, I think consciously echoing Hobbes, eschews the language of 'insecurity'. Hobbes believes that people must recognise their fear of violent death and organise themselves accordingly. 'It is through fear that men secure themselves' (*De Cive*, I.2-3). The fear of death at the hands of another becomes the basis of sovereignty and subjection. At the same time, however, this fear *remains present in that very state* erected to provide security. Despite the creation of the Leviathan, despite *Securitas* overlooking the city, we still lock our private doors and secure the public gates at night.

> I comprehend in this word *fear*, a certain foresight of future evil; neither do I conceive flight the sole property of fear, but to distrust, suspect, take heed, provide so that they may not fear, is also incident to the fearful. They who go to sleep, shut their doors; they who travel, carry their swords with them, because they fear thieves. Kingdoms guard their coasts and frontiers with forts and castles; cities are compact with walls.

The imagination of death in the state of nature as the most telling detail of our fundamental fear is carried over into the imagination of incalculable fears in the social order, as conflicts over even 'trifles' such as 'a word, a smile, a different opinion' can result in death (*Lev.*, XXIII). The natural fear of death takes on a social dimension, rendering security always already under threat: the police power always already liable to fail fear never leaves.

Moreover, every person must 'be restrained through fear of some coercive power' (*De Cive*, Preface). Here we come to the second dimension of *Securitas* which we saw in Lorenzetti's frescoes: 'the terrour of some punishment' must always exist. And for Hobbes, the good bourgeois, such terror must exist to ensure 'security of performance' (*Lev*, XV), so the creation of the Leviathan means that we come to fear death at the hands of the sovereign. In an earlier book *The Elements of Law*, Hobbes suggests that a person fears a death brought about by the 'displeasing of his superior', because behind this lies the 'fear of eternal death hereafter' (II.6.5), and in the later *Leviathan* the idea that 'there is no natural knowledge of man's estate after death' becomes the basis of political order, for the one way of 'gaining the secure and perpetuall felicity of Heaven' lies in the 'keeping of Covenant' (*Lev*, XV). To claim the power to preserve our life, the sovereign claims the power of death but also operates in such a way that is rooted in our continual fear of death. The state is a power to enforce the punishment of death to achieve a condition called 'security'. To be successful in its offer of protection, *Securitas* must also itself threaten death. The gallows rope always dangles before us.

This is why *Leviathan* needs to be read not simply for what it says or implies about security in the first two parts of the book, 'Of Man' and 'Of Commonwealth', in which he outlines the state of nature, man's drives, and the creation of a sovereign power offering security, but also, and more pertinently, for what it says about security in the fourth and final part, a political theology concerning 'The Kingdom of Darkness'. In that fourth part Hobbes imagines the Apostles after Jesus's Resurrection asking him whether he will restore the Kingdome of God. Hobbes offers us Jesus's answer:

> When the Apostles after our Saviour's Resurrection, and immediately before his Ascension, asked our Saviour, saying (Acts 1.6) *Wilt thou at this time restore again the Kingdome to Israel?* he answered them, *It is not for you to know the times and the seasons, which the Father hath put in his*

*own power; But ye shall receive power by the comming of the Holy Ghost upon you, and yee shall be my (Martyrs) witnesses both in Jerusalem, and in all Judaea, and in Samaria, and unto the uttermost part of the earth*: Which is as much as to say, My Kingdome is not yet come, nor shall you foreknow when it shall come; for it shall come as a theefe in the night; But I will send you the Holy Ghost, and by him you shall have power to bear witnesse to all the world (by your preaching) of my Resurrection, and the workes I have done, and the doctrine I have taught, that they may beleeve in me, and expect eternal life, at my comming againe (*Lev.*, XLIV).

Hobbes is lifting here the passage from *Thessalonians* cited above, but also referencing the more general Christian tradition, to the effect that when people say 'there is security' then destruction will be on them. What is in going on in Part 4 of *Leviathan* is thus a suggestion that the security constructed through the erection of a sovereign power in the opening parts of the book is not 'real' security. It cannot be real security because man is still ultimately a wolf to man, each threating the other with death; because Behemoth, the monster of revolution, is always a possibility; because despite the ever-present threat of the gallows, the obedience we learn is perpetually liable to dissipate; and because, after all, the Leviathan is not the City of God.

What this means is that the picture is far more complicated than the one which suggests that for Hobbes the sovereign is created in order to provide security. The security offered by the sovereign is a kind of holding power through which men must learn to 'acknowledge their owne Darknesse' (*Lev.*, XLIV). This is a darkness which generates fears about what Hobbes variously describes as 'Powers Invisible', 'Spirits Invisible', 'Invisible Agents' and 'Invisible Powers'.[25] 'This Feare of things invisible', from Witches to Fairies and from Ghosts to Goblins, 'is the natural Seed of that, which every one in himself calleth Religion'. But as well as driving us into the hands of the immortal God, our darkness and our fears also drive us into the hands of a mortal God. Power operates through our darkest fears, most obviously by peddling the idea that the Invisible Powers have a 'Kingdom on Earth'.

> This seed of Religion, having been observed by many; some of those that have observed it, have been enclined thereby so to nourish, dresse, and forme it into Lawes; and to adde to it of their own invention, any opinion of the causes of future events, by which they thought they should best be able to govern others, and to make unto themselves the greatest use of their Powers (*Lev.*, XI).

In other words, one of the main mechanisms of political obedience is the fear of death at the hands of some unknown 'Invisible Agents', a fear that is all the darker for being superstitious.

In this light, security is achieved only with and through the Kingdom of God restored by Christ at the end of historical time, at which point the political Leviathan created in the book's earlier parts disappears. The frontispiece of *De Cive* here becomes just as interesting as the more famous frontispiece of *Leviathan*. The image has three parts. On one side is 'Libertas', portrayed by a forlorn looking semi-naked Indian holding a bow and arrow with other Indians in the background hunting both animals and other humans. On the other side is 'Imperium', portrayed by the figure holding the scales of justice, bearing a sword and with work and industry taking place in the background. At the top of the frontispiece, above both Imperium and Libertas, is 'Religio', an image of the Last Judgement with people heading for either the perpetual security of Heaven or the perpetual misery of Hell.

Let me flesh out some of these ideas a little more with some observations about the work of Adam Smith, as a liberal and supposedly 'anti-Hobbist' counterpoint to the 'authoritarian' tendencies found in Hobbes. The first thing to note, however, is that a century on from Hobbes and despite the emergence of the word 'insecurity' in the mid-seventeenth century, as we noted, the word has still not yet become common. The first book with 'insecurity' in the title does not appear in English until 1706 (*The insecurity of a printed overture for an act for the Church's security*) and the second book, on *Insecurity against the small-pox*, takes another 100 years to appear (in 1806). It is therefore no surprise to find that 'insecurity' does not figure in Smith's work. In neither *The Theory of Moral Sentiments* (1759) nor *The Wealth of Nations* (1776) does 'insecurity' make an appearance, despite the former book being about human morality and the latter book containing descriptions of the negative effects of the division of labour on society. 'Insecure' appears once in *The Wealth of Nations*, but only in relation to the situation of a sovereign who has lost the support of the clergy (*WN*, V.i.g). In the *Lectures on Jurisprudence*,

delivered in the early 1760s, Smith makes reference to 'security' time and again in discussions of police, liberty and sovereignty, but 'insecurity' is nowhere to be found. In contrast to this complete absence of any interest in or use of 'insecurity' on Smith's part, 'fear' is as integral to his work as it is to Hobbes.

The fact that fear is central to a thinker widely understood to be one of the leading classical liberals thinkers and defenders of capital is perhaps telling, and is far from apparent in most accounts of fear. In contrast to Hobbes, Smith makes barely an appearance in intellectual histories of fear, such as Corey Robin's *Fear: The History of a Political Idea* (2004) or Geoffrey Skoll's *Social Theory of Fear* (2010). Smith likewise rarely makes an appearance in cultural histories of fear, despite how much his main work concerning competition, work and sympathy resonates with key cultural tropes in the West. Smith barely appears in Frank Furedi's *The Culture of Fear* (2002), Joanna Bourke's *Fear: A Cultural History* (2005), Barry Glassner's *The Culture of Fear* (1999) or Marc Mulholland's *Bourgeois Liberty and the Politics of Fear* (2012). This absence is really rather strange, given the centrality of fear and, in particular, the fear of death, to Smith's political economy of liberty.

A notable feature of the account of sympathy in *The Theory of Moral Sentiments* is that it begins with and relies on an argument about sympathy with the dead. 'We sympathise even with the dead', he says, and are affected by 'that awful futurity which awaits them'.

> It is miserable, we think, to be deprived of the light of the sun; to be shut out from life and conversation; to be laid in the cold grave, a prey to corruption and the reptiles of the earth; to be no more thought of in this world, but to be obliterated, in a little time, from the affections, and almost from the memory, of their dearest friends and relations (*TMS*, I.i.1.13).

In a later chapter he comments on our sympathy for someone being oppressed by another, but this quickly turns into a discussion of death. We sympathise with the injured party and rejoice when we see them attack their adversary. And yet 'if the injured should perish in the quarrel, we not only sympathise with the real resentment of his friends and relations, but with the imaginary resentment which in fancy we lend to the dead, who is no longer capable of feeling that or any other human sentiment':

> We put ourselves in his situation, as we enter, as it were, into his body, and in our imaginations, in some measure, animate anew the deformed and mangled carcass of the slain; when we bring home in this manner his case to our own bosoms, we feel upon this, as upon many other occasions, an emotion which the person principally concerned is incapable of feeling, and which yet we feel by an illusive sympathy with him. ... We feel that resentment which we imagine he ought to feel, and which he would feel, if in his cold and lifeless body there remained any consciousness of what passes upon earth. His blood, we think, calls aloud for vengeance. The very ashes of the dead seem to be disturbed at the thought that his injuries are to pass unrevenged.

The example is telling, for it concerns a person who has been killed by another and whose very death thus demands vengeance: 'the ghosts which, superstition imagines, rise from their graves to demand vengeance upon those who brought them to an untimely end, all take their origin from this natural sympathy with the imaginary resentment of the slain' (*TMS*, II.i.2.5).

All of this leads Smith to what he claims is 'one of the most important principles in human nature', namely the fear of death. This claim completes the opening chapter of *The Theory of Moral Sentiments* and is perhaps more important than the general logic of sympathy for which the book is better known. It is important for a number of reasons. First, our fear of death generates a 'foresight of our own dissolution so terrible to us', generating a sympathy for the dead which in turn forms the foundation of all other sympathy. Second, we feel sympathy for the dead yet also recognise that death is a 'safe and quiet harbour' (*TMS*, VII.ii.1.25). The *happiness* of the dead is not affected by their being dead. Why? Because of *the profound security of their condition*. Hence we identify with the dead, but we do so in such a way that differentiates and distances ourselves from them. In particular, we *differentiate our own lack of security with the security of the dead*. When Smith says that we 'lodge' our 'own living souls in their inanimated bodies', it may well be their security we are seeking, for this is something that we ourselves cannot have (*TMS*, I.i.1.13). Third, our fear of death propels us in turn into new forms of security. 'Death ... is the king of terrors', Smith says in one of his many Hobbesian moments (*TMS*, VI.iii.7). This psychology concerning the terror of death pushes us into the hands of a power that might then appear to offer security, or at least some version of it: the sovereign power. 'The dread of death ... [is] but the great restraint upon the injustice of mankind, which, while it afflicts and mortifies the individual, guards and protects the society' (*TMS*, I.i.2.13).

Smith is on the terrain of security as both moral psychology and political strategy, but this terrain is grounded not on 'insecurity' but on the fear surrounding death. Hence, into this picture comes the other dimension of fear about which we have already said a fair amount, namely the fear of death at the hands of the state. Smith says that 'we both punish and approve of punishment, merely from a view to the general interest of society, which, we imagine, cannot otherwise be secured' (*TMS*, II.ii.3.11). For Smith as for Hobbes, it is the *terror of punishment* that lies at the heart of social order (*TMS*, II.ii.2.3; II.ii.3.7; VII.iv.17). Recall the examples just given: those who have suffered a violent death at the hands of another demand vengeance, and we sympathise with their demand. The feeling that vengeance in the form of punishment is justice lies in the fact that resentment is a feature of the general sympathy around which Smith's theory of moral sentiments is organised. We readily 'sympathise with the natural resentment of the injured, and the offender becomes the object of ... hatred and indignation' (*TMS*, II.ii.2.1). The criminal, as 'the proper object of the resentment and indignation of mankind', must therefore accept the 'vengeance and punishment' that follows (*TMS*, II.ii.2.3). Because 'punishment, is the natural consequence of resentment', so mankind will always 'approve of the violence employed to avenge the hurt' (*TMS*, II.ii.1.5), *including the punishment of death*. This punishment applies especially to those crimes that damage not a particular person but, rather, the security of the whole society. 'Of this kind are all the punishments inflicted for breaches of what is called either civil police, or military discipline'. The 'severity' of the execution of these people is 'just and proper' (*TMS*, II.ii.3.11).

## 'By the scruff of the neck'

As is probably clear, despite important differences between their work, I am treating Hobbes and Smith as exemplary thinkers on the nature of a social order driven by a 'possessive individualism', whether that possessiveness comes in the form of an aggressive and antagonistic search for glory (Hobbes) or a self-regarding but sympathetic competitiveness (Smith). A fundamental feature of such an order for both thinkers is a sovereign power that reminds us time and again of the threat of death and uses this threat to underpin the security of order. The point appears to be the need for something that *might* act as a political condition of security, which might do so because of our fear of death, while also pointing to the fact that anything we might call 'real' security is possible only in death. These visions of politics consider both the public (political) and private (psychological) sides of security but also, simultaneously, the impossibility of security other than with death. Harping back to the Christian tradition, security is still in some sense divine, but divine only by virtue of being a feeling achieved with the divine. In the meantime, all that we have is the security offered by the sovereign power. This security plays heavily on the concept that will much later become something called 'insecurity', but about which these writers have absolutely nothing to say.

All of which is a kind of historico-theological backdrop to the political problem we face and which, for a number of reasons, points to a fundamental bind, touched upon by Jean Baudrillard when he observed that 'our obsessional compulsion for security can be interpreted as a gigantic collective ascesis, an anticipation of death in life itself'. Security, he suggests, is some kind of pact devised in opposition to death, which is precisely why it has come to stand as the basis of sovereignty.[26] What then is the bind?

First, the peace and security of being in the arms of God was no doubt once highly reassuring, but we are in the rather unfortunate position of having disillusioned man so that he no longer revolves around God, but without simultaneously abolishing the conditions of that illusion. A new secular God has emerged: Security. Our liberation from a *theology* of perpetual security has been used to reinforce our belief in a *politics* of Security, in the form of a security state which likes to reassure us that it can perform the task of God all the while knowing, and knowing that we know, that such a task is impossible. This is a problem that is in turn compounded by the fact that the one thing the modern state can and does guarantee is the perpetual 'insecurity' of the capitalist order.

Second, what this tells us is that Security wants to dispossess us of our own death. This might be the very reason that the term 'terror management', a term used by psychologists to understand our 'insecurity' in relation to death (following Ernst Becker's path-breaking *Denial of Death*), is also a term that describes perfectly what takes place in security politics; 'our work has ... suddenly been recognised to be relevant to current circumstances', note the leaders in the field following the attacks on the World Trade Centre.[27] The existential 'taming of terror' in the face of death coincides with the political 'taming of terror' offered to us by the security industry as the grounds of its power. To the extent that security wants to dispossess us of our death in this way, so it allows 'insecurity' to step in and consume our thinking. Instead of developing the critique of political economy and with it the critique of security, we are instead expected to fall back on the constant refrain of 'insecurity'. But the cry of 'insecurity' is impossible to disconnect from a cry for security. Aside from anything else, this is why 'insecurity' has absolutely no purchase as a critical idea.

Third, if there is one thing that might be said about security, it is that it is a death machine. Carol Cohn, commenting on her experience of working with security intellectuals, commented that she came to see herself as 'a feminist in the house of death'.[28] Security is a system for the manufacture of corpses. *Securitas* holding the gallows in Lorenzetti's fresco now takes the form of the images on our TV screens of piles of corpses created in the name of security. From the gallows to the drone: *I am security, I hold death in my hands*. And yet surviving through the manufacture of death and thriving on the spectacle that this creates, security has an easy time insisting that what it is doing is absolutely necessary because of our purported insecurity. The terror before the abyss of death, reconstituted as a series of never-ending insecurities, is expected to be removed by a consciousness of an abstract 'Security' and then a series of particular 'security measures'. Yet all that then transpires is a terrible insecurity, and in the face of those very same measures. Security as the sublimation of death, reducing us to terror management.

'Death has us by the scruff of the neck at every moment', Montaigne once reminded us, as if we needed reminding. But he added that a person who has learned how to die has unlearned how to be a slave: 'to practice death is to practice freedom'. Paraphrasing Montaigne, we might say that genuinely practicing death might be a way of learning how not to be a slave to security, and hence might be the basis of our liberation from the jargon of insecurity. My paraphrasing here might not be so far off of the mark, at least as regards Montaigne. According to Giovanni Botero's 1588 treatise *The Greatness of Cities*, the 'multitude of thieves and murderers' in France had led to an increasing number of 'confines, boundaries, ditches, hedges and enclosures' and the employment of large numbers of 'watchmen' to oversee the security of private estates and property, yet Montaigne employed one elderly doorkeeper and, contra Hobbes's knowing reminder to us of the everyday practices that are manifestations of our fear, such as locking our doors, Montaigne often did not lock his door, sensing perhaps that allowing our fears to dominate our world would push us into a plethora of fabricated 'security measures' and distract us from learning how to die.[29] Perhaps it is security rather than death that now has us by the scruff of the neck. Perhaps it does so because we have forgotten how to die. Perhaps 'the destruction of the ideology of death would involve an explosive transvaluation of social concepts',[30] *including the concept of security*.

To the extent that security wants to take our future from us in this way, it colonises any thinking about alternative futures. The future gets appropriated by the supreme concept of bourgeois society and the security industry's myth of its own power, which is then forced to acknowledge that it cannot offer anything remotely like 'perpetual security' and, as a way of sustaining the myth, peddles instead a jargon of insecurity and terror management. Death gets buried beneath the banal and seemingly never-ending performance of security and its insecurities, but also dangled before us as evidence of security's power.

'Perhaps the whole root of our trouble, the human trouble', James Baldwin once commented, 'is that we will sacrifice all the beauty of our lives, will imprison ourselves in totems, taboos, crosses, blood sacrifices, steeples, mosques, races, armies, flags, nations, in order to deny the fact of death'.[31] Among the most powerful of these prisons is now the prison of security, before which we sacrifice both life and death. This is why every discussion about security and insecurity is always tinged by a sense of melancholy: a reminder not of what we cannot have, but of what we have lost. To be free, we must renounce security.

*Mark Neocleous is Professor of the Critique of Political Theory at Brunel University. His book* The Fabrication of Social Order: A Critical Theory of Police Power, *originally published in 2000, is to be reissued in a new edition in 2020 by Verso.*

### Notes

1. Mark Neocleous, *Critique of Security* (Edinburgh University Press/McGill-Queens University Press, 2008); *War Power, Police Power* (Edinburgh University Press, 2014); *The Fabrication of Social Order: A Critical Theory of Police Power, Revised Edition* (London: Verso, 2020).
2. Mark Neocleous, 'War as peace, peace as pacification', *Radical Philosophy* 159 (Jan/Feb 2010), 8–17; Mark Neocleous, 'Against Security', *Radical Philosophy* 100 (March/April 2000), 7–15.
3. Norbert Elias, *The Loneliness of the Dying* (1982), trans. Edmund Jephcott (Oxford: Blackwell, 1985), 88–89.
4. Michael Dillon, *Politics of Security: Towards a Political Philosophy of Continental Thought* (London: Routledge, 1996), 120, 122, 127.
5. M. J. Williams, '(In)Security Studies, Reflexive Modernisation and the Risk Society', *Cooperation and Conflict* 43:1 (2008), 66.
6. R. B. J. Walker, 'The Subject of Security', in Keith Krause and Michael C. Williams (eds), *Critical Security Studies: Concepts and Cases* (London: UCL Press, 1997), 67.
7. Dillon, *Politics*, 127.
8. The untranslatability of *securitas* is why it appears as an entry in Barbara Cassin, *Dictionary of Untranslatables: A Philosophical Lexicon* (Princeton, NJ: Princeton University Press, 2014), 936–

8. The entry by John T. Hamilton is a very short version of the much longer argument in his book *Security: Politics, Humanity, and the Philology of Care* (Princeton, NJ: Princeton University Press, 2013). Also here see Dillon, *Politics of Security*, 16, 125; J. Frederik M. Arends, 'From Homer to Hobbes and Beyond – Aspects of "Security" in the European Tradition', in *Globalisation and Environmental Challenges: Reconceptualising Security in the 21st Century*, eds. Hans Günter Brauch et. al. (Berlin: Springer, 2008), 263–77.

9. I have adjusted the translation slightly, on the grounds that the translator renders *securitas* as 'freedom from care'. See Cicero, *De Officiis*, trans. Walter Miller (London: Heinemann, 1913).

10. Cicero does refer to statesmen doing well to also possess *securitas*, but this is still in reference to a calm soul: 'Statesmen too, no less than philosophers … should carry with them that greatness of spirit and indifference to outward circumstances to which I so often refer, together with a calmness of soul and security [*tranquillitas animi atque securitas*], if they are to be free from worries' (Cicero, *De Officiis*, Bk. I, Para 72). Hamilton, *Security*, 59.

11. Hamilton, *Security*, 58–59, 186.

12. Erika Manders, *Coining Images of Power: Patterns in the Representation of Roman Emperors on Imperial Coinage, A.D. 193-284* (Leiden: Brill, 2012), 205–11.

13. The standard English translation of *City of God* by Henry Bettenso (Penguin, 1972) has 'serenity' not security (864), but the original Latin is '*securitas*'.

14. Edwin Sandys, 'The Eleventh Sermon' (1585), in *The Sermons of Edwin Sandys* (Cambridge: Cambridge University Press, 1842), 210–12.

15. John Downame, *The Christian Warfare. Wherein is first generally shewed the malice, power and politike stratagems of the spirituall enemies of our salvation, etc.* (London, 1604).

16. The text is *Sermon XII* of *Thrēnoikos: The House of Mourning, Furnished with Directions For, Preparations To, Meditations Of, Consolations At, the Hour of Death: Delivered in LVI Sermons* (London: John Williams, 1672), 143–58.

17. Hamilton, *Security*, 63–4, 137.

18. William M. Bowsky, *A Medieval Italian Commune: Siena Under the Nine, 1287-1355* (Berkeley, CA: University of California Press, 1981), 283.

19. See, respectively, Nicolai Rubinstein, 'Political Ideas in Sienese Art: The Frescoes by Ambrogio Lorenzetti and Taddeo di Bartolo in the Palazzo Pubblico', *Journal of the Warburg and Courtauld Institutes* 21 (1958), 179–207, and two essays by Quentin Skinner: 'Ambrogio Lorenzetti: The Artist as Political Philosopher', *Proceedings of the British Academy* 72 (1987), 1–56, and 'Ambrogio Lorenzetti's Buon Governo Frescoes: Two Old Questions, Two New Answers', *Journal of the Warburg and Courtauld Institutes* 62 (1999), 1–28. Skinner's essays are reprinted in slightly altered form in *Visions of Politics, Vol. 2: Renaissance Virtues* (Cambridge: Cambridge University Press, 2002).

20. Uta Feldges-Henning, 'The Pictorial Programme of the Sala della Pace: A New Interpretation', *Journal of the Warburg and Courtauld Institutes* 35 (1972), 145–162; Jack M. Greenstein, 'The Vision of Peace: Meaning and Representation in Ambrogio Lorenzetti's *Sala Della Pace* Cityscapes', *Art History* 11:4 (1988), 492–510; Gerrit Jasper Schenk, 'Human Security in the Renaissance? *Securitas*, Infrastructure, Collective Goods and Natural Hazards in Tuscany and the Upper Rhine Valley', *Historical Social Research* 35:4, (2010), 209–33; Hamilton, *Security*, 138–46, 152–3.

21. Bowsky, *Medieval*, 120.

22. Jef Huysmans, *The Politics of Insecurity: Fear, Migration and Asylum in the EU* (Abingdon, Oxon: Routledge, 2006), 7.

23. Jacques Derrida, *The Death Penalty, Vol. 1* (2012), trans. Peggy Kamuf (Chicago: University of Chicago Press, 2014), 23.

24. Georg Christoph Lichtenberg, *The Waste Books* (1765-99), trans. R. J. Hollingdale (New York: New York Review of Books, 2000), Notebook L, 1796-99, No. 15. Compare the observation of Gregory Zilboorg: 'we like to read about executions. …What I would like to point out here is the less obvious unconscious reaction of egocentric self-delight which could be expressed by the exclamation: "It is not I who was executed last night"'. Gregory Zilboorg, 'Fear of Death', *The Psychoanalytic Quarterly* 12:4 (1943), 469.

25. See Mark Neocleous, *The Universal Adversary: Security, Capital, and 'The Enemies of All Mankind'* (Abingdon, Oxon: Routledge, 2016).

26. Jean Baudrillard, *Symbolic Exchange and Death* (1976), trans. Iain Hamilton Grant (London: Sage, 1993), 178. Also see Ernst Becker, *The Denial of Death* (New York: Free Press, 1973); Zygmunt Bauman, *Mortality, Immortality and Other Life Strategies* (Stanford, CA: Stanford University Press, 1992); Jeff Huysmans, 'Security! What Do You Mean? From Concept to Thick Signifier', *European Journal of International Relations* 4:2 (1998), 235–56.

27. Tom Pyszczynski, Sheldon Solomon and Jeff Greenberg, *In the Wake of 9/11: The Psychology of Terror* (Washington, DC: American Psychological Association, 2002), 8. For the popularisation, see Sheldon Solomon, Jeff Greenberg and Tom Pyszczynski, *The Worm at the Core: On the Role of Death in Life* (London: Penguin, 2016). Their starting point is Becker, *Denial*, 145.

28. Carol Cohn, 'Sex and Death in the Rational World of Defense Intellectuals', *Signs: Journal of Women in Culture and Society* 12:4 (1987), 691.

29. Montaigne, 'To Philosophise is to Learn how to Die', in *The Complete Essays*, trans. M. A. Screech (London: Penguin Books, 1987), 89–108; Giovanni Botero, *A Treatise Concerning the Causes of the Magnificency and Greatness of Cities* (1588), trans. Robert Peterson, in Giovanni Botero, *The Reason of State* and *The Greatness of Cities* (London: Routledge, 1956), 279.

30. Herbert Marcuse, 'The Ideology of Death' (1959), in *Philosophy, Psychoanalysis and Emancipation: Collected Papers of Herbert Marcuse, Vol 5*, ed. Douglas Kellner and Clayton Pierce (London: Routledge, 2011), 128.

31. James Baldwin, *The Fire Next Time* (London: Penguin Books, 1963), 79.

# The revival of Hegelian Marxism
## On Martin Hägglund's *This Life*
Nathan Brown

When a notable philosopher, having established a reputation for rigorous argumentation and scholarship, directs a major new book toward a popular audience, a certain skepticism may be forgiven among those familiar with the earlier work. However welcome an accessible style may be, popular address too often gives way to the *popularisation* of philosophical concepts and problems with results that are seldom adequate to the complexity of their history and significance. The general reader receives a bowdlerisation of conceptual difficulties, while the price of public reception is inconsequence at the level of philosophical intervention, and the demands of legibility offer an excuse for setting aside abstruse debates and technical details.

Martin Hägglund's third book, *This Life: Secular Faith and Spiritual Freedom*, may be met with varieties of such skepticism among seasoned readers of Marx, Hegel, Heidegger – and of the traditions from which their work emerges and to which it gives rise. But in fact *This Life* is a rare example philosophical writing that achieves conceptual rigour in the medium of a style open to anyone, regardless of academic training or theoretical persuasion, who wants to think about how life ought to be lived and about what we must do, collectively, to make it livable in common.* First and foremost, this is a book that revives and reconfigures an argument for the unity of Karl Marx's thought across the early and late phases of his career. Hägglund's arguments force a reconsideration of how concepts of freedom and equality traverse and ground Marx's entire oeuvre, as well as a reconsideration of how the critique of *both* religion and capitalism co-determine Marx's theoretical accomplishment. That Hägglund has been able to carry out this project with such accessible clarity is so unusual as to be disorienting.

Hägglund's book unfolds in two parts: the first articulating a concept of 'secular faith' as a condition of intelligibility for any form of care; the second articulating a concept of 'spiritual freedom' that demands for its actualisation the overcoming of capitalism and the determination of value in terms of socially available free time. The critique of religion in the first half of the book will be broadly familiar to readers of Hägglund's *Radical Atheism* (2008): across three chapters engaging most substantially with C.S. Lewis, Charles Taylor, Sören Kierkegaard, Saint Augustine and Karl Ove Knausgaard, Hägglund argues that the religious orientation of desire toward eternal life – in itself incompatible with care for *this* life – in fact obscures an implicit commitment to a secular form of faith grounding any and all commitments to the projects of finite existence. Defining as religious 'any ideal of being absolved from the pain of loss' (47) (here briefly engaging such philosophical ideals as Spinoza's *beatitude* and Nietzsche's *amor fati*), Hägglund seeks to show that the condition of intelligibility for the forms of finite care these frameworks also avow is a commitment to the fragility of mortal life incompatible with the religious logic of eternity and dependent upon the ineliminable finitude of time. He thus offers an immanent critique of religious appeals to the primacy of eternal life as grounded upon and inextricable from a more fundamental logic of constitutively finite time, a logic such appeals both disavow and rely upon for their ethics of care. I will return briefly to Hägglund's critique of religion toward the conclusion of this review –

---

* Martin Hägglund, *This Life: Secular Faith and Spiritual Freedom* (New York: Pantheon Books, 2019). 464pp., $29.95 hb., 978 1 10187 040 2. Subsequent references are given in the text.

to its relation to Hägglund's thinking of value and its consequences for his understanding of the unity of Marx's work. For the most part, however, I will leave readers to their own appraisal of this aspect of the book, focusing my own attention upon its second half, which I view as more theoretically and practically consequential.

Here, Hägglund applies his refined grasp of the existential stakes of temporal finitude to a breathtaking reconstruction of Marx as a thinker of freedom, re-grounding the conceptual priority of time and value within his critique of political economy. Indeed, the reading of Marx pursued in the second half of *This Life* may be the most important revival of Hegelian Marxism since Louis Althusser's critique of that orientation in the 1950s and '60s. In this respect, the book's importance lies in Hägglund's engagement with American readings of Hegel that have transformed the reception of his philosophy since the 1980s, especially those by Robert Pippin and Robert Brandom, which foreground Hegel's thinking of conditions of conceptual intelligibility, discursive normativity and social recognition. However one views these readings of Hegel, it has become necessary to take a position on their intervention. *This Life* is the first book to produce a major reading of Marx from a perspective systematically informed by this work, and to show how our understanding of both Marx and Hegel might be transformed by such an encounter. But to grasp the stakes of this move, we have to further complicate its framework by recognising that Hägglund's contemporary Hegelian Marxism is also saturated by his engagement with Heidegger's existential analytic.

## Spiritual and natural freedom

For the most part this engagement with Heidegger is implicit. Heidegger's name appears only twice in the book's endnotes, but the existential analytic is inextricable from Hägglund's understanding of finitude, and it is thus essential to his reading of Marx as a thinker of the relation between freedom and finite time. We must consider how Hägglund's Hegelian reading of Marx is transformed by the passage of Hegel through Heidegger that he performs. We can then consider what sort of *historical materialism* that transformation produces.

We see an implicit synthesis of these philosophical resources in the distinction between natural and spiritual freedom that opens the second half of *This Life*. Here Hägglund develops a distinction between human beings and other animals that, he notes, is neither biological nor anthropological. Rather, his account is grounded in the intelligibility of our specific relation to normative commitments. All animals are possessed of 'natural freedom' insofar as they are capable of self-movement and self-determination, and they are agents *for which* 'things appear *as* nourishing or damaging, appealing or threatening' (174). We could say that animals not only relate to an event *in itself*, as something that happens, but also *for themselves*, as something that matters to a living being in light of its own ends. Indeed, other animals are capable of norm-governed behaviour, insofar as they may acquire learned behaviours that are not instinctually innate. Thus, for Hägglund, what distinguishes the 'spiritual freedom' of human beings from the 'natural freedom' of other animals is not simply the distinction between norms and instincts, but rather our capacity to question, challenge and transform the norms to which we hold ourselves accountable (176). We are *intelligible* as spiritually free beings – it makes sense to understand ourselves in such terms – insofar as the validity of norms is always implicitly and potentially at issue for us, insofar as *who we should be* and *what we should do* can always be questioned and contested in a manner inseparable from our social practices and institutions.

Now this is already a theory of spiritual freedom that fuses Hegelian and Heideggerian concerns. We find in normative/pragmatic readings of Hegel an account of *Geist* conceiving of self-consciousness, sociality and collective reason in terms of conceptual, discursive and intersubjective *commitments* that depend upon structures of mutual recognition for their actuality. Moreover, these readings of Hegel emphasise his understanding of modernity as that epoch in which the intersubjective recognition of normative commitments, and the institutions in which they are actualised, become *in principle* open to a 'space of reasons' unbounded by the absolutism of divine law or sovereign authority. Hägglund builds upon this approach to Hegel through a theory of 'secular faith' as commitment to normative ideals that are *ungrounded* by any appeal to absolute authority, and of 'spiritual freedom' as commitment to the unbounded contingency of such norms, insofar as they must in principle remain open to questioning, contention, transformation. Spir-

itual freedom is distinct from natural freedom insofar as 'there is no natural way for us to be and no species requirements that can exhaustively determine the principles in light of which we act' (177). Thus commitments must be *sustained* insofar as they are never finally and fully achieved but rather finite and fragile; they must be held in the face of doubt, uncertainty and ineliminable anxiety.

It is this essential *finitude* of spiritual freedom – of the structures of collective recognition and existential commitment it entails – that renders Hägglund's account so powerfully consonant with Heidegger's existential analytic. We are *questioning* beings for whom the possibilities of our existence are constantly at issue, and we are thrown into a world whose history we can only belatedly take up, while our finitude projects us toward the anticipation of a death that may interrupt our commitments. In both the first and second half of his book, Hägglund emphasises that the finitude, fragility and anxiety of our temporal existence is a condition of intelligibility for any form of *care*, for any establishment of an order of priorities, any urgency of our actions, any effort to bring our projects to fruition or make our commitments matter. Hägglund's understanding of the relation between care and finite time is routed through Christine Korsgaard's theory of practical identities (188) and through Sebastian Rödl's work on self-consciousness and first-person perspective (194), but more fundamentally it is grounded in Heidegger's understanding of temporality as the meaning of care and in Heidegger's profound analysis of temporal structures such as historicity, thrownness, anticipation and resoluteness. We are spiritually free beings *because* our being-toward-death puts the finitude of our existence in question for us, such that what we ought to do with our time is never given but constantly at issue among possibilities that are taken up or left aside, commitments that may be held or broken.

In a note at the end of his Introduction, Hägglund

acknowledges that 'the most important sources for my thinking regarding freedom, finitude, and temporality are Hegel's *Phenomenology of Spirit* (as well as his *Science of Logic*) and Heidegger's *Being and Time*.' He holds 'that if we pursue the core insights of Hegel and Heidegger in the right way, we will grasp why their notions of freedom are mutually required' (394). Hägglund shows that we can do so by understanding *freedom* in terms of the relation between *spirit* and *existence* – or more precisely, between *Geist* and *Dasein*. Note that 'the self', for Heidegger, is not *prior* to care. On the contrary, 'the structure of care, conceived in full, includes the phenomenon of selfhood.'[1] It is our existence – our exteriority to ourselves, thrown into the world and riven by the temporality of anticipation – that makes temporality the meaning of care and grounds our being in *possibility*; and this exteriority of *what we are* throws us also into the situation that Hägglund gleans from Hegel: that our freedom is only actualised 'through our mutual recognition of one another as essentially social, historical, material, and finite beings' (36).

But this passage of freedom through the crux of *Geist* and *Dasein* would be empty without its passage through Marx, in whose work Hägglund finds 'the greatest resources for developing a secular notion of freedom' (212). For how can any serious reader of Marx traverse arguments concerning collective, institutionally objective reason in normative-pragmatic readings of Hegel without pondering the historical impossibility of an 'I that is We and a We that is I' within the structural conditions of capitalist wage labour? There can be no *Spirit of Trust*, to cite the title of Robert Brandom's major book on Hegel,[2] as long as all social wealth depends upon the extraction of surplus value from surplus labour time, a dependency that deeply structures our technological capacities and political institutions. *This Life* rescues normative-pragmatic readings of Hegel from their ideological dereliction by showing how their own conditions of intelligibility depend upon a critique of capitalism which they ignore, yet which Marx carries out in a manner that makes explicit the normative commitments liberal political philosophy would *have* to recognise to be consistent with its principles. Hägglund's immanent critique of liberalism is aimed at such figures as Keynes, Rawls and Piketty, who fail to recognise that the capitalist measure of value – socially necessary labour time –

renders structurally impossible a redistribution of social wealth that would enable the *actual* freedom of social subjects who require material resources (not only political rights) to determine, take up and enact existential possibilities. However, this critique applies also to the political liberalism of Hegelians like Pippin, Brandom and Pinkard, who do not confront the political and historical consequences of the understanding of Hegel they have helped to make legible. The institution of *ideals* of freedom and equality in democratic forms of political organisation may be an achievement of modernity but, as Hägglund argues, 'capitalism and actual democracy are incompatible' (271), since capitalism entails an objective, practical commitment to inequality. While the *distribution* of wealth may be at issue in modern democratic politics, the very production of that wealth relies upon a form of value and a system of wage labour that structurally *necessitate* unequal social relations that are in contradiction with the equal distribution of practical freedom. Like Jurgen Habermas, Pippin, Brandom and Pinkard at least implicitly understand modernity as an unfinished project. The same may be true of Hägglund, and indeed of Marx. But Hägglund follows Marx in thinking through the disarticulation of capitalism and modernity that is a minimal condition of possibility for the actualisation of such ideals as freedom and equality. He thus displaces the self-contradictory political horizon of normative-pragmatic readings of Hegel from which he also sets out.

Similarly, Hägglund participates in a lineage of deconstructive readings of Heidegger that have sought to delimit and displace Heidegger's reactionary politics while retaining key insights of the existential analytic. Jacques Derrida, Philippe Lacoue-Labarthe and Jean-Luc Nancy have each made valuable contributions to this project – including Nancy's effort in 'Of Being Singular Plural' to reframe the existential analytic through the priority of *Mitsein*, being-with, and on that basis to structure ontological reflection through the conceptual relation of singularity and plurality.[3] But in order to make these ontological reflections more than an evocation of ethical desiderata, Nancy would have to engage with the structural determinations of capitalism analysed by Marx, which foreclose the actualisation and recognition of singular plurality in the historical world. The challenge Hägglund takes up is to construct a coherent, systematic approach to Marx's critique of capital which is grounded in the core categories of the existential analytic: finitude, temporality, anxiety and care. This is what his deconstructive predecessors were unable to achieve, despite the interpretive and rhetorical brilliance of Derrida's *Specters of Marx*.[4] Indeed, this is also a task that had remained latent in Hägglund's earlier book on Derrida, where he does not confront the problem of how a commitment to 'radical democracy' is in contradiction with the historical actuality of capitalism. *This Life* realises the most important task of deconstructive engagements with Heidegger: to coherently articulate the compatibility of Heidegger's existential analytic with Marx's analysis of the relation between time and value. By doing so, Hägglund re-grounds the question of the political implications of the existential analytic – and that is an intervention in intellectual history of the first order.

So, while *This Life* mobilises Hegel and Heidegger toward an integral reading of the early and late Marx, it also deploys Marx's critique of political economy to expose and go beyond the limitations of Hägglund's Hegelian and Heideggerian sources. Let me now specify the implications of this double movement with respect to Althusser's theory of the epistemological break between the early and late Marx, and his associated critique of Hegelian Marxism. Althusser sharply divides Marx's theories of species being and alienation in his 1844 Manuscripts from his structural critique of political economy in *Capital*. In particular, he rejects all suppositions of a human essence, grounded in labour, *from which* man has become alienated under capitalist relations of production. Without mentioning Althusser directly, Hägglund's reading of Marx sets out from a critique of this position. He emphasises that for Marx 'the species-being of the human is precisely that we have no given nature or essence' (213), and he determines to 'show that there is no opposition between the appeal to "species-being" in the young Marx and the method of historical materialism in his mature work' (214). According to Hägglund, 'the key is to grasp that neither life nor species-being should primarily be understood in biological or anthropological terms' (214). While acknowledging that 'Marx himself tends to invite such a reading' (214), Hägglund notes that Marx's concepts can be deepened by grounding them in the distinction between natural and spiritual life he develops.

Again, this distinction is in turn grounded in Hägglund's synthesis of Hegel and Heidegger: it is because we are finite beings whose commitments are self-consciously subject to an economy of time that we not only follow normative behaviours to reproduce our existence but also question and justify the very norms to which we commit the time of our lives. It is the capacity to interrogate and justify the fundamental question of how *time* is spent from which proletarians are 'alienated' under capitalist relations of production – and from which we were differently divided by pre-capitalist social relations. Thus Marx's mature critique of capital is an exposition of the historically specific manner in which capitalism contradicts our capacity to question and transform our normative commitments, since we are structurally committed to inequality, whether we like it or not, through the extraction of surplus value from surplus labour time.

Hägglund thus constructs a formal, logical expressivist theory of social existence – integrally bound up with the economy of time – that places the concept of freedom back at the centre of Marx's mature theory. Although my own understanding of Marx has been strongly influenced by Althusser's critique of Marxist humanism, and although I tend to view the foregrounding of political ideals such as 'freedom' and 'equality' as idealist deviations from Marx's understanding of revolution in terms of class conflict, I must admit that I find Hägglund's reconstruction of the consistency of Marx's corpus highly persuasive, and it has forced me to reevaluate my own theoretical positions. His recuperation of the concept of alienation does not entail an ideological 'humanism' but rather a theoretically precise exposition of exactly why and how a commitment to freedom is implicit throughout Marx's structural critique of capitalism, and of how capitalism is in contradiction with the political ideals of modernity.

## Capitalism, time and history

If it is the relation between *time* and *freedom* that is at the core of Hägglund's reading of Marx, my critical question is whether his account of the *history* of capitalism is sufficiently robust to account for the collective conditions of possibility for overcoming it. Can Hägglund's account allow us to understand the historically mediated relation between *freedom* and *necessity* as it bears upon the theory of revolution? When considering the dialectical relation between freedom and necessity as it pertains to political struggle, it is typical to cite Marx's recognition that 'men make their own history, but not they do not make it just as they please; they do not make it under circumstances chosen by themselves, but under circumstances directly encountered, given and transmitted by the past.'[5] Note that this recognition is also at the core of Heidegger's thinking: we are thrown into this world, and our freedom to take up the possibilities of our existence is constrained by historical conditions we cannot choose. Marx offers an analysis of exactly how these historical possibilities are structured by capitalism, however else they make be structured. That structure is in one sense invariant; it is always grounded in the determination of value by socially necessary labour time, and the extraction of surplus value from surplus labour time. But the way in which that extraction proceeds, the particular intertwining of forces of production and relations of production upon which it depends, is historically variable. Thus we require, to understand the relation between freedom and necessity under capitalism, a precise understanding of how the structure of capitalism changes over time, though the value form is invariant. This relation between invariance and structural alteration changes the conditions of possibility for overcoming the capitalist measure of value.

In 'Contradiction and Overdetermination', Althusser makes an essential and permanent contribution to such understanding.[6] He shows that historical conditions of revolutionary possibility are *overdetermined*, beyond the level of individual wills, through the sharpening of economic contradictions by a multiplicity of other social contradictions that fuse into a 'ruptural unity'. Thus he obviates any recourse to economic determinism while also avoiding the idealism of voluntarist politics. That is, he theorises the historical mediation of freedom and necessity without recourse to historical determinism. But in addition to such a theory of overdetermined contradiction, Marxism also requires a theory of how the economic structure of capitalism itself changes over time, and of how these changes alter conditions of revolutionary possibility. Hägglund takes a strong position on a particular Marxist debate concerning this question, which bears upon crisis theory. Quite rightly, he notes that while 'many avowed Marxists continue to hinge their critique of capitalism on the prediction of a "terminal crisis" ... such a critique of capitalism is deeply misguided' (293).

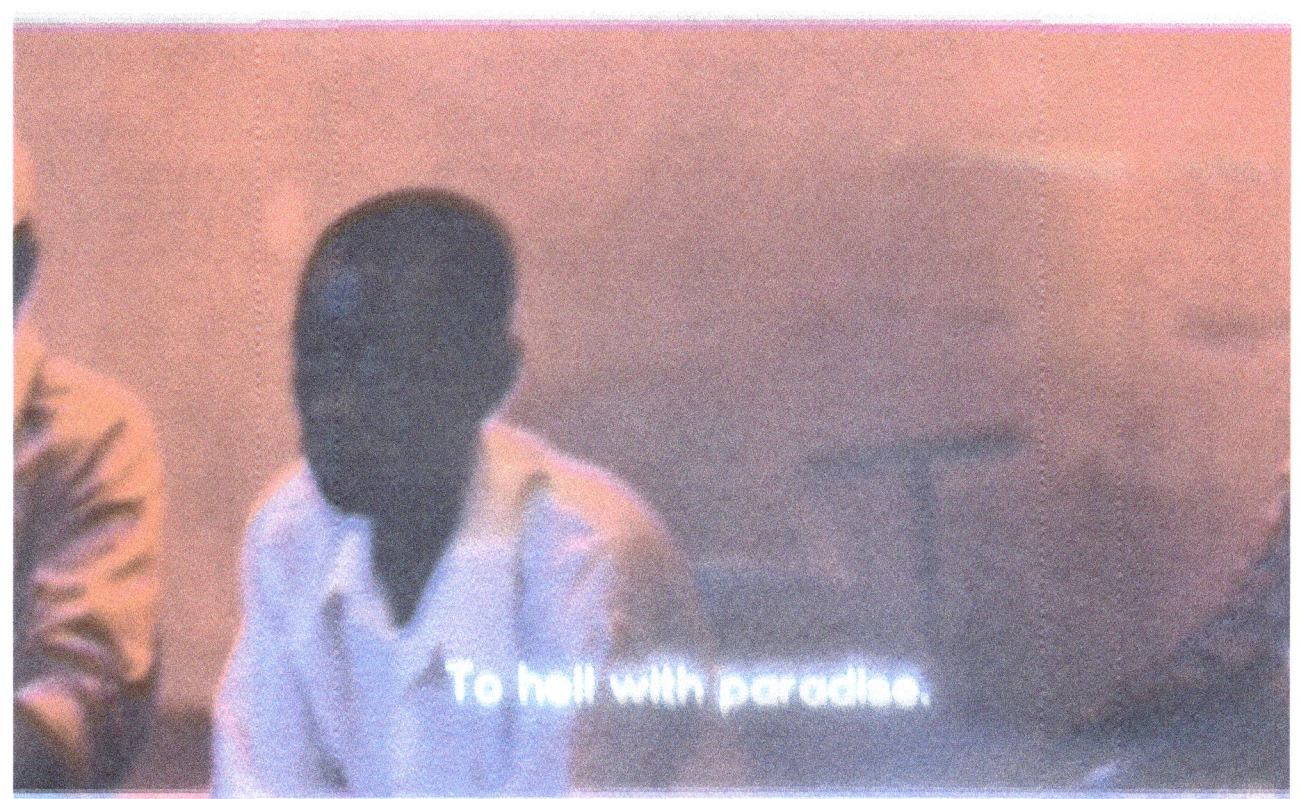

In rejecting that position, Hägglund implicitly agrees with Althusser: while the economy may condition class conflict 'in the last instance', the lonely hour of the last instance never comes. Hägglund argues that 'it is a grave mistake to think that the tendency toward crises heralds the end of capitalism', since 'crises are essential to cycles of capitalist accumulation and necessary for the continued production of capital wealth.' In this sense, crises are 'a condition of possibility for capitalism as a system to reproduce itself' (293). And this is true: the destruction of accumulated capital by crises opens new opportunities for accumulation such that new cycles of growth can begin.

But arriving at a correct position on the relation between crisis and revolution requires engaging with a second sense of the term 'secular', which may designate not only the worldly and temporal rather than the religious and eternal, but also refer to long periods of historical time, rather than shorter cycles. One cannot *only* consider crises in terms of cyclical phenomena of growth, destruction and renewed growth; one must also consider the *secular* crisis of accumulation with which the history of capitalism is tendentially bound up. Crises are different. And periods of renewed growth following crises are not equally robust or durable. Why? What is it that alters the conditions of possibility for capitalist accumulation in a *secular* rather than *cyclical* fashion, thus traversing and altering cycles of destruction and growth?

The crash of 1929 was followed by a massive period of growth in the real economy from the Second World War through the 1960s. But as Robert Brenner has shown, the crash of 1973 did not result in a such a period of dynamic growth;[7] rather, it has been followed by over forty years of tendentially declining profit rates, attended by a series of speculative bubbles. The reason is that there is indeed a *secular* decline in the capacity to extract relative surplus value through increasing productivity and increased surplus labour time, and this secular decline leads to increasingly fragile efforts to revive economic growth through financial speculation in contradiction with conditions of the real economy. Moreover, measures to avert catastrophic climate change are indeed in contradiction with the priority of profit seeking, and this is a *secular* crisis – a long term outcome of capitalist production – that the capitalist measure of value may not allow us to avert. These are the conditions under which history will be made in the twenty-first century, one way or another. That certainly does not mean that capitalism will abolish itself. But we need to differentiate capitalist crises; we need to periodise their structural differences according to secular tendencies as well as cyclical phenomena; and we need to understand the conditions of political possibility those differences entail.

In order to think through the conjunctural specificity of revolutionary struggle in the twenty-first century, Hägglund would need to expand his engagement with the tradition of Western Marxism, along with the history and present development of communist theory, beyond the parameters of *This Life*, in which such engagement is primarily polemical. While it may be true that 'many avowed Marxists continue to hinge their critique of capitalism on the prediction of a "terminal crisis"' (293), there are also avowed Marxists who have a complex, dialectical understanding of the relationship between crisis and revolutionary struggle, class composition and the changing structure of surplus value extraction, the diminishing returns of valorisation given the tendency of the rate of profit to fall, and the impact of climate change upon the geography of class conflict.

While he engages with and differentiates his position from Moishe Postone's reading of Marx, Hägglund's polemical characterisations of what Marxists have *not* done sometimes reveal a brusque indifference to the existing literature. Pointing out that 'everything in Marx's critique of capitalism stands or falls on his analysis of the concept of value', Hägglund notes that 'regarding this issue – the most seminal in all his work – Marxists have generally failed Marx' (252). That may *generally* be true (many Marxists have indeed accepted the error of attributing a 'labour theory of value' to Marx, with consequential misprisions), but this claim too easily assimilates the particular to the general, since there are certainly traditions which have not overlooked the primacy of value in Marx's theory. Michael Heinrich and David Harvey emphasise this point from different theoretical positions, while we have at our disposal Diane Elson's collection *Value: The Representation of Labour in Capitalism*, or the edited volume *Marxism and the Critique of Value*, along with the larger traditions of *Wertkritik* and *Neue Marx-Lektüre*, which Hägglund is equipped to assimilate in German.[8] Why not acknowledge these traditions and contemporary interlocutors, taking a position alongside and in distinction from them?

Hägglund's book does indeed make a fundamental contribution to considerations of Marx's theory of value. Arguing that value must be measured in terms of socially available free time (rather than socially necessary labour time) in order to be compatible with the actualisation of collective freedom, Hägglund grounds this claim in a fundamental reconstruction of temporal economy *in general*, thus opening what he calls "a fourth level of analysis" of value addressed to understanding "finite lifetime as the originary measure of value" (218-220). Drawing together the two halves of *This Life*, Hägglund brings to light the fundamental normative commitments of Marx's oeuvre in a manner overlooked by approaches that take these for granted. At issue is the question of *how* freedom is related to time, and *why* the capitalist measure of value is an inversion of the most basic dimension of human existence: the constitutive bond between possibility, time, and freedom that *is* value. For many Marxists, such a level of analysis may seem superfluous, since the critique of exploitation suffices to secure the normative grounds of the critique of capitalism. Yet Hägglund shows how much is at stake in understanding precisely why and how *temporal finitude* is at the very crux of Marx's work: with unprecedented clarity, his analysis shows that this is the dimension linking the early and late phases of Marx's career, and linking as well his critique of capitalism to his critique of religion.

However, Hägglund's critique of the religious *logic* or *desire* for eternity would be usefully informed by engagements with the *politics* of religion, including work by Talal Assad, Saba Mahmood, S. Sayyid, and Alberto Toscano.[9] For even if one agrees with his arguments (or Marx's) on this point, what is one to *do* with Hägglund's critique of religion – at the level of collective political practice? While one may mobilise the Marxist critique of capitalism toward an anti-capitalist and non-reformist politics, the practical suppression of religious traditions was, in my view, among the major errors of actually existing socialism in the twentieth century. Hägglund does not advocate any such practical suppression, and his political thinking would be incompatible with such measures. But nor does he address that history, and the question remains: what is the relation between the imperative to overcome capitalism in order to actualise ideals of freedom and equality and the practical *consequences* of the rationalist critique of religion carried out by Hägglund, or indeed by Marx? This is a question that bears upon a historical materialist perspective on religion. Here the relation between theory and practice is far more difficult to conceive, even from the side of theory, than imperatives to displace wage labour, collectivise the means of production, and reconceive the measure of value. This is particularly true under the present conditions of global politics, and not least the War on Terror. Like Marx, Hägglund views religion as ideology, and his implicit position would seem to be that it will eventually wither away under the lived conditions of democratic socialism. I don't think that's true.

In any case, these are instances (the need for a more precise reckoning with other approaches to the critique of value, or the politics of religion) in which the accessible style of Hägglund's volume may impede its theoretical articulation. Engagement with such work would likely tangle the clarity and the political stakes of Hägglund's account, but it might also have obviated objections among those cognisant of debates the book leaves aside. Hägglund's book has already received an extraordinary reception. But it will also be subject to superficial dismissals by radicals because it is too liberal, and by liberals because it is too radical. It will be praised by opponents of religion insensible to the parochialism of their politics, and it may be written off by opponents of radical enlightenment eager to disavow the real stakes of universalism. In further elaborating the stakes of his work, I would urge Hägglund to ignore the unproductive antinomy of such responses, and focus instead on developing the historical dimension of his theory through deeper engagements with Marxist economic historians (like Robert Brenner), thinkers of value (like Diane Elson and Michael Heinrich), theorists of communist revolution (like *Théorie Communiste*), and accounts of the politics of religion that mount a critique of secularism on historical and anthropological grounds. That would involve engaging more closely with positions that may not be directly opposed to his own, but both proximate and tangential to it. Doing so would allow Hägglund to bring the mediation of freedom and necessity to bear upon historical contradiction, and thus supplement his theory of time, finitude and freedom with a more robust theory of historical determination.

*Nathan Brown is Director of the Centre for Expanded Poetics at Concordia University in Canada, and author of* The Limits of Fabrication: Materials Science and Materialist Poetics *(2017).*

**Notes**

1. Martin Heidegger, *Being and Time*, trans. Joan Stambaugh (Albany: SUNY Press, 2010), 309.
2. Robert Brandom, *A Spirit of Trust: A Reading of Hegel's Phenomenology* (Cambridge, MA: Harvard University Press, 2019).
3. Jean-Luc Nancy, 'Of Being Singular Plural', in *Being Singular Plural*, trans. Robert D. Richardson and Anne E. O'Byrne (Palo Alto: Stanford University Press, 2000), 1–100.
4. Jacques Derrida, *Spectres of Marx*, trans. Peggy Kamuf (London: Routledge, 1994).
5. Karl Marx, *The 18th Brumaire of Louis Bonaparte* (New York: International Publishers, 1963), 15.
6. Louis Althusser, 'Contradiction and Overdetermination', in *For Marx*, trans. Ben Brewster (London: Verso, 2005), 87–128.
7. Robert Brenner, *The Economics of Global Turbulence* (London: Verso, 2006).
8. See Michael Heinrich, *An Introduction to the Three Volumes of Karl Marx's Capital*, trans. Alexander Locasio (New York: Monthly Review Press, 2012); David Harvey, *A Companion to Marx's Capital: The Complete Edition* (London: Verso, 2018); Diane Elson, ed., *Value: The Representation of Labour in Capitalism* (London: Verso, 2015); Neil Larson, Mathias Nilges, et al., eds, *Marxism and the Critique of Value* (Chicago: MCM' Publishing, 2014). See also Riccardo Bellofiore and Tommaso Redolfi Riva, 'The Neue Marx-Lektüre: Putting the Critique of Political Economy back into the Critique of Society', *Radical Philosophy* 189 (Jan-Feb 2015), 24–36.
9. See Talal Assad, *Formations of the Secular: Christianity, Islam, and Modernity* (Palo Alto: Stanford University Press, 2003); Saba Mahmood, *The Politics of Piety: The Islamic Revival and the Feminist Subject* (Princeton: Princeton University Press, 2011); S. Sayyid, *A Fundamental Fear: Eurocentrism and the Emergence of Islamism* (New York: Zed Books, 2015); Alberto Toscano, *Fanaticism: On the Uses of an Idea* (London: Verso, 2010). In particular, see Toscano's important chapter on Marx's critique of religion, 'The Clash of Abstractions: Revisiting Marx on Religion', 172–202.

# On the origins of Marx's general intellect

Matteo Pasquinelli

The general intellect of the whole community, male and female, is stunted or perverted in infancy, or more commonly both, by keeping from women the knowledge possessed by men. … The only and the simple remedy for the evils arising from these almost universal institutions of the domestic slavery of one half the human race, is utterly to eradicate them. Give men and women equal civil and political rights.

   William Thompson, *An Inquiry Into the Principles of the Distribution of Wealth*, London, 1824.

It is nearly twenty years since the first impulse was given to the general intellect of this country, by the introduction of a new mechanical system for teaching reading and writing, by cheaper and more efficacious methods than those previously in use. … The public mind has infinitely advanced: in despite of all the sneers at the phrase of the 'march of intellect', the fact is undeniable, that the general intellect of the country has greatly progressed. And one of the first fruits of extended intelligence has been the conviction, now fast becoming universal, that our system of law, so far from being the best in the world, is an exceedingly bad one; and stands in the most pressing need of revision and reform.

                           *The London Magazine*, 1828.

The development of fixed capital indicates to what degree general social knowledge has become a *direct force of production*, and to what degree, hence, the conditions of the process of social life itself have come under the control of the general intellect and been transformed in accordance with it.

                               Karl Marx, *Grundrisse*, 1858.

An 1828 caricature by cartoonist William Heath from the series 'March of Intellect' depicts a giant automaton advancing with long strides and holding a broom to sweep away a dusty mass of clerks, clergy and bureaucrats, representing figures of the old order and obsolete laws.[1] The automaton's belly is a steam engine, its head is made of books of history, philosophy and (importantly) mechanics. Its crown reads 'London University'. In the background the goddess of justice lies in ruins summoning the automaton: 'Oh Come and Deliver Me!!!' Upon closer observation, the caricature appears to ridicule the belief that the technologies of industrial automation (already looking like robots) might become a true agent of political change and social emancipation under the command of public education. Heath's series of satirical engravings was originally commissioned by the Tories to voice their sarcasm regarding a potential democratisation of knowledge and technology across all classes. Nonetheless, by dint of his visionary pen, they became an accidental manifesto for the progressive camp and the invention of the future.[2]

Initiated as a campaign in England during the Industrial Revolution, the March of Intellect, or 'March of Mind', demanded the amelioration of society's ills through programmes of public education for the lower classes.[3] The expression 'March of Intellect' was introduced by the industrialist and utopian socialist Robert Owen in a letter to *The Times* in 1824, remarking that in recent years 'the human mind has made the most rapid and extensive strides in the knowledge of human nature, and in general knowledge.'[4] The campaign triggered a reactionary and not surprisingly racist backlash: *The Times* started to mock the ambitions of the working class under headlines such as 'The March of Intellect in Africa'.[5]

As a campaign for progress in both literacy and technology, the March of Intellect was part of the so-called 'Machinery Question', that is, the public debate in England on the massive replacement of workers by industrial machines in the first half of the nineteenth century.

William Heath, *The March of Intellect* (1828) © The Trustees of the British Museum

The response to the employment of machines and workers' subsequent unemployment was also the demand for more education about machines, which took the form of initiatives such as the Mechanics' Institute Movement. 1823 saw the establishment of the London Mechanics' Institute (later to become known as Birkbeck College). In 1826, Henry Brougham, future Lord Chancellor, founded the Society for the Diffusion of Useful Knowledge to help those without access to schooling. In the same year the London University (later University College London) was founded. Though often going unacknowledged, a good part of the British academic landscape as it stands today emerged out of the epistemic acceleration of the industrial revolution.

In 1828 *The London Magazine* endorsed the March of Intellect for the benefit of the 'general intellect of the country', a country which, thanks to mass education, would understand the need to reform a decaying legislative system.[6] When in 1858 Marx used the expression (in English) 'general intellect', in the famous 'Fragment on Machines' of the *Grundrisse*, he was echoing the political climate of the March of Intellect and the power of 'general social knowledge' to, in his reading, weaken and subvert the chains of capitalism rather than those of old institutions.[7]

But it was specifically in a book of the utopian socialist, William Thompson, that Marx encountered the idea of the general intellect and, more importantly, the argument that knowledge may become a power inimical to workers, once it has been alienated by machines. Thompson's book carried the optimistic title *An Inquiry Into the Principles of the Distribution of Wealth Most Conducive to Humane Happiness Applied to the Newly Proposed System of Voluntary Equality of Wealth* and was published in 1824, the same year in which Owen launched the March of Intellect.[8] The book contains probably the first systematic account of mental labour – followed by Thomas Hodgskin's own account in *Popular Political Eco-*

*nomy* (1827) and Charles Babbage's project to mechanise mental labour in *On the Economy of Machinery and Manufactures* (1832).[9] Afterwards, because of the decline of the Mechanics' Institutes and tactical decisions within the workers' movement, the notion of mental labour encountered a hostile destiny in the Machinery Question.[10]

So when in the twentieth century authors began to analyse the so-called knowledge society and thought they were discussing for the first time forms of symbolic, informational and digital labour, they were actually operating in an area of political amnesia. Marx was partly responsible for bringing about this amnesia.[11] He engaged with Thompson's and Hodgskin's political economy, but considered their emphasis on mental labour as the celebration of individual creativity – as the cult of the gifted artisan, the ingenious toolmaker and the brave engineer – *against* labour in common: in *Capital*, Marx intentionally replaced the mental labourer with the 'collective worker' or *Gesamtarbeiter*. Marx's refusal to employ the concept of mental labour was due to the difficulty of mobilising collective knowledge into campaigns on the side of workers. The substance of knowledge and education is such that they can only be summoned for universalist battles (for the 'general intellect of the country') rather than partisan ones on the side the proletariat. Besides, since *The German Ideology,* Hegel's notion of absolute spirit appeared to be the antagonist of Marx's method of historical materialism: Marx transposed his famous anti-Hegelian passage 'life is not determined by consciousness, but consciousness by life' to industrial England, in order to claim that labour is not determined by knowledge, but knowledge by labour.[12]

Traditionally, for Marxism, the distinction between manual and mental labour evaporates in the face of capital insofar as any kind of labour is *abstract labour*, that is, labour measured and monetised for the benefit of producing surplus value. What follows shares this traditional starting point, but goes on to depart from orthodox Marxist positions. I wish to consider that any machinic interface of labour is a social relation, as much as capital, and that the machine, as much as money, mediates the relation between labour and capital – what could be termed a *labour theory of value mediated by machines*. Thinking with, as well as beyond, Marx, I want to stress that any technology influences the metrics of abstract labour. For this purpose, this essay traces the origins of Marx's general intellect in order to reconsider unresolved issues of early political economy, such as the econometrics of knowledge, that are increasingly relevant today.[13] In the current debates on the alienation of collective knowledge into corporate AI we are, in fact, still hearing the clunky echoes of the nineteenth-century Machinery Question.

## The discovery of Marx's 'Fragment on Machines'

Sophisticated, materialistic notions of mental labour and knowledge economy were already offered at the dawn of the Victorian age and they were already given very radical interpretations. Marx addressed the economic roles of skill, knowledge and science in his *Grundrisse,* specifically in the section that has become known as the 'Fragment on Machines'. There Marx explored an unorthodox hypothesis which was not to be reiterated in *Capital*: that because of the accumulation of the general intellect (particularly as scientific and technical knowledge embodied in machinery), labour will become secondary to capitalist accumulation, causing a crisis of the labour theory of value and blowing the foundations of capitalism skywards.[14] After 1989 Marx's 'Fragment on Machines' was rediscovered by Italian *post-operaismo* as a prescient critique of the transition to post-Fordism and the paradigms of a knowledge society and an information economy.[15] Since then this esoteric fragment has been mobilised by many authors, including those outside Marxism, as a prophecy of different economic crises, especially since the Internet bubble and 2000 Nasdaq stock market crash. The way Marx's 'Fragment on Machines' has reached even the debate on artificial intelligence and post-capitalism is a philological adventure that is worth recapitulating.[16]

The *Grundrisse* is 'a series of seven notebooks rough-drafted by Marx, chiefly with the purpose of self-clarification, during the winter of 1857–8'.[17] The notebooks frequently reveal the method of inquiry and subtext of *Capital*, published a decade later. Yet the *Grundrisse* remained unpublished until the twentieth century, which means that its reception entered Marxist debates almost a century after the publication of *Capital*. The *Grundrisse* was published for the first time in Moscow in 1939 and then in Berlin in 1953. A partial Italian translation started to circulate in 1956. The complete English translation was to become available only in 1973, twenty years after the German edition.[18] The denomination 'Fragment on Machines', to define specifically notebooks 6 and 7 of the *Grundrisse*, became canonical due to the editorial choice of Raniero Panzieri, who published their translation under the title 'Frammento sulle macchine' in the 1964 issue of *Quaderni Rossi*, the journal of Italian *operaismo*.[19] In the same year Herbert Marcuse drew upon notebooks 6 and 7 in his *One Dimensional Man*, while discussing the emancipatory potential of automation.[20] In 1972, in a footnote in *Anti-Oedipus*, Gilles Deleuze and Felix Guattari also refer to them as the 'chapter on automation'.[21] In 1972 they were partially published in English as 'Notes on Machines' in the journal *Economy and Society*.[22] In 1978 Antonio Negri gave an extended commentary on the 'chapter on machines' in his *Marx Beyond Marx* seminar in Paris (on the invitation of Louis Althusser), reading it against the background of the social antagonism of the 1970s. But it was only after the Fall of the Berlin Wall that Italian *operaismo* rediscovered and promoted the 'Fragment on Machines.' In 1990 the Italian philosopher Paolo Virno drew attention to the notion of general intellect in the journal *Luogo comune*. Paying ironic tribute to the Spaghetti Western, he was already warning about the cycles of the concept's revival:

> Often in westerns the hero, when faced by the most concrete of dilemmas, cites a passage from the Old Testament. ... This is how Karl Marx's 'Fragment on machines' has been read and cited from the early 1960s onwards. We have referred back many times to these pages ... in order to make some sense out of the unprecedented quality of workers' strikes, of the introduction of robots into the assembly lines and computers into the offices, and of certain kinds of youth behaviour. The history of the 'Fragment's' successive interpretations is a history of crises and of new beginnings.[23]

Virno explained that the 'Fragment on Machines' was quoted in the 1960s to question the supposed neutrality of science in industrial production, in the 1970s as a critique of the ideology of labour in state socialism and, finally, in the 1980s as a recognition of the tendencies of post-Fordism, yet without any emancipatory or conflictual reversal, as Marx would have wished. Whilst Marxist scholars aimed for greater philological rigour in their reading of the general intellect, militants updated its interpretation in the context of current social transformations and struggles.[24] *Post-operaismo* famously forged new antagonistic concepts out of Marx's general intellect, such as 'immaterial labour', 'mass intellectuality' and 'cognitive capitalism', stressing the autonomy of 'living knowledge' against capital. A lesson worth recalling from the Machinery Question, however, is that the issue of collective knowledge should never be separated from its embodiment in machines, instruments of measurement and *Kulturtechniken*. The employment of artificial intelligence in the twentieth century has abruptly reminded everyone that knowledge can be analysed, measured and automated as successfully as manual labour.

Scholars have wondered where the expression 'general intellect' came from, as it appears only once, in English, in the *Grundrisse*. Virno thought he detected the echo of Aristotle's *nous poietikos* and Rousseau's *volonté générale*.[25] As the 'Fragment on Machines' follows strains of argumentation that are similar to chapters 14 and 15 of *Capital* on the division of labour and machinery, it is not surprising that the missing sources can be found in the footnotes to these chapters of *Capital*. These common strains of argumentation are, fundamentally, Babbage's theory of machinery, and it is by following Marx's reading of Babbage in chapter 14 of *Capital* that the notion of general intellect can be reliably traced back to William Thompson's notion of 'knowledge labour'.

## Marx's Interpretation of Babbage

'The workshops of [England] contain within them a rich mine of knowledge, too generally neglected by the wealthier classes', Babbage advised his fellow industrialists in 1832.[26] Following the invitation to the industrial workshops as 'mundane places of intelligence', the historian of science, Simon Schaffer, finds that 'Babbage's most penetrating London reader' was Marx.[27] Marx had already quoted Babbage in *The Poverty of Philosophy* during his exile in Brussels in 1847 and, since then, adopted two analytical principles that were to become pivotal in *Capital* in drawing a robust theory of the machine and in grounding the theory of relative surplus value.

The first is what could be defined as 'the labour theory of the machine', which states that a new machine comes to imitate and replace a previous division of labour. This is an idea already formulated by Adam Smith, but better articulated by Babbage due to his greater technical experience.

The second analytical principle is usually called the 'Babbage principle' and is here renamed 'the principle of surplus labour modulation'. It states that the organisation of a production process in small tasks (division of labour) allows exactly the necessary quantity of labour to be purchased for each task (division of value). In this respect the division of labour provides not only the design of machinery but also an economic configuration to calibrate and calculate surplus labour extraction. In complex forms of management such as Taylorism, the principle of surplus labour modulation opens onto a clockwork view of labour, which can be further subdivided and recomposed into algorithmic assemblages. The synthesis of both analytical principles ideally describes the machine as an apparatus that actively projects back a new articulation and metrics of labour. In the pages of *Capital* the industrial machine appears to be not just a regulator to discipline labour but also a calculator to measure relative surplus value, echoing the numerical exactitude of Babbage's calculating engines.

I aim to read the *Grundrisse* and *Capital* through the lens of Babbage's two analytical principles. It will be shown how Babbage's labour theory of the machine is used by Marx to raise the figure of the collective worker as a sort of reincarnation of the general intellect, and furthermore, how Babbage's principle of modulation of surplus labour is used to sketch the idea of relative surplus value. Taken together, Babbage's two principles show that the general intellect of the *Grundrisse* evolves in *Capital* into a machinic collective worker, almost with the features of a proto-cybernetic organism, and the industrial machine becomes a calculator of the relative surplus value that this cyborg produces.

In discussing the relation between labour and machinery, knowledge and capital, Marx found himself embedded in a hybrid dialectics between German idealism and British political economy. The similar argumentation in the *Grundrisse* and *Capital* in the sections on machinery and division of labour follows four movements to which I will turn now: (1) the invention of machinery through the division of labour, (2) the alienation of knowledge by machinery, (3) the devaluation of capital by knowledge accumulation and (4) the rise of the collective worker.

## The invention of machinery through the division of labour

Who is the inventor of the machine? The worker, the engineer or the factory's master? Science, cunning or labour? As a fellow of the Royal Society, Babbage publicly praised the gifts of science, but theoretically maintained that machinery emerges as a replacement of the division of labour. Babbage's theory could be defined as a *labour theory of the machine*, since for him the design of a new machine always imitates the design of a previous division of labour. In *The Poverty of Philosophy* (1847), Marx already mobilised Babbage against Proudhon, who thought that machinery is the *antithesis* of the division of labour. Marx argued the opposite, that machinery emerges as the *synthesis of the division of labour*: '[W]hen, by the division of labour, each particular operation has been simplified to the use of a single instrument, the linking up of all these instruments, set in motion by a single engine, constitutes = a machine.'[28] Later, in the *Grundrisse*, Marx kept on drawing on Babbage to remark that technology is not created by the 'analysis' of nature by science, but by the 'analysis' of labour:

> It is, firstly, the analysis [*Analyse*] and application of mechanical and chemical laws, arising directly out of science, which enables the machine to perform the same labour as that previously performed by the worker. However, the development of machinery along this path occurs only when large industry has already reached a higher stage, and all the sciences have been pressed into the service of capital.... Invention then becomes a business, and the application of science to direct production itself becomes a prospect which determines and solicits it. But this is not the road along which machinery, by and large, arose, and even less the road on which it progresses in detail. This road is, rather, dissection [*Analyse*] = through the division of labour, which gradually transforms the workers' operations into more and more mechanical ones, so that at a certain point a mechanism can step into their places.[29]

Marx adopted Babbage's theory also methodologically: in *Capital*, the chapter on machinery follows after the chapter on the division of labour. There a structural homology between the design of machinery and the division of labour is highlighted: 'The machine is a mechanism that, after being set in motion, performs with its tools the same operations as the worker formerly did with similar tools.'[30] In a footnote Marx refers to Babbage's synthetic definition of machine ('The union of all these simple instruments, set in motion by a motor, constitutes a machine') and offers his own paraphrase:

> The machine, which is the starting-point of the industrial revolution, replaces the worker, who handles a single tool, by a mechanism operating with a number of similar tools and set in motion by a single motive power, whatever the form of that power.[31]

It is at this point of *Capital* that Marx advances a further analytical principle that will have enormous influence on the methodology of the history of science and technology in the twentieth century.[32] After challenging the belief that science, rather than labour, is the origin of the machine, Marx reverses the perception of the steam engine as prime catalyst of the Industrial Revolution. Marx contends that it is the growth of the division of labour, its tools and 'tooling machines', that 'requires a mightier moving power than that of man', a source of energy that will be found in steam.[33] It was not the invention of the steam engine (*means of production*) that triggered the industrial revolution (as it is popular to theorise in ecological discourse), but rather the developments of capital and labour (*relations of production*) demanding a more powerful source of energy.[34]

> The steam-engine itself, such as it was at its invention during the manufacturing period at the close of the seventeenth century, and such as it continued to be down to 1780, did not give rise to any industrial revolution. It was, on the contrary, the invention of [tooling] machines [*Werkzeugmaschinen*] that made a revolution in the form of steam-engines necessary.[35]

The 'mechanical monster' of the industrial factory was summoned first by labour and then accelerated by steam power, not the other way around.[36] Marx was clear: the genesis of technology is an *emergent process* driven by the division of labour. It is from the materiality of collective labour, from conscious and unconscious forms of cooperation, that extended apparatuses of machines emerge. Intelligence, here, resides in the ramifications of human cooperation rather than in individual mental labour. Machine intelligence mirrors, embodies and amplifies the analytical intelligence of collective labour.[37]

## The alienation of knowledge by machinery

'What distinguishes the worst architect from the best of bees is that the architect builds the cell in his mind before he constructs it in wax.'[38] This is Marx's recognition, in *Capital,* of labour as a mental and individual activity: the collective division of labour, or labour in common, however, remains the *political inventor* of the machine.[39] A process of alienation of skill and knowledge starts as soon as machinery appears in front and in place of labour. Tools pass from the hands of the worker to the hands of the machine, and the same process happens to workers' knowledge. 'Along with the tool, the skill of the worker in handling it passes over to the machine.'[40] The machine is but a crystallisation of collective knowledge. Marx condemns this alienation of the human mind, seconding Owen: 'Since the general introduction of soulless mechanism in British manufactures, people have with rare exceptions been treated as a secondary and subordinate machine, and far more attention has been given to the perfection of the raw materials of wood and metals than to those of body and spirit.'[41] The introduction of machinery marks a dramatic dialectical turn in the history of labour, whereby the worker ceases being the *subject* of the machine and becomes the *object* of capital: 'The hand tool makes the worker independent – posits him as proprietor. Machinery – as fixed capital – posits him as dependent, posits him as appropriated.'[42] This shift in power between human and machine in the Victorian age is also the inception of a new imagery, in which machines acquire features of the living and workers that of automata.[43] Let's compare two similar passages from the *Grundrisse* and *Capital*, respectively, in which Marx describes the alienation of science from workers.

> [It] is the machine which possesses skill and strength in place of the worker, is itself the virtuoso, with a soul of its own in the mechanical laws acting through it …. The worker's activity, reduced to a mere abstraction of activity, is determined and regulated on all sides by the movement of the machinery, and not the opposite. The science which compels the inanimate limbs of the machinery, by their construction, to act purposefully, as an automaton, does not exist in the worker's consciousness, but rather acts upon him through the machine as an alien power, as the power of the machine itself.[44]

This reflection on the alienation of knowledge from

workers continues in *Capital*, where Marx makes the process of knowledge extraction culminate in the full separation of science as productive agent from labour.

> The knowledge, judgement and will which, even though to a small extent, are exercised by the independent peasant or handicraftsman, in the same way as the savage makes the whole art of war consist in the exercise of his personal cunning, are faculties now required only for the workshop as a whole. The possibility of an intelligent direction of production expands in one direction, because it vanishes in many others. What is lost by the specialised workers is concentrated in the capital which confronts them. It is a result of the division of labour in manufacture that the worker is brought face to face with the intellectual potentialities [*geistige Potenzen*] of the material process of production as the property of another and as a power which rules over him. This process of separation starts in simple co-operation, where the capitalist represents to the individual workers the unity and the will of the whole body of social labour. It is developed in manufacture, which mutilates the worker, turning him into a fragment of himself. It is completed in large-scale industry, which makes science a potentiality for production which is distinct from labour and presses it into the service of capital.[45]

Marx comments upon the latter passage from *Capital* with a footnote to William Thompson's book *An Inquiry Into the Principles of the Distribution of Wealth*. Thompson claims, as quoted by Marx:

> 'The man of knowledge and the productive labourer come to be widely divided from each other, and knowledge, instead of remaining the handmaid of labour in the hand of the labourer to increase his productive powers ... has almost everywhere arrayed itself against labour.' 'Knowledge' becomes 'an instrument, capable of being detached from labour and opposed to it.'[46]

Thompson provided a definition of knowledge labour that predates the twentieth-century theorists of the knowledge society and cognitive labour: 'In speaking of labour, we have always included in that term the quantity of knowledge requisite for its direction. Without this knowledge, it would be no more than brute force directed to no useful purpose.'[47] Presciently, he recognized that the economy of knowledge follows different rules of diffusion than the economy of capital: 'Wealth, the produce of labor, is necessarily limited in its supply .... Not so with the pleasure derived from the acquisition, the possession, and diffusion of knowledge. The supply of knowledge is unlimited .... The more it is diffused, the more it multiplies itself.'[48] In a polemic typical of

Owenism, Thompson described machinery humiliating the '*general intellectual powers*' of the workers reduced to 'drilled automata'. The factory is an apparatus to keep the workers 'ignorant of the secret springs which regulated the machine and to repress the general powers of their minds' so 'that the fruits of their own labors were by a hundred contrivances taken away from them'.[49] In different passages Thompson used the expressions 'general intellect', 'general intellectual power', 'general knowledge' and 'general power of the minds' (often in italics) in direct resonance with identical or equivalent terms used by Marx in the *Grundrisse*, such as 'general social labour', 'general scientific labour', 'general productive forces of the human brain', 'general social knowledge' and 'social intellect'.[50] Importantly, as remembered in the opening quote, Thompson drew a direct link between the construction of a primarily white male general intellect and issues of gender and race discrimination. In Thompson's utopian view, people are racist and chauvinist due to the lack of proper knowledge and education:

> Why also, it may be asked in reply, has the slavery of the blacks, and of women, been established? Because the whites in the one case, because the men in the other, made the laws: because knowledge had not been obtained on these subjects, the whites and the men erroneously conceiving it to be their interest to oppress blacks and women.[51]

Marx, too, recognised the psychopathologies of industrial labour and the tactics to keep the workforce as illiterate as possible. Adam Smith's mentor, Adam Ferguson, wrote: 'Ignorance is the mother of industry as well as of superstition. Reflection and fancy are subject to err; but a habit of moving the hand or the foot is independent of either. Manufactures, accordingly, prosper most where the mind is least consulted, and where the workshop may … be considered as an engine, the parts of which are men.'[52] This all reminds us that the public mythology of artificial intelligence has always operated on the side of capital with a hidden agenda to foster human stupidity, including racism and sexism.

## The devaluation of capital by knowledge accumulation

What is the economic value of knowledge and science? Which role do they play in capitalist accumulation? Marx explored these questions in an age that was flourishing with mechanical ingenuity, technical intelligence and large infrastructures, such as railway and telegraph networks. In the passage on the general intellect Marx considered knowledge in three ways: first, as a 'direct force of production' [*unmittelbaren Produktivkraft*]; second, under the form of 'social forces of production' [*gesellschaftlichen Produktivkrafte*]; and, third, as social practice [*gesellschaftlichen Praxis*], which is obviously not abstract knowledge *per se*.

> Nature builds no machines, no locomotives, railways, *electric telegraphs*, *self-acting mules* etc. These are products of human industry; natural material transformed into organs of the human will over nature, or of human participation in nature. They are *organs of the human brain, created by the human hand*; the power of knowledge, objectified. / The development of fixed capital indicates to what degree general social *knowledge* has become a *direct force of production*, and to what degree, hence, the conditions of the process of social life itself have come under the control of the *general intellect* and been transformed in accordance with it[s measure]. / To what degree the powers of social production have been produced, not only in the form of knowledge, but also as immediate organs of social practice, of the real life process.[53]

The general intellect becomes a transformative agent of society in a way that clearly echoes Thompson's optimism about the 'distribution of knowledge' as conducive to 'voluntary equality in the distribution of wealth'. The 'Fragment on Machines' contains an unresolved tension between *knowledge objectified in machinery* (as 'development of fixed capital') and *knowledge expressed by social production* (as 'development of the social individual'). Marx considers the primacy of knowledge in the production process and, then, the primacy of praxis over knowledge itself. The same thesis emerges in *Capital*, where Marx registers the stress of industrial labour on the workers' nervous system. Marx compares the economic value of individual skill against that of science. The competition between the two is deemed unfair, since after a long process of 'separation of the intellectual faculties', the special skills of the worker vanish before the magnitude of the science, natural energy and social labour that animates machinery:

> The separation of the intellectual faculties of the production process from manual labour, and the transformation

of those faculties into powers exercised by capital over labour, is ... finally completed by large-scale industry erected on the foundation of machinery. The special skill of each individual machine-operator, who has now been deprived of all significance, vanishes as an infinitesimal quantity in the face of the science, the gigantic natural forces, and the mass of social labour embodied in the system of machinery, which, together with those three forces, constitutes the power of the 'master'.[54]

In the 'Fragment on Machines', we have not only the recognition of knowledge as an alien power embodied in machinery (as found in Thompson) but also the attempt to assess the magnitude of its valorisation (which is missing in Thompson). Here Marx uses a criterion to assess knowledge from the work of Thomas Hodgskin, a Ricardian socialist of libertarian tendency and a rationalist optimist who believed in the progress of collective knowledge and the autonomy of society from both capital and state intervention. Hodgskin was one of the founders of the London Mechanics Institute, where in 1826 he presented the lecture 'On the Influence of Knowledge', later to be published as part of his book *Popular Political Economy* (1827). Marx often quoted this book and also praised his *Labour Defended Against the Claims of Capital* (1825). Hodgskin pits a positive emphasis on fixed capital as a concrete accumulation of past labour, knowledge and science, against the 'fiction' of circulating capital. In the *Grundrisse*, there is an echo of Hodgskin's ideas in Marx's claim that machinery is the 'most adequate form of fixed capital':

> The accumulation of knowledge and of skill, of the general productive forces of the social brain, is thus absorbed into capital, as opposed to labour, and hence appears as an attribute of capital, and more specifically of fixed capital, in so far as it enters into the production process as a means of production proper. Machinery appears, then, as the most adequate form of fixed capital, and fixed capital ... appears as the most adequate form of capital as such.[55]

Modernising the Baconian motto 'knowledge is power', authors of the industrial age such as Babbage, Thompson and Hodgskin argue that knowledge is without doubt a productive and economic force. Knowledge is so crucial to Hodgskin that he even complained that Adam Smith did not dedicate a proper treatment to the subject: 'Those books, therefore, called Elements, Principles, or Systems of Political Economy, which do not embrace and fully develop ... the whole influence of knowledge on productive power, and do not explain the natural laws which regulate the progress of society in knowledge, are and must, as treatises on Political Economy, be essentially incomplete.'[56]

For Hodgskin, as much as for Thompson, labour is primarily mental labour, that is, knowledge. 'Mental labour' is 'the labour of observing and ascertaining by what means the material world will give us the most wealth'. 'Unless there be mental labour, there can be no manual dexterity; and no capability of inventing machines. It therefore is essential to production.'[57] Hodgskin relates the growth of knowledge to the material substrate of population growth: 'Necessity is the mother of invention; and the continual existence of necessity can only be explained by the continual increase of people.'[58] Population growth demands increased skill in producing and distributing wealth, thereby generating advanced knowledge. 'As the world grows older, and as men increase and multiply, there is a constant, natural, and necessary tendency to an increase in their knowledge, and consequently in their productive power.'[59] But Hodgskin remarks that the economy of knowledge follows different laws than the economy of capital: 'the laws which regulate the accumulation and employment of capital are quite dissimilar to and unconnected with the laws regulating the progress of knowledge.'[60]

Importantly, in Hodgskin's view of society, there are neither intellectual hierarchies, nor division of hand and mind, nor a labour aristocracy in need of promotion: 'both mental and bodily labour are practised by almost every individual.'[61] In fact, Marx quotes Hodgskin in *Capital* to stress that skill is a common resource that is shared among workers and passes from one generation to the next.[62] Knowledge is a power that is collectively produced and shared, and this power constitutes (together with machinery and infrastructures) the core of fixed capital that must be re-appropriated by workers (against the 'fiction' of circulating capital).[63]

The most visionary passages of the *Grundrisse* refer to the crisis of capitalism due to the crisis of the centrality of labour, and therefore of the labour theory of value, which is to say, due to the fact that 'direct labour and its quantity disappear as the determinant principle of production ... compared to general scientific labour, technological application of natural sciences ... and to the general productive force arising from social combination [*Gliederung*]'.[64] Further, says Marx:

> Capital itself is the moving contradiction, [in] that it presses to reduce labour time to a minimum, while it posits labour time, on the other side, as sole measure and source of wealth. ... On the one side, then, it calls to life all the powers of science and of nature, as of social combination and of social intercourse, in order to make the creation of wealth independent (relatively) of the labour time employed on it. On the other side, it wants to use labour time as the measuring rod for the giant social forces thereby created, and to confine them within the limits required to maintain the already created value as value. Forces of production and social relations – two different sides of the development of the social individual – appear to capital as mere means, and are merely means for it to produce on its limited foundation. In fact, however, they are the material conditions to blow this foundation sky-high.[65]

What looks like a contradiction in Marx's system (the obliteration of the political centrality of labour) is actually the consequence of such centrality. Everywhere in the world workers have been working enough! They have been producing so much and for so long that their past accumulated labour (under the forms of machinery, infrastructures and collective knowledge) affects the rate of profit and slows down the economy. This is the thesis of the productivity of labour pitted against the unproductivity of capital that is found specifically in Hodgskin's *Labour Defended Against Capital*. Marx tries to prove that the accumulation of fixed capital (as machinery, infrastructures, collective knowledge and science) could have profound side-effects on the side of circulating capital (beside the chance of an overproduction crisis). In the *Grundrisse* Marx explores the hypothesis that a growth of collective and technical knowledge could undermine capital's dominance, as Thompson and Hodgskin envisioned. The utopian enthusiasms of the *Grundrisse* are reabsorbed in *Capital* by a realistic calculation of relative surplus value, which is adopted as the metrics of machinery and implicit metrics of knowledge value as well.

## The rise of the collective worker

In *Capital* Marx replies to the Machinery Question by casting an extended social actor, the collective worker (*Gesamtarbeiter*), at the centre of the industrial theatre, whereas for the bourgeoisie it was an engineer with a steam engine. The figure of the collective worker replaces the personality cult of the inventor (individual mental labour) but also the idea of the general intellect (collective mental labour). Drawing on Babbage's labour theory of the machine, which explains the machine as the embodiment of the division of labour, Marx asserts the collective worker as the true *political inventor* of technology. The ambiguous hypothesis of the *knowledge theory of value* of the *Grundrisse*, is finally grounded on an empirical basis: intelligence is logically materialised in the ramifications of the division of labour. The collective worker is a personification of the general intellect and, precisely, of its mechanisation.

Marx follows closely Babbage's labour theory of the machine in both the *Grundrisse* and *Capital*, but only in the latter does he make use of Babbage's principle of surplus labour modulation, which helps Marx to sketch the concept of relative surplus value and to measure the productivity of labour and machinery. Babbage's principle as quoted by Marx is as follows:

> The master manufacturer, by dividing the work to be executed into different processes, each requiring different degrees of skill or of force, can purchase exactly that precise quantity of both which is necessary for each process; whereas, if the whole work were executed by one workman, that person must possess sufficient skill to perform the most difficult, and sufficient strength to execute the most laborious of the operations into which the art is divided.[66]

Marx reverses the mystification of 'the master manufacturer' by restoring at the centre of the Babbage principle the collective worker who, needless to say, becomes now the main actor of the division of labour. The collective worker acquires features of a super-organism:

> The collective worker, formed out of the combination of a number of individual specialized workers, is the item of machinery specifically characteristic of the manufacturing period. ... In one operation he must exert more strength, in another more skill, in another more attention; and the same individual does not possess all these qualities in an equal degree. ... After the various operations have been separated, made independent and isolated, the workers are divided, classified and grouped according to their predominant qualities. ... The collective worker now possesses all the qualities necessary for production in an equal degree of excellence, and expends

them in the most economical way by exclusively employing all his organs, individualised in particular workers or groups of workers, in performing their special functions.[67]

In Marx's language the collective worker becomes an 'item of machinery', a 'social mechanism', a 'collective working organism'.[68] Vivid machinic metaphors accompany the reincarnation of the general intellect as collective worker. The prehistory of the cyborg can be read between the lines of *Capital*: 'The social mechanism of production, which is made up of numerous individual specialized workers, belongs to the capitalist. ... Not only is the specialised work distributed among the different individuals, but the individual himself is divided up, and transformed into the automatic motor of a detail operation.'[69]

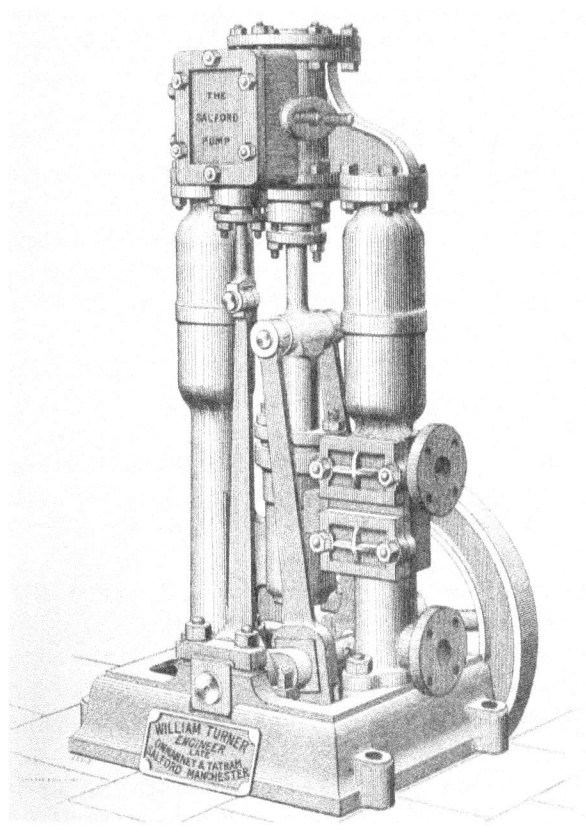

The 'Fragment on Machines' did not just emphasise the growing economic role of knowledge and science but also the role of social cooperation, that is, the growing role of the *general machinery* of social relations beyond the factory system. In a movement that resembles that of the construction of the *Gesamtarbeiter* within the factory, in the *Grundrisse* Marx sets 'the social individual ... as the great foundation-stone of production and of wealth' in the society to come:

[The worker] steps to the side of the production process instead of being its chief actor. In this transformation, it is neither the direct human labour he himself performs, nor the time during which he works, but rather the appropriation of his own general productive power, his understanding of nature and his mastery over it by virtue of his presence as a social body – it is, in a word, the development of the social individual which appears as the great foundation-stone of production and of wealth.[70]

It seems that, with the transmutation of the general intellect into the collective worker, the prediction of capitalism's implosion due to the overproduction of knowledge as fixed capital is abandoned by Marx. Capitalism will no longer collapse due to the accumulation of knowledge, because knowledge itself helps new apparatuses to improve the extraction of surplus value. Michael Heinrich has noted that in *Capital* 'when dealing with the production of relative surplus value, we can find an implicit critique of the "Fragment on machines"'.[71] In *Capital* Marx appears to employ Babbage's principle of the modulation of surplus labour to design a theory of relative surplus value that recognises capitalism's capacity to maintain exploitation in equilibrium. According to Marx, surplus value can be augmented not just by reducing wages and material costs but also by increasing the productivity of labour in general, that is, by redesigning the division of labour and machines. If, according to Babbage's principle, the division of labour is an apparatus to modulate regimes of skill and therefore different regimes of salary according to skill, the division of labour becomes a modulation of relative surplus value. Being itself an embodiment of the division of labour, the machine then becomes the apparatus to discipline labour and regulate the extraction of relative surplus value.[72] As in Babbage's vision, the machine becomes a calculating engine – in this case, an instrument for the measurement of surplus value.

## The machine is a social relation, not a thing

In the twentieth century Harry Braverman was probably the first Marxist to rediscover Babbage's pioneering experiments in computation and influence on Marx's theory of the division of labour.[73] Marx read Thompson, Hodgskin and Babbage, but never employed the notion of mental labour, probably in order to avoid supporting a labour aristocracy of skilled artisans as a political subject separate from the working class. For Marx, labour is always collective: there is no individual labour that is more prestigious than others and, therefore, mental labour is always general; the mind is by definition social. Rather than a *knowledge theory of labour* that grants primacy to conscious activity, like the one in Thompson and Hodgskin, Marx maintains a *labour theory of knowledge* that recognises the cognitive import of forms of labour that are social, distributed, spontaneous and unconscious. Intelligence emerges from the abstract assemblage of workers' simple gestures and micro-decisions, even and especially the unconscious ones.[74] In the general intellect studies and the history of technology, these are the in-between worlds of collective intelligence and unconscious cooperation but also of 'mechanised knowledge' and 'mindful mechanics'.[75] It ends up being Babbage who provides Marx with an operative paradigm to overcome Hegel's *Geist* and imbricate knowledge, science and the general intellect into production.

As already stressed, the distinction between manual and mental labour disappears in Marxism because, from the abstract point of view of capital, all waged labour, without distinction, produces surplus value; all labour is abstract labour. However, the abstract eye of capital that regulates the labour theory of value employs a specific instrument to measure labour: the clock. In this way, what looks like a universal law has to deal with the metrics of a very mundane technology: clocks are not universal.[76] Machines can impose a metrics of labour other than time, as has recently happened with social data analytics. As much as new instruments define new domains of science, likewise they define new domains of labour after being invented by labour itself.[77] Any new machine is a new configuration of space, time and social relations, and it projects new metrics of such diagrams.[78] In the Victorian age, a metrology of mental labour existed only in an embryonic state. A rudimentary econometrics of knowledge begins to emerge only in the twentieth century with the first theory of information. The thesis of this text is that Marx's labour theory of value did not resolve the metrics for the domains of knowledge and intelligence, which had to be explored in the articulation of the machine design and in the Babbage principle.

Following Braverman and Schaffer, one could add that Babbage provided not just a labour theory of the machine but a *labour theory of machine intelligence*.[79]

Babbage's calculating engines ('intelligent machines' of the age) were an implementation of the analytical eye of the factory's master. Cousins of Bentham's panopticon, they were instruments, simultaneously, of surveillance and measurement of labour. It is this idea that we should consider and apply to the age of artificial intelligence and its political critique, although reversing its polarisation, in order to declare computing infrastructures a concretion of labour in common.[80]

*Matteo Pasquinelli is Professor in Media Philosophy at the University of Arts and Design, Karlsruhe, and editor of* Alleys of Your Mind: Augmented Intelligence and Its Traumas *(2015).*

**Notes**

1. The author would like to thank Henning Schmidgen, Jon Beller, Max Stadler, Manuel Disegni, Wietske Maas, Ariana Dongus, Sami Khatib, Jason King and Ben Seymour for their comments and feedback on this essay.
2. 'Even though Heath was satirising the movement, his posters include some wonderful future ideas for transport, including a steam horse and a steam coach, a vacuum tube, a bridge to Cape Town, and various forms of flight, including a flying postman.' Mike Ashley, 'Inventing the Future', British Library blog, 15 May 2014, www.bl.uk/romantics-and-victorians/articles/inventing-the-future.
3. See Don Herzog, *Poisoning the Minds of the Lower Order* (Princeton: Princeton University Press, 2000).
4. Ashley, 'Inventing the Future'.
5. See Michael Hancher, 'Penny Magazine: March of Intellect in the Butchering Line', in *Nineteenth-century Media and the Construction of Identities*, eds. Laurel Brake, Bill Bell and David Finkelstein (London: Palgrave, 2016), 93.
6. Author unknown, *The London Magazine*, April and June 1828 issues. See opening quote.
7. Karl Marx, *Grundrisse der Kritik der politischen Ökonomie* (Moscow: Verlag für fremdsprachige Literatur, 1939); *Grundrisse: Foundations of the Critique of Political Economy*, trans. Martin Nicolaus (London: Penguin, 1993).
8. William Thompson, *An Inquiry Into the Principles of the Distribution of Wealth Most Conducive to Humane Happiness Applied to the Newly Proposed System of Voluntary Equality of Wealth* (London: Longman, 1824).
9. Thomas Hodgskin, *Popular Political Economy: Four lectures delivered at the London Mechanics Institution* (London: Tait, 1827). Charles Babbage, *On the Economy of Machinery and Manufactures* (London: Charles Knight, 1832).
10. Edward Royle, 'Mechanics' Institutes and the Working Classes, 1840-1860', *The Historical Journal* 14:2 (June 1971).
11. In *Capital* Marx refers to Wilhelm Schulz's distinction between tool and machine, yet without commenting on Schulz's account of 'mental production' (*geistige Produktion*) from *Die Be-*

*wegung der Produktion* (Zurich, 1843). He adds: 'In many respects a book to be recommended'. Karl Marx, *Das Kapital. Kritik der politischen Ökonomie*, vol. 1 (Hamburg: Meissner, 1867); *Capital: A Critique of Political Economy*, vol. 1, trans. Ben Fowkes (London: Penguin, 1981), 493. See Walter Grab, *Dr. Wilhelm Schulz aus Darmstadt. Weggefährte von Georg Büchner und Inspirator von Karl Marx* (Frankfurt am Main: Gutenberg, 1987). Thanks to Henning Schmidgen for this reference.

12. Karl Marx and Friedrich Engels, *Die deutsche Ideologie* (1846) (first edition: Moscow: Marx-Engels Institute, 1932); *The German Ideology*, ed. C.J. Arthur (New York: International Publishers, 1970). But argumentarguing against Malthus.nd linear logic. tion, visual a or an age of algorithn.istical models) but on the process, a

13. In the nineteenth century, physiologists and political economists tried to figure out a 'metrology' of 'cerebral labour': according to Schaffer, the attempts to quantify intelligence with the aid of instruments contributed to the project of artificial intelligence in the following century. See Simon Schaffer, 'OK Computer', in Michael Hagner, ed., *Ecce Cortex: Beitraege zur Geschichte des modernen Gehirns* (Göttingen, Wallstein Verlag, 1999), 254–85.

14. This visionary hypothesis did not emerge again in *Capital*, again as a result of historical circumstances. Notebooks 6 and 7 were written in the winter 1857–1858, amid a financial crisis, whereas *Capital* was published after the crisis was over.

15. The primary sources of the complex debate on Marx's general intellect can be succinctly reconstructed as follows: Paolo Virno, 'Citazioni di fronte al pericolo', *Luogo comune* 1 (November 1990); translated as 'Notes on the general intellect', trans. Cesare Casarino, in *Marxism beyond Marxism*, eds. Saree Makdisi et al. (New York: Routledge, 1996), 265–272. Christian Marazzi, *Il posto dei calzini. La svolta linguistica dell'economia e i suoi effetti sulla politica* (Torino: Bollati Boringhieri, 1994); translated as *Capital and Affects: The Politics of the Language Economy*, trans. Giuseppina Mecchia (New York: Semiotexte, 2011). Maurizio Lazzarato and Antonio Negri, 'Travail immatériel et subjectivité', *Futur antérieur* 6 (1991), 86–99. Paolo Virno, *Grammatica della Moltitudine* (Rome: Derive Approdi, 2002); translated as *A Grammar of the Multitude*, trans. Isabella Bertoletti et al. (New York: Semiotexte, 2004). Carlo Vercellone, 'From formal subsumption to general intellect: Elements for a Marxist reading of the thesis of cognitive capitalism', *Historical Materialism* 15:1 (2007), 13–36. Probably the first reception of this debate in English is Nick Dyer-Witheford, *Cyber-Marx: Cycles and Circuits of Struggle in High-Technology Capitalism* (University of Illinois Press, 1999). See also, of course, Michal Hardt and Antonio Negri, *Empire* (Cambridge, MA: Harvard Univ. Press, 2000). For a critique of *operaismo*'s interpretation, see Michael Heinrich, 'The Fragment on Machines: A Marxian Misconception in the *Grundrisse* and its Overcoming in *Capital*', and Tony Smith, 'The General Intellect in the *Grundrisse* and Beyond', in *In Marx's Laboratory: Critical Interpretations of the Grundrisse*, eds. Riccardo Bellofiore et al. (Leiden: Brill, 2013), 195–212 and 213–231.

16. See Paul Mason, 'The end of capitalism has begun', *The Guardian*, 17 July 2015, and Paul Mason, *Postcapitalism: A Guide to Our Future* (London: Macmillan, 2016). See also MacKenzie Wark, *General Intellects* (London: Verso, 2017).

17. Martin Nicolaus, 'Foreword', in Marx, *Grundrisse*, 7.

18. Marcello Musto, 'Dissemination and reception of the Grundrisse in the world', in *Karl Marx's Grundrisse*, ed. Marcello Musto (London: Routledge, 2008), 207–216.

19. Karl Marx, 'Frammento sulle macchine', trans. Renato Solmi, *Quaderni Rossi* 4 (1964).

20. Herbert Marcuse, *One Dimensional Man* (Boston: Beacon Press, 1964), 39.

21. Gilles Deleuze and Félix Guattari, *Anti-Oedipus: Capitalism and Schizophrenia*, vol. 1, trans. Robert Hurley et al. (Minneapolis: University of Minnesota Press, 1983), 232, n. 76. See also Matteo Pasquinelli, 'Italian Operaismo and the Information Machine', *Theory, Culture & Society* 32:3 (2015).

22. Karl Marx, 'Notes on Machines', *Economy and Society* 1:3 (1972), 244–254.

23. Virno, 'Notes', 265.

24. Wolfgang Fritz Haug has warned that the nebulous origins of the general intellect contributed to a sloganistic use 'at the cost of theoretical arbitrariness'. The general intellect belongs, Haug asserts, to a galaxy of similar Marxian terms to be taken into consideration, such as 'general social labour', 'general scientific labour', 'accumulation of knowledge and of skill, the general productive forces of the human brain', 'general progress', 'development of the general powers of the human head', 'general social knowledge', 'social intellect'. See Wolfgang Fritz Haug, 'Historical-Critical Dictionary of Marxism: General Intellect', *Historical Materialism* 18:2 (2010), 209–216.

25. Virno, 'Notes'.

26. Babbage, *On the Economy of Machinery*, vi.

27. Simon Schaffer, 'Babbage's Intelligence: Calculating Engines and the Factory System', *Critical Inquiry* 21:1 (1994), 203–227.

28. Babbage, *On the Economy of Machinery*, as quoted in Karl Marx, *The Poverty of Philosophy*, trans. Harry Quelch, in *Marx-Engels Collected Works*, vol. 6 (New York: International Publishers, 1976). Marx translated Babbage from French.

29. Marx, *Grundrisse*, 704.

30. Marx, *Capital*, 495.

31. Ibid., 497.

32. See Gideon Freudenthal and Peter McLaughlin, eds. *The Social and Economic Roots of the Scientific Revolution: Texts by Boris Hessen and Henryk Grossmann* (Springer Science & Business Media, 2009).

33. 'An increase in the size of the machine and the number of its working tools calls for a more massive mechanism to drive it; and this mechanism, in order to overcome its own inertia, requires a mightier moving power than that of man' (Marx, *Capital*, 497).

34. Marx is mistakenly considered a *techno-determinist* for the prominence he grants to machinery in capitalism, but if he is determinist at all, he is a determinist of the *relations of production* and not of the *means of production*, as the division of labour, and not technology, is the driving force of capital. 'The inclusion of labor power as a force of production thus admits conscious human agency as a determinant of history: it is people, as much as or more than the machine, that make history.' Donald MacK-

enzie, 'Marx and Machine', *Knowing Machines* (Cambridge, MA: MIT Press, 1998), 26.

35. Marx, *Capital*, 496.

36. Ibid., 507.

37. For the idea of analytical intelligence see Lorraine Daston, 'Calculation and the Division of Labour, 1750–1950', *Bulletin of the German Historical Institute*, 62 tafter being invented by labour itselffinellintence that links them well, I think.(Spring), 9–30.

38. Marx, *Capital*, 284.

39. Hodgskin gave great importance to observation (i.e. mental design) in the invention of machinery.

40. Marx, *Capital*, 545.

41. Robert Owen, 'Essays on the Formation of the Human Character' (London, 1840). As quoted in Marx, *Grundrisse*, 711.

42. Marx, *Grundrisse*, 702. Marx quotes Hodgskin also at 709: 'As soon as the division of labour is developed, almost every piece of work done by a single individual is a part of a whole, having no value or utility of itself. There is nothing on which the labourer can seize: this is my produce, this I will keep to myself' (*Labour Defended*, 25, 1, 2, XI).

43. Simon Schaffer, 'Babbage's Dancer and the Impresarios of Mechanism', in *Cultural Babbage*, eds. Francis Spufford and Jenny Uglow (London: Faber & Faber, 1997), 53–80.

44. Marx, *Grundrisse*, 692–93.

45. Marx, *Capital*, 482.

46. Ibid., 483. Thompson, *Principles of the Distribution of Wealth*, 274.

47. Thompson, *Principles of the Distribution of Wealth*, 272.

48. Ibid., 274–290.

49. Ibid., 292.

50. Ibid., 272–362.

51. Ibid., 303.

52. Ferguson as quoted by Marx in *Capital*, 483. Marx cites Ferguson also for recognising as early as 1767 that 'thinking itself, in this age of separations, may become a peculiar craft'. Marx, *Capital*, 484.

53. Marx, *Grundrisse*, 706. The terms marked by asterisks appear in English in the original manuscript.

54. Marx, *Capital*, 549.

55. Marx, *Grundrisse*, 694.

56. Hodgskin, *Popular Political Economy*, 97.

57. Ibid., 45, 47.

58. Ibid., 86. This is clearly an anti-Malthusian argument. See Malthus' elitist account of knowledge in 'An Essay on the Principle of Population' (1798).

59. Hodgskin, *Popular Political Economy*, 95.

60. Ibid., 78.

61. Ibid., 47.

62. 'Easy labour is transmitted skill.' Ibid., 48.

63. 'Hodgskin called circulating capital a "fiction". Fixed capital was the stored-up skill of past labour'. Maxine Berg, *The Machinery Question and the Making of Political Economy* (Cambridge: Cambridge University Press, 1980), 274.

64. Marx, *Grundrisse*, 700.

65. Ibid., 706.

66. Marx, *Capital*, 469. The Penguin edition wrongly says 'Ch. 19, pp. 175' of Babbage's book: it is chapter 18, page 137.

67. Marx, *Capital*, 468–69.

68. See Henning Schmidgen, '1818: Der Frankenstein-Komplex', afterword to Bruno Latour, *Aramis: oder Die Liebe zur Technik*, trans. Gustav Roßler (Heidelberg: Mohr Siebeck, 2018), 303–319.

69. Marx, *Capital*, 481.

70. Marx, *Grundrisse*, 705.

71. Michael Heinrich, 'The Fragment on Machines', 197.

72. 'One great advantage which we may derive from machinery is from the check which it affords against the inattention, the idleness, or the dishonesty of human agents.' Babbage, *On the Economy of Machinery*, 54.

73. Harry Braverman, *Labor and Monopoly Capital: The Degradation of Work in the Twentieth Century* (New York: Monthly Review Press, 1974).

74. For the notion of micro-decision, see Romano Alquati, 'Composizione organica del capitale e forza-lavoro alla Olivetti', Part 2, *Quaderni Rossi* 3 (1963); partially translated in Matteo Pasquinelli, 'Italian Operaismo and the Information Machine', *Theory, Culture & Society* 32:3 (2015), 55.

75. What in the following century will become the core of operationalism: management, logistics and computer science. See Sandro Mezzadra and Brett Neilson, *The Politics of Operations: Excavating Contemporary Capitalism* (Durham: Duke University Press, 2019).

76. See Antonio Negri, *Time for Revolution* (London: Continuum, 2003), 27.

77. See Peter Damerow and Wolfgang Lefèvre, 'Tools of Science', in *Abstraction and Representation: Essays on the Cultural Evolution of Thinking*, ed. Peter Damerow (Dordrecht: Kluver, 1996), 395–404.

78. The idea that each machine establishes its own labour unit of measure constitutes a *machine theory of labour* which cannot be expanded here.

79. See Schaffer, 'Babbage's Intelligence'.

80. See Antonio Negri, 'The Re-Appropriation of Fixed Capital: A Metaphor?', in *Digital Objects, Digital Subjects*, eds. David Chandler and Christian Fuchs (London: University of Westminster Press, 2019), 205–214; and Fredric Jameson, *An American Utopia: Dual Power and the Universal Army* (London: Verso, 2016).

# The racial regime of aesthetics
## On David Lloyd's *Under Representation*
Lucie Kim-Chi Mercier

One of the persistent difficulties of attending to race in the history of philosophy is the equivocal nature of this object. Long ignored by philosophers, 'race' has no clear status or obvious place in the history of philosophy, cutting across different areas of philosophical inquiry. Although in recent years historians of philosophy have been increasingly interested in the question of race, they hold the effects of their discoveries in check by narrowing down its concept to the extreme. In particular, with a few notable exceptions, they tend to keep the problem within tight limits by restricting their analyses to those *texts* by Leibniz, Kant, Fichte or Hegel in which the concept of 'race' – whether the scientific notion or the word – actually *appears*.

A different strand of reflections on the historico-philosophical underpinnings of race has emerged from cultural studies and literary scholars. While for historians of philosophy the notion of 'race' tends to detach itself from the problem it is supposed to register through an extreme historical segmentation of its concept, for the latter 'race' often becomes ubiquitous through an uncheckable proliferation of its effects and root causes. Less concerned with the crisis faced by philosophy as a discipline, they tend thus to view philosophical writings as part of a generalisable *discursive production* which, following the Foucauldian quandary, can hardly be kept within bounds. Consequently, we find ourselves in the paradoxical situation that, although the constitutive bind between Enlightenment philosophy and racialism is understood as irrevocable, the precise nature of their articulation remains hard to determine, as if race and racism were either deemed too foreign to philosophical discourse, or as too germane to it, without ever being able to strike the right balance between the two.

Here as in other matters, the scholarship on Kant proves exemplary, for in Kant the presence-absence of 'race' comports immense architectonic subtleties, in particular regarding the relationship between the critical works and the less 'noble' corpus constituted by the historical, geographical and anthropological writings. Moreover, in the micrology of each of the *Critiques* and in every essay, this relationship may always be questioned anew.

David Lloyd's last book *Under Representation: the Racial Regime of Aesthetics* (2018) invites us to confront the question of race in Kant's philosophy – and in the *Critique of the Power of Judgement* in particular – not directly but through a mediating term, that is, through the problem of representation.* The five essays that comprise the book constitute neither a denunciation of Kant's racism, nor a philological investigation into the historico-textual underpinnings of the Third Critique, but a reflection on the *unrepresentability* of race and racialised subjects which emerges from the aesthetic paradigm set up by Kant's *Critique of the Power of Judgement*. The problem of representation has long been a crucial one in black studies and postcolonial theory, but it takes an unusual turn here: rather than borrowing its terminology from post-structuralism, Lloyd's critique of representation stems from a long-standing engagement with Marxist cultural theory, and especially from a reflection on the hidden links between political representation and aesthetic 'culture'.

---

* David Lloyd, *Under Representation: The Racial Regime of Aesthetics* (New York: Fordham University Press, 2018). 240pp., £79.00 hb., £21.99 pb., 978 0 82328 238 8 hb., 978 0 82328 237 1 pb.

## Abolishing culture?

The book comprises five essays, the composition of which span from the early 1990s to the present. As he states in the Preface, Lloyd's project emerged in the midst of the so-called culture wars of the 1980s, and expands on the theses previously developed with Paul Thomas in a first book, *Culture and the State* (1999), which investigated the rapport between culture and state in the writings of the English romantics. Looking at the advent of the figure of the 'citizen-subject' in nineteenth-century England, *Culture and the State* emphasised the fundamental role played by pedagogy and education in the process of consolidation of the state, developing an account of the emergence of governmentality that could function as an alternative to what they criticised as Foucault's 'virtual positivism', and asking instead: 'how do state institutions come to seem evident within the common sense of a population?'[1] The concept of representation was already at the crux of this project, since the state was analysed as an engine of cultural *assimilation*: 'It is within the concept of representation that we trace the manner in which an apparent parallelism between state and cultural theory gives way to a relationship of substitution or supplementation in which culture comes to mediate between a disenfranchised populace and a state to which they must in time be assimilated.'[2]

As Lloyd investigates the entanglements of race and aesthetics in *Under Representation*, the concept of 'culture' remains similarly central. Importantly, and against its recodification in various strands of cultural studies, 'culture' is to be taken in its largely polysemic, nineteenth-century sense, of 'formation' or 'education', 'civilisation' or 'civility', but also art and refinement. In other words, Lloyd reads Kant through a decidedly Schillerian lens, by emphasising the idea that common sense is the 'foundation equally of the aesthetic and the public sphere';[3] a conception that would be taken up and shared by the likes of Wordsworth, Coleridge and Matthew Arnold. At the crossing point of a critical history of 'culture' and the problematic of race, *Under Representation* performs, then, a critique of both so-called 'Left aesthetics' and postcolonial theory. For Lloyd, neither field has sufficiently taken stock of the constitutive link binding together state violence and aesthetic culture, a link that stretches from nineteenth-century European nationalisms to postcolonial nationalisms. Any hasty recovery of the 'emancipatory' power of aesthetic philosophy thus skips over a critique of *Bildung* philosophy that hasn't yet been completed, especially in institutions that are still seamlessly reproducing its underlying model, such as the university.

Put otherwise, *Under Representation* grapples with one of the enduring heritages of Enlightenment philosophy: the assumption that aesthetics constitutes a domain of authentic freedom, the persisting bind between aesthetics and emancipation. By focusing on the political subtext of the Third Critique, Lloyd occupies a similar terrain to Hannah Arendt's late *Lectures on Kant's Political Philosophy*,[4] but his perspective is diametrically opposed. If paragraphs §39 and §40 of the *Critique of the Power of Judgement*, where the concept of 'sensus communis' appears, are indeed a key to Kant's political philosophy, it is this that enables us to understand the fundamentally exclusionary dimension of aesthetics and politics, not their democratic foundation. Furthermore, Lloyd interprets this political subtext *simultaneously* at the level of the formation of the 'citizen-subject' and at the level of 'race'. In this way, he grounds the analysis of the passages in which Kant's racialism emerges (for example, the evanescent figures of 'New Hollanders and inhabitants of Tierra de Fuego', the Savage and the Savoyards) in a systemic reflection on the racial politics of aesthetics. Or, in other words, he offers a systemic analysis of what Spivak, for one, has addressed as 'casual remarks' and 'foreclosures' in the textual economy of the Critique.[5] For Lloyd, 'Kant's work is saturated with politics even, and perhaps especially where it is ostensibly not at all political' (33).

To speak of a 'regime' rather than a 'discourse' or 'apparatus' precisely serves to highlight that 'the aesthetic' has a constitutively masked political dimension. Indeed, Lloyd goes back to Marx's description of German philosophy as *forestalled* politics: aesthetic philosophy would have both realised and closed off the potentialities of political revolution, translating its representational stance into pedagogical institutions (34–35). 'In the process of translation, the terms of aesthetic culture established by writers like Kant and Schiller continue to work as a template, allowing one to formalise in general terms the continuing relationship of the aesthetic to the political through the longer history of liberal cultural formations' (35). In turn, race is nested in this representational structure, whereby the subject's freedom is deferred into the ideal of 'free aesthetic judgements'.

Paradoxically, then, it is what seems least 'interested' that is in fact most *interested* – since for Lloyd there is no distinction anymore between the formalism of Kant's move to *sensus communis* and the need to root the aesthetic domain outside of, and yet in constant rapport with, politics. The culture of disinterest becomes the emblem of a typically liberal versatility in politics. As Lloyd writes, '[t]he aesthetic sphere is held to transcend all contingent differences, and, with less paradox than might at first appear, it is in defining this domain as beyond political interest that the formal terms of bourgeois or liberal ideology are constituted' (24).

## The logic of exemplarity

Lloyd seeks nothing less than a redefinition of *race* through this aesthetic regime of representation, arguing that 'aesthetic culture itself constitutes the formal principles of racist discourse, that the indices of difference on which racism relies gain their meaning from a distribution of values determined by an aesthetic philosophy that founds the idea of a universal common sense and its space of articulation, the public sphere' (91). The originality of his project lies in its attempt at grasping race in neither a sociological, phenomenological or psychoanalytical register, but in a typically *critical* and post-critical register in which the logical defines the categories of experience. It is precisely *because* of Kant's puzzlement with regard to the (possible) formalisation of aesthetic experience and the elaboration on 'reflective judgement' that the Third Critique is a particularly interesting place to start. Indeed, this uncertainty would manifest the presence of concurrent or competing movements of generalisation / universalisation, between the formal equality of judgement and the empirical diversity of the human. At the heart of this conflict lies the empirico-transcendental doubling that captivated Foucault, but which the latter failed to investigate from the standpoint of racial difference. Like Denise Ferreira da Silva, who draws abundantly on the Kantian corpus,[6] Lloyd understands that it is on such a hypothesis that our ability to offer an analysis of the representation mechanisms at the root of racialisation and racial judgement depends. Focusing on the various movements of universalisation and generalisation at play in the Third Critique, the difficulty for Lloyd is to correlate the process of 'formalisation' taking place in the communal (*Gemeinschaftlich*) foundation of aesthetic judgement with the production of racial(ised) subjects, i.e. with the production of subjects that are coded at once anthropologically and historically.

The key is to divide 'the Kantian universal in order to analyse the working of different modes of generalisation, universalisation and formalisation but also the related literary tropes of metaphor and analogy at stake in the Third Critique. Here, as in a previous article,[7] Lloyd discusses, in particular, the crucial importance of Kant's use of examples and the dynamics of *exemplarity*. Unlike subsumption, exemplarity has a temporal logic attached to it:[8] an 'exemplary' case, by virtue of being a 'model' (*Muster*), turns into a law of development. This means that the passage from the example to the model or the exemplary, although it seems formal, immediately harbours historical and political dimensions. Exemplarity turns out to be a pivotal element in the articulation of the racial problematic with the broader question of representation. Indeed, it is because the temporality of the formation of the aesthetic subject becomes a model for cultural progress at the level of world-history, and communication through the *sensus communis* becomes a model of 'lawful sociability' (§60), that racial hierarchy re-emerges at the heart of Kant's Third Critique. *Under Representation* points to the importance of further unpacking this temporality of universalisation, which, unlike Hegel, Kant didn't fully explicate.

Lloyd's project demonstrates the inadequacy of some recent attacks on the 'postcolonial' made in the name of universalism. For the point is not to oppose universalism and particularism or singularity *in abstracto*, but first and foremost to unpack the variety of universalisation processes, in theory and in practice, that have grounded, and reproduced, the logics of race. This is a larger project to which Lloyd provides an important contribution. However, the relationship between the formal, on the one hand, and the historical, on the other, is not as fully fleshed out as we might hope, for Lloyd doesn't venture into the Kantian texts devoted to history and progress, nor into Kant's *Anthropology*, and instead draws mainly on a notion of progress analysed through the prism of pedagogy and via other authors such as Schiller.

At the level of methodology, Lloyd's undertaking shows that thinking 'representation', race and aesthetics within a single theoretical figure requires us to move quickly through various steps of generalisation, starting with the general term 'aesthetic' itself. By nominalising aesthetic into 'the aesthetic', Lloyd chooses to bypass some pivotal moments in the history of post-Kantian aesthetics, preferring to assume the continuity of a tradition running from Schiller to Rancière over discontinuities brought about in this history by Romanticism and the Frankfurt School, under the heading of art theory. (Spivak's own reflections on 'aesthetic education',[9] though so wonderfully at odds with Lloyd's argumentative trajectory, are also strangely absent from this book.) Whilst Lloyd strives to distinguish the notion of 'regime' from that of 'discourse', we might wonder whether the former does not encounter the same methodological difficulties as the latter, when it seeks to offer itself as a coherent theory. For although Lloyd is adamant that we should bring back the 'aesthetic regime' to regulations and forms of subjection emanating from the *state*, and thus to its material underpinnings, such a 'regime' also depends on the epistemological naturalisation of representation by aesthetics, that is, on the generalisation and systematisation of the activity of representation, 'from the most fundamental acts of perception and reflection to the relation of the subject to the political and the economic, or to the social as a whole' (7). However, to show that aesthetic discourse, or that philosophical aesthetics, is permeated by the operations of race does not require us to account for the singularity of 'aesthetic' over other Enlightenment discourses about the 'human'. Unfortunately, a justification as to why this all-encompassing matrix of representation is *aesthetic* – rather than anthropological or historical, or a particular constellation of these different theoretical fields – is missing from Lloyd's book.

## Whiteness of the citizen-subject: Kant/Fanon

While Kant may be the central reference of *Under Representation*, it is Frantz Fanon who remains Lloyd's principal (if sometimes implicit) interlocutor, thus generating an unusual dialogue between Kant(-ianisms) and Fanon(-isms). The triumph of representation in the aesthetic sphere is contrasted here to what Fanon analyses as the failure of the anticolonial claims to representativity. In targeting the 'racism of culture' (70), Lloyd pursues an early Fanonian, typically post-war line. Indeed, in the 1950s one of the difficulties of theoretical anticolonialism was precisely to demonstrate that claims to cultural or civilisational development would do nothing to emancipate the people subjected to colonial violence. As Fanon famously explained during the First Congress of Black Writers and Artists (1956), any claim to culture is suspicious and contains a half-masked racism.[10] At the crux of this debate lay the thorny question of the role of the intellectual in decolonisation, since the intellectual vanguard was also the most 'assimilated' section among the colonised population, and hence, in David Lloyd's conception, those who were most integrated within the state mechanisms of representation.

In the central and best-known chapter of the book, 'Race Under Representation', it is the notion of 'assimilation' that operates as the conceptual connexion between *Bildung* philosophies and Fanon's theory of racial subjection. Lloyd thereby establishes an unusual bridge between the nineteenth-century figure of the citizen-subject and the production of colonised subjects in the 'French Imperial nation-state' (Gary Wilder); a connexion that, we may hypothesise, probably emerged through Lloyd's work on Ireland, since the Irish case was uniquely structured by an ensemble of pedagogic and institutional measures, on the one hand, and by a singular racial order, on the other.[11] As is well-known, the nineteenth-century ideologies of European emerging nation-states were carried over into anticolonial discourse. Contrasting with this 'black Bildung', or what Pheng Cheah has described as the 'organismic' narratives of anticolonial nationalism,[12] the end of Fanon's Bildung is 'not identity but the discovery of the culturally constitutive function of racism; it reveals the insistence of a splitting rather than the fulfillment of a developed subject' (91). Importantly, Lloyd claims that the persistence of racial formations to this day indicates the state's failure to 'totalise the domain of the subject', be it under the umbrella of assimilation or multiculturalism. Without fully thematising it, he develops a theory of the split S/subject. The chapter's pivotal contention is that the existence of the Subject as the ideal-type subject of aesthetic judgement and citizen-subject of a unified public sphere irremediably gives rise to its twin figure; that is, the subject of race. In other words, the regime of representation, by instituting the Subject, institutes itself immediately as a regime of assimilation, and thus as an essentially racial regime. This racial regime does not only prevent certain populations from being *adequately* represented (*vertreten*, *Vertretbarkeit*), it also bars their access to representation itself (*vorstellen*).

Lloyd reinterprets Fanon's own analysis of the pathological subject (of race) through the prism of representation. Throughout *Black Skin White Masks*, Fanon describes various ways in which the white or the coloniser, for the black subject, functions as a *third* person, an observer, a fictional eye. This is for instance the case in Fanon's rewriting of Adler's theory in chapter 7 of *Black Skin White Masks*. Drawing on Adler's analysis of the inferiority complex as the root of neurosis, Fanon emphatically claims that 'Antillean society is a neurotic society'.[13] In the Antilles, one needs to supplement Adler's comparison mechanism with a third term, the 'White', which constitutes the fiction of self-identity and mastery, and the projected locus of the black's judgement. Whiteness, then, doesn't simply designate a 'Subject without properties', but encapsulates the very capacity of representation (*Vorstellung*), that capacity for inscribing a difference within the human. Lloyd's theorem is that 'it is impossible for the racialised individual to enter the domain of representation except as that Subject that negates difference and therefore the racialised subject itself. Assimilation is self-negation, "renunciation" as Fanon puts it' (92). This is one of the senses in which race is *under* representation: it lies underneath the threshold of representation, because it is constitutive of its regime. In this sense there can be no 'racial democracy' (12–13). This is Lloyd's radical way of intervening within the debates on multiculturalism and curricula transformation in the university, which, as he explains, provides the political backdrop for the book as a whole.

Lloyd underscores the fact that both Kantian aesthetics and racialism posit 'indifference' and the 'un-marked', but also dis-interest and impartiality as the high point of the civilisational scale and the telos of human development. Furthermore the very idea of *sensus communis*, by establishing as norm a 'subject without properties', a purely formal and exchangeable subject, produces whiteness: 'The white assumes the position of universally representative man within the narrative of representation itself. That is not to say that the white man is (yet) identical with the position of pure, universal identity that is the Subject without properties but rather that he stands as its representative' (89). Crucially, Lloyd holds that race is no 'ontological or essential quality but is constructed in differential relation to the normative culture of the state' (93). What separates the positions of whiteness and blackness, then, cannot be 'difference', but instead the chasm between self-identity (through representability), on the one hand, and non-identity, on the other.

For Lloyd, the typically aesthetic 'as if' judgement, the possibility of a common sense, determines the logical and ethical foundation of social relations in the civic-bourgeois order. By drawing an itinerary from the production of the citizen-subject to the problematic of race, Lloyd interestingly follows a similar thought trajectory to that of Étienne Balibar in his work on anthropological differences. But whereas Balibar considers 'anthropological differences' to be the unavoidable excess of civic-bourgeois universality and the irresolvable consequence of political modernity,[14] Lloyd's suggestion is that the mechanisms of racialisation are intrinsic to the very category of the subject. Indeed, while Balibar seeks to maintain the philosophical polysemy and political ambivalence of the modern concept of subject, Lloyd's notion of S/subject is embedded in *representation* in a fundamental way, ideologically and materially, through what he describes as the 'normative culture of the state'. Their bifurcation highlights the difference between a critique of racial violence that saves the integrity of philosophical conceptuality, and one which understands philosophy as yet another mechanism of representation, directly sustaining, and sustained by, the mechanisms of racial violence.

The final chapters of the book, 'Representation's Coup' and 'The Aesthetic Taboo: Aura, Magic, and the Primitive', explore two figures that stand beyond, or outside of, the regime of representation: the subaltern (in Spivak's account) and the work of art (in Adorno's). They constitute not so much upbeat conclusions or resolutions to the quandary of representation, as aporetic developments of the problem set in place. Although Lloyd is sympathetic to Spivak's arguments in 'Can the Subaltern Speak?', he highlights the consternation and paralysis, or even the aura of melancholia, that surround her figure of the Subaltern (96). Lloyd's qualm about Spivak, then, is that by characterising the Subaltern as the very limit of representation, by making of the Subaltern subject an unrepresentable figure, she transforms it into an ethical dilemma. Such 'partial analysis of the system of representation has the unintended effect of positing the unrepresentability of the Subaltern as a problem of the individual positioning of the intellectual and therefore as an ethical or an epistemological rather than a political matter' (118). Instead, Lloyd advocates an examination of the intellectual's constitutive role in the 'representative formations against which the subaltern emerges differentially' (ibid.). Likewise, Lloyd remains ambivalent about Adorno's considerations on the artwork, arguing that his theory is at once embedded within the racial regime of aesthetics when it comes to his dismissal of 'magic', but also provides a way out of it, through his analysis of the non-identity of the work of art as a materiality that resists formalisation (156). These aporetic endings indicate that such theoretical attempts to move outside representation remain, as 'countermovement within the system of representation' (158), bound up with what they negate. For Lloyd, our task continues to be to adopt the standpoint of these excessive figures, and to 'think again the history of the present from the place of the subaltern subject of affectability and with the irreducible element of art that is its abundance even in the poverty of means' (158). Nonetheless, assessing the possibility of redemptory art forms beyond the racial regime of aesthetics is not a central concern of this volume. Instead, the book's main virtue is to keep us in this zone of discomfort, where the racial problematic springs out from the very core of 'our' Western philosophical and political modernity, that is, in the genealogy of the 'subject'.

*Lucie Kim-Chi Mercier is a member of the editorial collective of* Radical Philosophy.

**Notes**

1. David Lloyd and Paul Thomas, *Culture and the State* (New York: Routledge, 1998), 4.
2. Ibid., 5.
3. Ibid., 5.
4. Hannah Arendt, *Lectures on Kant's Political Philosophy* (Chicago: University of Chicago Press, 1992).
5. Gayatri Chakravorty Spivak, *A Critique of Postcolonial Reason: Toward a History of the Vanishing Present* (Cambridge, MA: Harvard University Press, 1999), 26–35.
6. Denise Ferreira da Silva, *Toward a Global Idea of Race* (Minneapolis: University of Minnesota Press, 2007).
7. David Lloyd, 'Kant's Examples', *Representations* 28 (Autumn 1988), 34–54.
8. Ibid.
9. Gayatri Chakravorty Spivak, *An Aesthetic Education in the Era of Globalization* (Cambridge, MA: Harvard University Press, 2013).
10. Frantz Fanon, 'Racism and Culture', in *Towards the African Revolution: Political Essays* (New York: Grove Press, [1956] 1988), 31–44.
11. See David Lloyd, *Irish Culture and Colonial Modernity 1800-2000: The Transformation of Oral Space* (Cambridge: Cambridge University Press, 2011).
12. Pheng Cheah, *Spectral Nationality: Passages of Freedom from Kant to Postcolonial Literatures of Liberation* (New York: Columbia University Press, 2013).
13. Frantz Fanon, *Black Skin White Masks*, trans. Richard Philcox (New York: Grove Press, 2008), 188.
14. See Étienne Balibar, *Citizen Subject: Foundations for Philosophical Anthropology*, trans. Steven Miller (New York: Fordham University Press, 2017), 275–302.

# Critical theory and lived experience

## Interview with Detlev Claussen

Detlev Claussen with Jordi Maiso

Detlev Claussen (b. 1948) is Professor Emeritus of Social Theory, Culture and Sociology at Leibniz Universität Hannover. In the mid-sixties he moved to Frankfurt to study with Theodor W. Adorno and Max Horkheimer, where he was actively involved in the protest movements associated with the political upheavals of 1968. In the seventies, Claussen worked as Oskar Negt's assistant, with whom he shared the common project of opening up new avenues for critical theory without renouncing the thought of their intellectual mentors. Since then, Claussen has argued that instead of offering an overarching theory that can be applied from 'outside' of existing social reality, critical theory offers a variety of strategies that allow us simultaneously to disentangle and invigorate present experience. Claussen has written on a wide range of themes, including social theory, psychoanalysis, the sociology of science and culture, as well as anti-Semitism, racism, nationalism and migration. His biography of the legendary Jewish coach and footballer Béla Guttmann, yet to be translated into English, offers a prime example of how his published work cannot be separated from the wider context of his intellectual biography. Both an essayist and Adorno's biographer, Claussen is one of the leading lights of critical theory today.

**Jordi Maiso:** How did you come to critical theory?[1]

**Detlev Claussen:** The need to transform the society in which one lives: that led me to critical theory. For me it wasn't present from the start, but the other way around, as is often the case with normal citizens lacking in intellectual self-awareness: they arrive at the theory after encountering obstacles in their attempt to change society. They begin to reflect on why such a transformation is so hard; and, when they come up against the failures that lived experience presents in the process, cannot help but ask what went wrong. Critical theory offers the means to understand this process because it was conceived from the outset as a reflection on a failed revolution. That is, while trying to understand society from the point of view of its transformation, critical theory participates in the Marxian theoretical tradition. However, how it thinks of its historical genesis is different. For critical theory it makes no sense to talk about the supposed 'revolutionary optimism of the twenties', as certain intellectual historians have put it. Rather, it was a desperate situation in which nobody knew if the attempt to transform society would have any effect or outcome whatsoever. It is this reflexive concern for historical experience that characterises critical theory, requiring it to constantly renew itself under the imperative of immanence. At the time, this imperative meant the incorporation of psychoanalysis. Yet this need for immanent renewal also means that one cannot focus exclusively on Adorno and Horkheimer's project.

**JM:** As a student, you moved to Frankfurt with the intention of transforming society. Why Frankfurt? Were you already familiar with Horkheimer and Adorno's work?

**DC:** I moved to Frankfurt in 1966. In Bremen, the city where I grew up, I'd listened Adorno's 'Progress' lecture as a student, and was completely convinced by it.[2] Immediately I knew I wanted to study with him. Until then I had only read one book by him, *The Jargon of Authenticity*, but gathered in it was everything I'd had to suffer intellectually as student; namely, the trivialised Heideggerianism that marked the intellectual climate in the Federal Republic of Germany. Today, I would say that it was a post-national-socialist climate, Nazi-lite, so to speak, that manifested itself in an omnipresent language: from radio stations and evangelical academia through to the 'Popular University' [*Volkshochschule*], etc. This jargon was omnipresent, and it had a sinister element, because as a teenager you didn't have the least idea of where it all came from. Then I read *The Jargon of Authenticity*, that blue pocket book which demonstrated the direct relation such language had to Nazism. The whole atmosphere was terribly oppressive, and behind its apparent naivety the ideology of 'national community' or *Volksgemeinschaft* persisted. Today the fifties are idealised, but that era was terrible. The Cold War was frightful: that narrowness that penetrated everyday life, the persecution of all remotely divergent behaviour. It was a totally conformist society. Likewise, if for some reason you disagreed, you were told to 'get lost to the other side!', to the German Democratic Republic. That's the environment we grew up in. The meanness and narrowness of the dominant mentality was unbearable. When you encountered the likes of Adorno, it was as if the blindfold had been lifted.

**JM:** Adorno was therefore a way out of this oppressive provincialism and post-national-socialist regime. Was Frankfurt also an appropriate place to leave behind the narrow mentality of the Federal Republic?

**DC:** Yes, Frankfurt was ideal. There, the student bodies were the product of the post-war re-education programmes. Student halls of residence were self-governing and had to offer something to different to the traditions of the German student fraternities [*Burschenschaften*]. We had for example a self-run film studio, where we could watch the whole gamut of contemporary films: from French New Wave to the new 'third' Polish cinema and American movies, etc. Similarly there was also the self-managed student magazine *Diskus*; a magnificent magazine for which I became editor of the culture section. At the time, the most important writers interested in democratic initiatives (for example, Günther Grass, Peter Weiss, Heinrich Böll, Martin Walser or Hans Magnus Enzensberger) had a great interest in writing in student publications because they knew that their future readers were there. As a student in Frankfurt there were many activities on offer, and that greatly expanded our intellectual horizon: it was like an explosion that took you out of the old Federal Republic. And all these institutions existed thanks to Horkheimer's work as rector, thanks to what he'd made possible on both a practical and a political level. It should not be forgotten that at the time in the Federal Republic people only ever talked about the wall and the division of Germany, accompanied by the constant lament that painted Germany as the victim of universal history: 'What a disgrace, everyone always against us Germans, why, such injustice', etc. On the other hand, Frankfurt offered another perspective, among other things because it was the city of the Auschwitz trials. Nevertheless, in general Frankfurt allowed a totally different relationship to society outside. There were many American students, but also some Israelis, and in this way we were suddenly confronted with realities which until then we hadn't had the slightest idea about. The media and the press were worse than they are today.

There was no news of conflict in the Middle East, for example, nothing was known about the Palestine Liberation Organisation (PLO), because in the media it was not mentioned at all. Yet, in Frankfurt, the Six-Day War was acutely felt as it affected our Israeli friends and their families.

**JM:** And in this broader Frankfurt context you began to study with Adorno. What do you remember about his lectures?

**DC:** When I arrived in Frankfurt, in the winter of 1966-67, Adorno was on a sabbatical term during which he finished writing *Negative Dialectics*. Instead I had the opportunity to attend an introductory course by Horkheimer, which influenced me decisively. At that point Adorno was totally overwhelmed with work, by the enormous effort that writing *Negative Dialectics* entailed, and which contributed to his early death. Actually you could argue that *Negative Dialectics* is a kind of extension of *The Jargon of Authenticity*: Although many people do not take it into account, they contain the same political impulse. In my second term I attended a series of seminars by Adorno on *Negative Dialectics*. I attended despite being only nineteen years of age because Hans-Jürgen Krahl, who was doing his doctorate with Adorno, thought that I had to learn everything as soon as possible, so he took me with him and said: 'You come with me, sit in the seat next to me, and nobody will dare question why you are here.' For this reason I ended up attending the seminar alongside twenty-seven-year-olds and doctoral students. I also met Angela Davis there, and that's how our friendship, which has lasted to this day, began.

**JM:** Did guests also attend the seminars from time to time?

**DC:** Of course. When there were two upholstered chairs it meant that Horkheimer had come from Montagnola, and if there were three, Horkheimer and Pollock. When Horkheimer was there, Adorno didn't talk to any of us. He was simply trying to present his ideas in order to hear what Horkheimer thought of them. That was enormously interesting. For example, sometimes they ended up arguing about the Freudian concept of sublimation, and Adorno was at the end of his tether as Horkheimer saw things completely differently. Then he would say: 'But Max, you have always said the same!' That's why it's so ridiculous that certain historical studies speak presumptuously of 'paradigmatic differences', asking whether or not one viewed a problem in one manner and the other in another: all that is nothing but pseudo-historiography. They discussed among themselves a variety of subjects as normal intellectuals do, albeit vastly learned ones. In any case they would usually agree on a joint formulation in the end. Later, these experiences prompted me to write about the real context in which critical theory was actually produced, and of course the Adorno biography offered the ideal opportunity to present my observations.

**JM:** What was Adorno's relationship with his students like?

**DC:** At first, Adorno seemed very elusive, but once you got past that he was very interested in his students and their individual progress. He always spoke of 'my students', and all those who were his disciples in the fifties and sixties had a very close and personal relationship with him. Many ended up in the media or in radio station newsrooms, that's why there are so many pieces for radio by Adorno. There was nothing better for an editor with a script at her disposal than the chance to invite Adorno on, because he spoke so well that you could print it directly. What's more, he always had something interesting to say. He often brought along some of the most distinguished protagonists of the German art and theatre worlds. There are some simply excellent radio broadcasts, of which a good many were ad-libbed. For example, the comments on

Proust collected in *Notes on Literature* are improvised glosses that Adorno made as Marianne Hoppe read his text live on air. It's amazing what can be gained from that text, and it was all off-the-cuff! You can read it five or six times and always discover new takes.

**JM:** And yet the academic situation for Adorno and his students was not easy, am I correct?

**DC:** It was not easy at all. Adorno followed his student's professional development closely, as for those who had done their doctorates with him it was not easy to find an academic placement. At the time it was very difficult to find a place in the university system and, contrary to what some argue again and again (all these stories about the 'Frankfurt School' as the 'second foundation of the Federal Republic' and other nonsense), Frankfurt was in fact very isolated, and Adorno himself was isolated in the University of Frankfurt until the end of the fifties. Working with Horkheimer and Adorno meant fewer professional opportunities. For example, Ralph Dahrendorf soon latched onto this and quickly disappeared from the Institute for Social Research because his stay in Frankfurt did not help him at all to promote his academic career. Habermas's relationship with the Institute is an unfortunate story, but it also highlights a typical impasse. This is what I wanted to document with the publication of Horkheimer's letter to Adorno in 1958 as it demonstrates very clearly what a university position meant for Horkheimer.[3] Horkheimer institutionally rejected the approximation of academic and political radicalism, because for him this necessarily led to a merely verbal radicalism. I think that in this context, rather than accuse Horkheimer of political cowardice for having dropped Habermas from the *Institute*, it is important to reflect on the veracity of those claims, given that ten years later Habermas' arguments against the students would be quite similar, but not exactly the same either.

**JM:** Was Horkheimer still the 'political brains' of the *Institute*?

**DC:** Without a doubt; to tell the truth, more so even than Adorno. While gathering information for my Adorno biography I found many things in the Horkheimer Archive that I could not use in the book. There I found for example a huge file on Iraq. I discovered that Horkheimer had dealt extensively with the coup in Iraq in 1958, as well as the Chinese Cultural Revolution. Many people simply did not understand just what drove him to study these events so devotedly, but he certainly had a good instinct. For him it was not solely about Iraq, rather that something terrible had happened there: it was a paradigmatic case of what I have called an 'ill-fated revolution'. And he had to study and reflect on it, because he saw that it was an absolutely fundamental issue.

**JM:** Yet one often gets the impression that Horkheimer is not taken into account. One might say that he is studied even less today. What was your impression of him?

**DC:** In Horkheimer, one met with a *grand seigneur*. For me, that's highly appealing and enormously likeable. Among today's academics you no longer see that at all. Even at the time Horkheimer had an elegance that few could match. He lived the good life: good food, good drink, good hotels, and the others, more or less, tried to follow his lead. There is a very nice memo of a conversation between Horkheimer and Pollock, in which they argue about what they want to do with the Institute and what rules they want to establish. Horkheimer writes to him: 'never do expenses'. His noble instinct was already evident in that for him there were much more important things than a career. For Horkheimer, as for many socialists of the twenties, the term 'upstart' was an insult: he did not want such people in the Institute. It is a completely different attitude to today's, from another culture, even. When in my first term I attended an introductory course taught by him, he impressed me deeply: his enormous intelligence and sharpness, his experience, the serenity with which he explained to students who were only eighteen years old *The Phenomenology of the Spirit*. I immediately wanted to find out more about him, and I soon discovered that without him there would have been no critical theory and no Institute for Social Research as we know it today.

**JM:** However, his later interpretations are often oversimplified or misinterpreted, which may have to do with his relatively scarce output, productively speaking, after his return to Europe. It would seem that *Dialectic of Enlightenment* signalled some sort of end for Horkheimer, at least for his writing, while Adorno's return spurred him to take on a frenetic work-rate. How would you explain this situation?

**DC:** When we talk about Horkheimer's apparent lack of productivity, we should not forget that few men have understood so quickly and synchronically that which came to pass after 1941. Once that is accepted, we see that the question of his output, not to mention that of an academic career, is ultimately not the most important thing. One is not especially motivated to pursue these directions either. However, Horkheimer's late annotations, the only things he came to write after 1945, are an inexhaustible source of interest since they contain excellent analyses. Many of them stem from conversations. Horkheimer and Pollock lived in Montagnola, and Pollock realised that he ought to write down the conversations he'd had with Horkheimer next to the fireplace over a glass of red wine. This is how *Splinters: Notes on a Conversation with Max Horkheimer* happened [*Späne: Notizen über Gespräche mit Max Horkheimer*], in which there are extremely intelligent reflections to be found.[4] It is a text that can be read again and again and one will always discover something new. Much the same can be said for the piles of correspondence. Horkheimer was a prodigious letter writer, and these letters have a lot of substance. The letters themselves provide excellent commentaries on specific situations of the time, and bear witness to the intelligence and precision with which he approached his subject matter. Nevertheless, it is fundamental to keep in mind that Horkheimer recognised and understood the significance of the fragment for the philosophy of history. Faced with the supremacy of political systems and conceptual disintegration, the fragment offered an appropriate response. Therefore, although it hadn't been planned that way, *Dialectic of the Enlightenment* passed down as a collection of fragments, a torso, a work in progress. That's why it can't be read as an exclusively academic text: it does not represent the last word on any given matter; rather it attempts to capture a particular historical moment, specifically the state of the world from 1944-47. The great contribution of the book is that Horkheimer and Adorno managed to recognise and express the epochal quality of the historical-social transformations they were examining precisely as they were taking place. Normally, the meaning of a particular shift is only ever understood twenty years later. Today, our understanding of the epochal change that took place in 1989 still has a long way to go, yet *Dialectic of Enlightenment* managed to recognise what was changing contemporaneously.

**JM:** Hence your insistence on the 'temporal kernel of truth' …

**DC:** Exactly. The legacy of critical theory, which I aspire to in my own theoretical work, is that we must understand the present. That doesn't mean that the past isn't important. What it means is that our conception of the past has to be continually renewed, but always from the perspective of the present. I would say that critical theory is a critique of the present and that the past is constantly transformed by this criticism. Therefore, it is absurd to try and establish a particular set of axioms or to try and marginalise a certain theoretical orientation by denouncing it as 'orthodox critical theory'. There can be no orthodoxy in the first place, as critical theory is not a doctrine that can be found in this or that book. Rather, it is the attempt to articulate historical and social experience by way of theory. That's why it was so important to Horkheimer to only publish those writings of his that met the demands of the present. In them, his capacity for historical differentiation is evident: a text written in 1966 has to be different than one written in 1944. Hence also his irritation with Habermas' text in his letter to Adorno: in 1958 you could not establish continuity with Marx's early writings without some kind of rupture. It is something people experience in their development: when you're young, you read the *Economic and Philosophical Manuscripts* with great excitement. What you have initially is that very enthusiasm: the encounter has yet to incorporate a moment of reflection. First, you have to keep in mind when the text was written, why it was written like that, what Marx understood by 'work', what relation that has to work today, etc. Of course the impulse behind the pre-1848 era that guides the early writings, known as the *Vormärz*, is very appealing, and that's why one deals with historical issues. However, to understand all that one needs much more than enthusiasm. Hence Horkheimer's distrust of pure enthusiasm and verbal radicalism. He had seen everything. Today I can understand it much better: I abhor verbal radicalism given my own experience. When you reflect critically on the sixties, it becomes clear that verbal radicalism often ends up accepting the conformism of protest. And that has dangerous consequences both theoretically and practically, for example when pre-fascism is confused with fascism.

## Critical theory and the student movement

**JM:** I would like to ask you some questions about your relationship with the anti-authoritarian protest movement of the second half of the sixties. You played an important role in Frankfurt's SDS [Socialist Federation of German Students] and had close contact with key figures in the movement like Hans-Jürgen Krahl and Angela Davis, who also had a strong link to critical theory. What was the historical and biographical situation which led you to the student movement?

**DC:** When I went to Frankfurt to study with Adorno, it was accepted everywhere that something had to give socially. It was in the air. There was great dissatisfaction with West Germany's post-Nazi situation. Shortly before, there'd been the 'Spiegel scandal', which posed a dangerous threat to the freedom of the press.[5] For my generation, which had been exposed to the benign influence of the re-education programmes, in a progressive intellectual climate, this situation became intolerable. A strong impulse to transform society emerged from the contradiction between the democratic aims we'd been educated in and the day-to-day reality of the Federal Republic. This was compounded by my first experience abroad, to England, where daily life seemed to be marked by a basic democratic outlook that simply fascinated me. It was not merely a democracy without content, where one just goes to vote every four years. Instead, there was a permanent spirit of debate: there were people on the streets that approached citizens for their views on the political issues of the day, asking for example what they thought about atomic war and things like that. Yet the decisive factor in understanding this drive for transformation was obviously Germany's past. In this sense, the Auschwitz and Eichmann trials were enormously important in my upbringing. We mustn't forget that nobody in the Federal Republic ever spoke about such things; it was as if they had never happened. And suddenly both trials could be followed on television. Naturally, this led to conversations within the family: we wanted to know who this Eichmann was, what he had done, and when we read something about him or discovered a new fact we were completely shocked. Little by little we began to understand why Germany was not particularly well-regarded in Europe and to see through the ideological construct that rendered Germany a victim of world history. As you can imagine, given the historical, social and generational situation, the SDS was very attractive. For example, in the mid-sixties the SDS campaigned for Nazi justice reparations, which for me was enormously important. My father was a solicitor who would've liked to have made it as a judge, however his examiner deemed him insufficiently national-socialist, fortunately. I remember that in the early fifties, from time to time my father would see old faces at the court entrance; sometimes, when I asked him what they'd done he'd simply say: 'he used to be a judge'. Only later did I come to understand the situation: as judges they'd handed down death sentences over nothing, over trivialities. During this campaign, we discovered things that somehow we could have intuited but could not demonstrate. That was decisive for my entry into the SDS. The more you dealt with the subject, the more you felt your blood curdle. Besides, what was really mobilising was that not only did you come up against the events of 1933-1945, but also with everything that happened after. For us this didn't represent an attempt to rake up the past, on the contrary, such events were inseparable from our childhood and youth, from this totally enforced silence. It was as if we were covered in muck: there were issues that simply couldn't be touched, as it were, and if one did, the result was immediate social exclusion. In this context, the SDS played a very important role.

**JM:** That was also one of the main points of agreement between the SDS and critical theory, was it not?

**DC:** Yes, but in general the Frankfurt SDS had close ties to critical theory. Horkheimer and above all Adorno were regular guests at the SDS headquarters. With Adorno we saw each other very often and we argued a lot. He tried to convince us that it was somewhat imprudent to compare West German society with fascism: one could speak of a survival of national-socialism in the Federal Republic, even of a potential for fascism, but always stressing the fundamental difference between democracy, even in its authoritarian forms, and fascism. In spite of this, there was always the possibility of a reversal back to an authoritarian state, and this was a view that everyone shared, including Adorno. That's why he always referred to us as 'my students', because we represented the possibility of continuing the work he had done. We saw things in much the same light. For us it was a question of identifying a space in which to articulate a critical theory that understands society from the perspective of its transformability. By then, it wasn't possible to talk about a revolutionary movement of workers, let alone of a vanguard formation that would attempt a 'substitute revolution' of the proletariat, on their behalf and for them, so to speak. That's why we thought that the student milieu was a terrain where transformation could take place. For this reason, as potential intellectuals, the task of the students was to understand society – to understand it, but also to transform it. In this way, we tried to reflect on the problem of students and their social privilege: the intention was not to suppress privileges, but to extend them. The desire to reach beyond the university, to communicate what critical theory knew to the whole of society, all this had to be informed by such an intention. This was what the student movement in the second half of the sixties originally set out to do.

**JM:** And therefore, when you arrived in Frankfurt, you made the decision to join the SDS.

**DC:** Yes, in my first week I went to the SDS office on Wilhelm Hauff Street to sign up. Coincidentally Krahl was there, that's how we met, and immediately we went together to the printers to prepare pamphlets. I was quickly accepted into the group. Back then the bars were the heart of the SDS social scene. Krahl drank a lot. He set the pace with his doubles, a nightmare for the liver. Yet there was also much talk and discussion and I learned a lot. First of all, they insisted I read *The Phenomenology of Spirit*. I bought the book right away, but of course I didn't understand a thing, and so it was clear to me that I should join Krahl's research group as soon as possible. They were the ones who took me with them to the seminars: Adorno, Alfred Schmidt and, above all, Oskar Negt – that's how I met him. Negt did many things with us and took great care of our theoretico-political development. He was decisive in our learning: he was extraordinarily well-grounded theoretically and also very interested in working with us. He realised immediately that if he was able to convince Krahl to collaborate with his seminar, then he would bring all of his friends with him and in this way he could bring together the great critical potential there was in Frankfurt. The quality of the discussions in those seminars was excellent, first-class. His seminar on the philosophy of right, which lasted several for years, was also a great mainstay. In 1967 we began with twenty people and by 1968 we were two hundred and fifty, and there were also people like Alexander Kluge and his sister Alexandra. It was thanks to that seminar that Negt met Kluge. In 1968 it was fantastic to see.[6]

**JM:** What was the relationship with the older critical theorists like? Did they also collaborate closely, as did Negt?

**DC:** It was of a different kind, though of course very respectful and cooperative, too. They were extremely influential. Adorno was first of all our teacher, for us he was a figure of authority; Horkheimer was slightly secondary, but he was always available, on-hand, and we often bumped into one another. With Marcuse it was different; more of a friendship, and that was a decisive experience for my own personal development. In spite of an age difference of forty years, he was able to cultivate true friendships – that's a quality few people have, and Herbert had it. He always wanted to meet young people and had an enormous interest in what they thought, what they did, etc. On the other hand, his advice helped us a lot in various difficult moments, for example in our discrepancies with Adorno. We invited him again and again to Frankfurt, and from 1967 until his death he came every year, and we also went to visit him in San Diego. We saw each other often and so we could maintain our friendship. His presence was enormously important for me.

**JM:** Given the context of the relation between critical theory and the student movement, how did things stand with Jürgen Habermas?

**DC:** With Habermas there were also intense debates and very incisive discussions, but back then Habermas was much more political as an intellectual. His seminar was held on Saturday mornings. His assistants were the ones who prepared the discussion and, as Negt was his assistant, he also participated in the seminar; the discussions with him were simply great, because he was incredibly well prepared. Then there was also Krahl and our group, whose level of preparation was also high. We discussed Habermas' ideas and texts. There were also, of course, some of Habermas's favourite students, such as Albrecht Wellmer and Claus Offe, who generally had little to do with us, but actively participated in debates of an extraordinarily high quality. I remember that there were some enormously interesting discussions, for example on the essay 'Science and Technology as Ideology' [published by Habermas in 1968], and all that was also fundamental to our learning process.

**JM:** When in this case you speak of 'us', to whom are you referring exactly?

**DC:** I'm talking a relatively small group of people. In a way, I'm referring to the group that coalesced around Krahl and a handful of students who wanted to do their doctorate with Adorno. As Adorno's doctoral student, Krahl was exemplary. When Horkheimer said that Adorno was proud of 'his students', he was referring to this group of people around Krahl, since, of course, they were not the dimmest and you could expect a lot from them.

**JM:** Yet this group of people also played a fundamental role in the occupation of the Institute for Social Research in January 1969, is that correct?

**DC:** Undoubtedly the occupation of the Institute was the stupidest action we undertook. Few situations are more deserving of the label 'idiotic'. Besides, to top it off, I was the spokesperson for the action and had to try to sell it to the press. In my opinion, Adorno understood everything perfectly: our strike movement was collapsing and we needed a new twist; 'they've done so because they were running out of breath, for propagandistic aims', he said at the time.[7] In fact, it had been Krahl's idea and we agreed to see it through, against our better judgment. It's also true that we already felt it wasn't the right course of action to take. Krahl's obituary for Adorno was shot through with guilt,[8] and when the funeral took place, he said: 'If anyone is out of order, if it occurs to anyone to do anything, I will kill them.' Everybody was on their best behaviour, and usually this only works when the feeling of guilt is widespread. However, at the time we simply hadn't understood the severity of the situation. Not for a moment had we been aware of the terrible strain Adorno and the Institute were under. Walter Rüegg, who was the rector of the university at the time, a sociologist of the Faculty of Economic and Social Sciences, was not exactly a friend of critical theory. He had put Adorno under enormous pressure, and it was clear that they were going make him personally responsible for anything that may have happened during the occupation of the Institute. That way they could get the Federal State of Hessen to end their financial support to the Institute for Social Research, so that the sociological model of the Faculty of Economic and Social Sciences could occupy the whole field, thus eradicating critical theory from the University of Frankfurt. Yet we did not take all that into account, we behaved like apolitical ignoramuses. We were only interested in how our 'assassination of the father' looked to those outside the university, and indeed in that respect it worked well.

**JM:** Notwithstanding, wasn't the occupation of the Institute an attempt to stop the further disintegration of the protest movement?

**DC:** Strictly speaking, that process had not yet begun, but of course the occupation was a decisive contribution to it. What you could already notice then was that little by little militants were becoming increasingly competitive. I do not want to psychologise the facts, but for a period Krahl was afraid that he would be overtaken on the left by exclusively militant forces. There were for example the so-called 'leather jackets' lot that caught everyone's eye because they were totally anti-intellectual and opposed to theory. For example, in our shared flat they assaulted and destroyed a friend's bedroom, and some of the traces of this incident are to be found in Adorno's 'Marginalia to Theory and Praxis'.[9] In the desolate atmosphere after the occupation of the Institute, Krahl tried to smooth things over with them, but that only lasted for two or three weeks. In the end he had to distance himself because these were people who were completely hostile to theory and reflection, and Krahl was the epitome of a reflective, theoretically-oriented individual. In the summer of 1969, Krahl turned his attention towards theoretical questions with renewed intensity, and in this last phase he wrote very interesting things about the new problems faced by critical theory in its relation to protest movements.

**JM:** It is difficult to avoid the impression that Krahl has been unjustly forgotten, especially at a time when movements associated with '1968' are given great historical weight.

**DC:** Yes, in that respect many things are overlooked. I remember that at the time, Krahl seemed to me to be older, a fully-rounded adult, but he was only twenty-five or -six, like Rudi Dutschke: that's what's incredible! Rudi led a terrible life, travelling constantly from one place to another, and meanwhile he read, read and read like a madman, and that was only possible by sacrificing hours of sleep. That has to be taken into account when his writings are commented on today: it was a lifestyle that had nothing to do with academia or the university. The writings of Krahl or Dutschke available today are texts that have been either taken from notes or transcribed from recordings: they can't be considered in the same way as a piece of writing composed over several years! Yet at that point two thousand people were listening to these texts. Perhaps some half-grasped a couple of their ideas. Today we lack the sensitivity to understand the enormous potential these people had. Krahl was undoubtedly one of the most intelligent and astute people I ever met, who nevertheless had a miserable life-story and an untimely, terrible death.

## After Adorno's death

**JM:** Adorno died in August 1969 and Krahl in February 1970. The working context of critical theory in Frankfurt, in which different teachers from the University of Frankfurt collaborate with one another and with some groups of students, little by little dissolves. You have identified Adorno's death as the key moment in this process. How did this dissolution take place and why? Why did a large number of your circle end up moving to Hannover with Oskar Negt?

**DC:** Without a doubt, Adorno was the figure around which everything had crystallised. Adorno exerted a very strong pull, and not only in the Federal Republic of Germany – that's why Angela Davis came to Frankfurt, through Marcuse. Although in the first analysis we saw ourselves as his disciples, critical theory was for us a collective project that ought to be continued, not a kind of 'unitary paradigm' or anything like that. We considered our work an elaboration of critical theory in the manner that Adorno intended, and our aim was to continue in this direction. Nevertheless, after Adorno's death we found ourselves confronted with the unavoidable question: 'How do we do something new now? From where do we glean new impulses?' To this was added the whole dispute over who was to get Adorno's chair at the University of Frankfurt. First of all, some considered whether Leszek Kolakowski ought to be his successor, but we could not allow it. Habermas' ambivalence towards Adorno's critical theory can already be seen in the fact that he was the one to propose Kolakowski in the first place: he was not interested in a continuation of the old style of critical theory. However, as long as we had the right to our say and a vote, we did our best to make sure that his chair wasn't occupied by someone who was openly anti-Adorno. There were those who attacked us for our lack of sympathy for those persecuted by communist regimes in Eastern Europe, but anyone who has even glanced at the three volumes of Kolakowski's *Main Currents of Marxism* knows to what extent this book is defamatory against critical theory. For example, it claims that Herbert Marcuse had demanded that libraries be burned, as if he were a Nazi book-burner himself! Those assertions are indisputably false, simply defamatory: we could not allow someone with that kind of attitude to occupy Adorno's post at the University of Frankfurt. It would have been more logical then for Oskar Negt to have occupied the chair. Everything seemed to point in this direction, and I think it would have been the best outcome. Negt was surrounded by the most promising young students, and without a doubt was perfectly qualified both intellectually and professionally for the post. However, even though Negt was an extraordinarily political man, he ended up declining the offer. He was afraid that pressure from the Ministry of Culture would be too great, that he'd be involved in a permanent struggle, but also taking into account the fact that it was not yet clear which direction the student movement would take. In the end he preferred a change of environment and moved to Hannover. His intention was to create a centre for critical theory there, and I have been involved in this project for almost twenty years. After Adorno's death it was undoubtedly one of Oskar Negt's merits to have created this space where one could reflect and re-examine the situation. We could no longer continue what we had done in Frankfurt without some sort of interregnum. The point was to ask how we might appropriate a legacy of thought that was so fragmented, and also establish something new, and this transfer to Hannover forced us to resituate ourselves, to rethink our circumstances. This whole process of reflection, which attempted to develop critical theory in a political and not merely academic sense, is documented in my book *With a Heart of Stone* [*Mit steinerem Herzen*].[10]

**JM:** And where did the renewed impulse to continue with critical theory stem from? By then there wasn't much to be hoped for from the protest movement, am I right?

**DC:** Certainly not. After 1970, with the dissolution of the SDS, we no longer knew what to do politically. Everything broke down quickly into small groups, the majority of which were of a Marxist-Leninist character, which also reveals the backlash of the movement as a whole. All these Marxist-Leninist groups were really repulsive. To this day I associate them with feelings of disgust. Their anti-intellectualism, their aversion to pleasure and art, their bad asceticism, as if what we needed in the West was the misery of real socialism: all that was frankly repugnant to me. These groups detested critical theory from the beginning, it was their number one enemy, but in reality they were unable to say anything other than 'Critical theory is bourgeois, and you are all bourgeois because you are critical theorists.' Yet what I thought really dangerous was the way such groups enforced conformism in their own ranks: anything that deviated from the norm was threatened and persecuted highly aggressively. That is the most terrible thing of all. And when all these people are expelled or become ex-Marxist-Leninist, the majority of them do not change. Perhaps the outline of what they once defended changes a little, but in any case, anyone who is not mainstream, who does things on their own terms, continues to be a target of hatred. That's why I had to leave Germany – to find something new, new leads, a new well of experience with which to water the theory.

In those years there were several factors and experiences that were very relevant to my development. In the first place, Italy was enormously important. After 1969, the most significant thing that remained of the protest movement was the Italian situation and, through friendships and personal relationships, I myself ended up going there. In the seventies I spent a lot of time in Italy, especially in Milan, later in Rome, and there I met some really intelligent and fascinating people. This is how I met Adriano Sofri, one of the founders of Potere Operaio, an incredibly smart guy, and through him I came round to the idea of examining Eastern modes of production. Unfortunately Sofri has been imprisoned unjustly for years in connection with the events of Piazza Fontana: he has paid a terrible price having done absolutely nothing; and that people like Berlusconi, who are the ones who should truly go to jail, should be re-elected and return to lock Sofri up is simply unspeakable.[11] What has happened in Italian society in recent years is something that I simply cannot understand.

**JM:** In the Italy of the seventies you must have found a political situation that bore little resemblance to the one you'd encountered in Germany. Is that so?

**DC:** As an outsider, what quickly caught my attention was that even though friends were clearly distancing themselves from the Italian Communist Party, it was obvious that the PCI was at the heart of the entire Italian political environment, both positively and negatively: the presence of communism was simply stronger and also had institutional support. In those years in Italy I also worked heavily on Eurocommunism, which at that time was enormously important. New friendships emerged from the confrontation with Eurocommunism, especially Luciana Castellina and, through her, Rossana Rossanda. Thanks to them we were also able to get in touch with Eastern European dissidents. That impressed me and affected me a lot, because they were people and intellectuals of a very special order. In 1977 I met some of these dissidents at a conference in Venice [organised by Il Manifesto].[12] Among them were [Ukrainian mathematician and cybernetician] Leonid Pljuschtsch, who had just left the Gulag, Edmund Baluka, one of the leaders of the Szczecin strikes, a movement that preceded Solidarnosc, and, above all, Franz

Marek, thanks to whom I was better able to understand the processes of transformation at work in Hungary and Czechoslovakia.[13] Experience of the Italian situation and contact with Eastern European dissidents enabled me to better understand the divided situation in Germany. On the other hand, thanks to Franz Marek I heard for the first time about the Hakoah football team in Vienna, and also of the enormous role they played in raising Jewish awareness up until the mid-thirties. This discovery would lead me several years later to occupy myself extensively with Béla Guttmann and Jewish football.[14]

**JM:** The problem of anti-Semitism would also be one of the fundamental concerns of your later work. Was your own biographical experience influential in this regard?

**DC:** Yes, initially it was thanks to the Jewish and Israeli friends I had met in Frankfurt. However

it eventually became a central issue that was to shape the next ten years. In Frankfurt I was in close contact with a Jewish support group, and I learned a lot from how it was established and progressed over time. From then on the situation in Israel-Palestine became a fundamental problem. From there arose the friendship with Dan Diner, who was enormously constructive.[15] Thanks to him, I learned many things about Israel-Palestine, but also about the meaning of the Middle East, in the widest sense. Finally, I became aware of wanting to continue working on the dispute between anti-Semitism and critical theory, since the 'Elements of anti-Semitism' chapter in *Dialectic of Enlightenment* was not the final word on the matter, but a point of departure that required elaboration. Out of these political experiences, I came to view my theoretical work as an attempt to articulate this problem and think it anew with pin-point accuracy.[16]

**JM:** What other experiences of this era were important for your intellectual development?

**DC:** In 1971-1972 Angela Davis was arrested, and that affected me a lot personally. The Sozialistische Büro was willing to start a campaign in favour of Angela's release and I was actively involved in it and I went to tour with them for a year.[17] On my part, the trip to the United States in 1978 was also undoubtedly a key experience. I visited the country to see friends and acquaintances, and so I acquired a panoramic view of the whole. Above all, I was impressed by the democratic character of daily life in America. Of course, racism, violence and white supremacy are deeply rooted in American society, and without a doubt there are crude adversaries of democracy, such as rednecks or the awful anti-abortionists. However, in spite of everything, it is a country that airs its discussions out in the open. Its basic structures are democratic, everything must be discussed, and that gives rise to a sort of *éducation sentimentale*. Definitively, all these experiences from the seventies were not only thought processes, but vital processes of experience, and that helped me enormously in reflecting on how to continue the tradition of critical theory. That's because critical theory needs the articulation of new experiences to fill it, and that's what I did then. The most important thing about such experiences was acting within a framework of relations alongside people who were working on similar issues, which represented a breakthrough in my own trajectory, and that is why we did our best to maintain contact; back then establishing such connections was not as simple as it is now. Therefore each encounter carried with it a tremendous broadening of horizons. This whole process of experience was fundamental for understanding the significance of social awareness and behaviour, including that of daily life. Later, in the nineties, I developed a whole theory of daily life, which was completely new territory for me, informed by all these prominent experiences.

**JM:** In 1978 you returned to Germany. Your return coincides with the so-called 'years of lead' of the Federal Republic, which today has become the subject of numerous publications and even some movies. What was your impression of the socio-political predicament Germany faced at the time?

**DC:** This period in Germany was unbearable, especially the whole issue with the Red Army Faction (RAF). I got to know everyone personally from the first generation of the RAF. They were all stupid and politically useless. You could say, with Walter Laqueur (with whom I disagree on almost everything else), that there has never been a group of more insignificant people about whom so much has been written. Fundamentally, all that was intended as a strategic backlash against '68, and there are still echoes of it today. The fact is that society had changed for the better, albeit indirectly, but this is how social transformation actually takes place: not because a couple of individuals make their wishes a reality, but through social conflicts and their development. For example, the level of social intolerance significantly decreased. In 1970, if a girl was wearing a short skirt or a boy had long hair, his hair would be pulled or they'd have things thrown at them in the street. Already by 1977 that was unimaginable. However, this process of transformation was counteracted at a political level. A frightening victim mentality emerged. If you made certain comments, that was enough to see you suddenly involved in a disciplinary procedure. If the social and political climate after the kidnapping of Schleyer and the events in Mogadishu had lasted for three further weeks, nobody knows how democracy would have ended up in Germany. That is something that is completely forgotten when talking about the RAF today. Heinrich Böll understood this victim mentality very well when he observed that something was not right in German society given that it had to mobilise sixty million inhabitants against six people. Similarly, among some there was the total idealisation of the RAF, which was completely insignificant with regard to the real social dynamic, with what was actually going on in German society. The RAF was simply a repulsive organisation of truly stupid people. You could not take them seriously, not even one of them was able to think politically. Even Ulrike Meinhof was totally apolitical; she did little else but moralise – not to mention Horst Mahler. And today they are styled as if they had been something extraordinary. The public is fascinated that there are people who go around with hand grenades and weapons! I cannot have the slightest respect for something like that, and I cannot take it seriously politically either. The members of the RAF were ideal victims for the secret services and, if they had not played their own game, they would have finished with them in four weeks: it was very easy to find them! Half the city of Hannover knew when Ulrike was there, because there were people who went around asking everyone if they could crash at hers. And the police, who had special units dedicated only and exclusively to finding her, do not know where she is? Those are the issues that need to be clarified, and not whether Karl-Heinz Kurras received some money from the Stasi or not.[18] What is certain is that the Stasi did not say: 'shoot Ohnesorg in order to trigger the rise of a protest movement in Germany', because the student movement disrupted the entire strategy of the SED [the governing party of the German Democratic Republic]. The illegal leaders of the KPD [German Communist

Party] tried time and again to exert influence on the SDS, but from the opposite direction. They said: 'You mustn't do this, you mustn't do that – you are only going to irritate people!', and things like that. In fact the anti-authoritarian protest movement was a real nightmare for authoritarian communists: they wanted something very different! That's why it's incredible, the nonsense you read in the newspapers today, and nobody dares contradict them.

## The actuality of critical theory

**JM:** From the end of the seventies, some academic volumes began to present the history of critical theory as the unified development of a project of 'interdisciplinary materialism'. In the eighties, with the publication of the theory of communicative action, the so-called 'paradigm shift' in critical theory was proclaimed. Since then the term 'critical theory' is often associated primarily with the name Jürgen Habermas, and Adorno's work is abstractly declared to have been 'superseded'. In this context you have spoken of an 'invention of tradition'. What consequences has this had for the reception of critical theory and for attempts to develop it?

**DC:** To understand the meaning of this whole process, an analogy could be established with the development of psychoanalysis. Psychoanalytic theory and praxis have remained completely at the mercy of the associations of psychoanalysts, and the implications of this development have already been criticised, for example by Paul Parin, who recently passed away. On the other hand, there have also been attempts to re-appropriate psychoanalysis for science, especially from the perspective of literary theory. Nevertheless, such attempts cling to psychoanalysis as a simple mode of representation, as if it were a purely academic theory in which contradictions and drives are no longer recognised, so to speak; that is, psychoanalysis as such is preserved, but its contribution to knowledge and self-knowledge, that which made it worthwhile, is eliminated. Something similar has happened with critical theory. The 'invention of tradition' has academicised it completely, and with this it has eliminated its principal attraction: it has made it one theory among others, a rung on the career ladder. However, according to my experience, critical theory is informed above all by a non-academic impulse. Critical theory requires an interest in emancipation and, to put it crudely, in human happiness. I understand emancipation to be the movement of a social totality that runs within each and every individual. Yet the interest in emancipation also requires reflection on the contradictions that hinder it; that is to say, it refers to what Parin has called 'the contradictions of the subject'. Experiencing these contradictions in the subject and wanting to understand them is the driving force that leads one to dedicate oneself to critical theory – that is why those who present critical theory as some kind of apocalyptic fantasy completely confuse its meaning. Every individual, if she is not psychically damaged, tries to close the gulf between her predicament and happiness. The attempt to overcome suffering is constantly renewed. Theoretical activity is therefore a moment in the articulation of a vital force, it is a union of the 'ego' and 'superego', and the 'super-ego' is not just an enemy soldier who watches over the occupied territory of the 'ego', but must also help the 'ego' to achieve satisfaction. Nevertheless, this is all completely neglected by the 'invention of tradition'.

**JM:** Sometimes you have the feeling that the so-called 'paradigm shift', with its turn towards the purely procedural, has finally emptied critical theory of all substance and experience.

**DC:** That's right. Actually this 'invention of tradition', with its merely instrumental understanding of knowledge, falls well below the level of *Dialectic of Enlightenment*. Enlightenment resorts to a focus on what is crudely instrumental, and in the end we have many great instruments, but we cannot build anything with them. In this sense the 'linguistic turn' has led to a dead end. Critical theory is now without an object, without content, without any experience that reflection requires in order to function. That is why the 'linguistic turn' has left a desolate intellectual landscape: everything consists of theoretical collections in which some things are hoarded alongside others, everything is deemed equivalent, everything is reconstructed, reformulated; it's enough to make you weep. That has nothing to do with critical theory; it is simply adaptation to a conformist academic culture. From those premises you can perhaps build an academic career or direct an editorial line, but of course it has little to do with the possibility of gaining knowledge about a society in transformation. Critical theory can only be renewed if one thinks with reference to new objects, and that also means referring to new contradictions. And in this sense I am an optimist, because there is now a need to restore substance to thought and that is why Adorno is being read again.

**JM:** Yet if critical theory is understood as elaboration of social experience by means of thought, is it not problematic to include Habermas in this theoretical tradition?

**DC:** First of all, we can't forget that Habermas represents a leap forward for German intellectuals: Habermas has been for the Federal Republic what Max Weber was for Wilhelmine Germany. He is a tremendously sharp and intelligent individual who has not shied away from political dispute; he is someone who has consistently opposed the reactionary tendencies that crop up again and again in German society. As a deeply democratic intellectual, Habermas is undoubtedly a very important figure for Germany, and also for Europe. However, the critical theory that I was attracted to was different. I think Habermas is actually closer to the tradition of Weber than of critical theory – hence the division of his writing along the lines of 'grand theory' and 'politics'.

The critical theory of Horkheimer and Adorno was closely linked to their experience of emigration and exile, and of course one cannot claim a similar background and say 'I belong to this tradition.' Nevertheless one should try to make such experiences bear fruit in the work itself. It is about making visible the experience of the present from the experience of the past. That's why I deal with issues such as those linked to migration. Today we no longer live in ethnically homogeneous societies and that raises new problems. In this sense, the critical theorist's experience of exile qualifies the understanding that these issues are not only problems of language acquisition or of integration, but that they require a new concept of culture. Culture is not like a billiard ball that is solid and sealed; rather the cultural process is a very complex issue that is in continual flux. That's why I think it is disingenuous when certain authors speak of a 'German' or 'Anglo-Saxon' tradition, as if they were fixed and separate entities that could be theoretically reconciled with the right array of tools.

**JM:** So, how can the reference to 'tradition' be understood today? In an anti-traditional sense, as Adorno would have said? As the search for the new in the old from the viewpoint of the present?

**DC:** For me, the book *The Invention of Tradition* by Eric Hobsbawm and Terence Ranger was very stimulating because from the German perspective England has always been admired for having an unbroken and accessible sense of tradition. In France, in England, and in the United States, bourgeois society was something real, but in Germany around 1800 there was nothing of the sort; that's why you had to think about it, and that's how the German intellectual tradition came about: without German misery there would have been no German idealism. Be that as it may, today we no longer have a tradition that we may call a whole, instead we have only broken continuities. Today we have to create our traditions, because tradition is not simply the transmission of the old, but the foundation of something new. In this sense you might say that Germany has a head start because we do not have the illusion of continuity that dominates in Anglo-Saxon countries. However, what is true is that we have such a strong rejection of the new that we are not capable of conceiving it as such. In 1989, a new reality was created in Germany, but we have termed it 'reunification', as if it represented the reestablishment of something from the past. In opposition, critical theory wants to understand the new and, after the Cold War, this can no longer be attempted from within national borders, rather it must take into account what has become of society globally. That is the current challenge: we live in a transformed society, but we lack the adequate concepts with which to grasp it. That's why critical theory is not simply 'there', it is not something available to us to inherit; instead it is something that we must develop.

**JM:** How would you explain the relationship between the inevitably historical character of the work of Adorno, Horkheimer and Marcuse and the relevance of their approaches? What's the significance of this 'tradition of thought' today?

**DC:** Critical theory is part of the great theoretical tradition of German idealism, in which the big themes were thought, freedom and action. However, it can no longer settle for idealism, as it has become aware of the limits of the Enlightenment, the limitations of spirit, of material contradictions – and that requires consciousness of the most terrible events in history and society. Critical theory states from the outset that these atrocities cannot be cancelled out by intellectual progress or the development of consciousness. And that means that critical theory is only possible by acts of remembrance. That's why I wrote Adorno's biography: for me Adorno is the nucleus of the 20th century, and only following his example can we continue to develop critical theory. The experiences he gives voice to in his thinking cannot be marginalised, one cannot say: 'that was simply a dark chapter of history'. Such experiences were not just a German adventure, but part of world history, and that is why we must reflect on national-socialism, on the gulag archipelago, and also, for example, on Chinese history, which in the past hundred years has been nothing but an accumulation of catastrophes. Crucially, all these experiences are deposited in today's subjects: the terror of the past is the fear of the present, that's why individuals no longer trust in their abilities, and the whole world has concluded in one way or another that human life is of little value or consequence, and you don't need to be a critical theorist to realise that.

**JM:** You have also pointed out that today we are no longer in a position to carry out an immanent critique of bourgeois society, since it no longer exists as such. What is there to draw on that could take critical social theory in the direction you propose?

**DC:** That's the subject of the book that will follow the one I'm working on right now. It is titled *Changes*, and it will thematise the relationship between the 'long nineteenth century', the 'short twentieth century' and the present. It will therefore constitute an attempt to read history and society as a palimpsest. Today the nexus of experience is no longer given: contemporary society is fragmented, everything appears disconnected. The Internet is a magnificent example: there are millions of perspectives, but in reality, the only thing that holds them together is the computer screen. That is, today the nexus has to be built out of the different fragments of experience. The dissolution of received experience, of inherited context, happened over time. Marx could still count on a lot of received knowledge, hence the prominence of Hegel and Ricardo in his work. For critical theory the situation was already more difficult, but nevertheless they attempted to analyse contemporary thought as part of a whole, for example in *The Critique of Instrumental Reason* by Horkheimer. That's no longer available to us, and, given the decline of academia and the university, probably won't be possible in the future either. That's why I'm interested in building an experiential totality, and *Changes* will do it by addressing food, sports, television or art, and also how the different fragments superimpose and overlap with one another. Due to the fact that today the totality of the 'spirit', as it were, or culture, is no longer a unity as it had been during the 'long nineteenth century', this whole is no longer so powerful and it does not subject individuals to such an overwhelming extent. And this also opens up new possibilities. There are those whose listening capacity is pseudo-deformed after a lifetime of being raised on a compromised musical language. Such people become very irritated when listening to Schönberg as his music doesn't have a melody. Nevertheless, current generations of students are free of these prejudices, they encounter Schönberg and are able to listen; for them this music is also sound in which something interesting might be found. Those are the moments in which you can begin to build anew the connections that make critique possible. In this sense, one might say that by doing theory you strengthen the subject, showing that it needn't be as fragile as it currently is. In fact what takes place, generally speaking, is that the subject encounters a series of socially enforced prohibitions and obstacles. These mechanisms prevent subjects from realising their social experience in an emphatic sense. Our job is to work against this tendency.

**JM:** How do you foster this emphatic intellectual experience? Is it possible to give voice to something like that in universities today?

**DC:** For the time being, I try to make these experiences possible in the shadow of the university.

With the current set-up of degree and master's degree, as exists in Germany and many other European countries, the possibility of having formative experiences during one's period of study is greatly hindered if not completely destroyed. Universities have become exam machines: your work-rate is monitored, but not what you learn. I think that the future for universities is pretty dismal as I get the impression that educational policy is directed by financial interests and a misunderstood utilitarianism. With regard to how intellectual wealth is produced, a completely mistaken approach predominates. This is because one can only have wealth when one has abundance, when other variables are allowed to come into play. What's useful from a practical point of view is generally the product of abundance, of a surplus, and not the product of attempting to obtain something directly. There are so many tests that demonstrate this that it's not necessary give any further detail. On the other hand, I don't know if universities are at all suitable places for critical theory. What I was able to experience was that it not only hinders the work of those who carry out critical theory in its most authentic sense, but to a certain extent it also persecutes them for doing so – just as anything that deviates from the norm is also pursued, and which in one way or another has to do with freedom and independence. That's why old-fashioned concepts like 'academic freedom' are today enormously important, because currently the university mostly tends to inhibit freedom rather than enable it.

However we needn't be so grim. In the past ten years I have met excellent groups of students all over the world, even in universities where one expects only to meet students from elite institutions who have been completely hot-housed and know exactly which career path they're on. I found that even in those universities there exist critical theory reading groups that look to maintain and encourage discussions that often go on for hours – such is the liveliness of their interest. When in discussion with them, you sense that their needs come up against the institution, and they thus find themselves called to take up themes and issues that are beyond the mainstream, and that is a good substrate for critical theory. After having been so isolated throughout the nineties and early noughties, seeing this new interest resonate even at a global level has filled me with optimism. This isn't to say that I am naïve. Instead, I would like to think that I am true to the maxim of my mentor, old Horkheimer: 'Pessimism in big matters, optimism in the small.'

## Translated by Alex Alvarez Taylor

### Notes

1. This interview was held on the 12 June 2009 in Frankfurt am Main. The transposition from spoken conversation to legible text would not have been possible were it not for the work of Arne Kellerman.
2. The transcript is included in Theodor W. Adorno, 'Fortschritt', *Gesammelte Schriften* 10.1.
3. Claussen is referring to Max Horkheimer's letter to Adorno of September 27 1958. After having read Habermas' 'On the Philosophical Question of Marx and Marxism', Horkheimer wrote to Adorno wanting to clarify Adorno's relationship to the Institute and, more generally, to introduce certain changes inside the Institute. The letter, which bears annotations by Adorno, is reproduced in Claussen's biography of the latter.
4. See Max Horkheimer, *Späne: Notizen über Gespräche mit Max Horkheimer*, in *Gesammelte Schriften 14: Nachgelassene Schriften 1949-1972, 5. Notizen* (Frankfurt a. M.: Fischer, 1988). [An English translation is currently unavailable.]
5. The Spiegel-Affäre concerned the freedom of the press in the Federal Republic of Germany. Following the publication of a critical article in the magazine, several editors and contributors to *Der Spiegel* were arrested and accused of national treason. Finally, in 1965 the court of appeal decided not to pursue the case.
6. See Johan Hartle's interview with Oskar Negt, 'Critical Theory's contexts of cooperation', *Radical Philosophy* 2.04 (Spring 2009), 73-85.
7. 'Now they are all contrite, but Krahl organised the

whole action so as to enter preventive detention and keep the Frankfurt SDS – which is breaking down – together, and for the moment it has succeeded. In their propaganda they turn things upside down completely, as if we were the ones to have taken repressive measures and not the students who told us to shut up, who told us we weren't welcome.' Theodor W. Adorno, letter to Herbert Marcuse 14th February 1969, in *Frankfurter Schule und Studentenbewegung*, ed.Wolfgang Kraushaar (Hamburg: Hamburger Edition, 1998), S. 575.

8. See Hans-Jürgen Krahl, 'The Political Contradiction in Adorno's Critical Theory', *Telos* 21 (Fall 1974), 164–67. Originally published in *Konstitution und Klassenkampf* (Frankfurt a M.: Neue Kritik, 2008), 291–94.

9. 'Today once again the antithesis between theory and praxis is being misused to denounce theory. When a student's room was smashed because he preferred to work rather than join in actions, on the wall was scrawled: "Whoever occupies himself with theory, without acting practically, is a traitor to socialism".' Theodor W. Adorno, 'Marginalia to Theory and Praxis', in *Critical Models: Interventions and Catchwords*, trans. Henry W. Pickford (New York: Columbia University Press, 2005), 259–78.

10. Detlev Claussen, *Mit steinerem Herzen. Politische: Essays 1969-1989* (Bremen: Bettina Wassman Verlag, 1989).

11. In January 1997 Adriano Sofri was sentenced to 22 years in prison for allegedly participating in the murder of police officer Luigi Calabresi. Calabresi was one of the officers whose responsibility it was to investigate the massacre that took place at Piazza Fontana. In December 1969, while investigations were underway, one of the suspects, a railworker named Giusepe Pinelli, died in custody after falling out of the window of an office that belonged to Calabresi. The circumstances surrounding Pinelli's death have yet to be clarified; however the conditions under which he was detained strained the limits of legality. At one point, Sofri held Calabresi responsible for Pinelli's death. Calabresi was assassinated in Milan in May 1972 and in 1990 Adriano Sofri was convicted. Sofri has always insisted on his innocence.

12. The minutes from this conference were published in *Potere e opposizione nelle società postrivoluzionarie* (Rome: Alfani editore, 1978).

13. Born to a family of Polish Jews, Franz Marek was one of the intellectual leaders of the Austrian Communist Party (KPÖ). In the 1960s the party shifted towards reformist positions. After the Prague spring he adopted a decidedly critical attitude towards Soviet communism and soon became one of the principal representatives of Eurocommunism. Unable to convince the KPÖ to follow suit, in the 1970s he tried to encourage an independent stream of thought as editor of the Wiener Tagebuch.

14. See Detlev Claussen, *Bela Guttmann. Weltgeschichte des Fußballs in einer Person* (Berlin: Berenberg, 2006).

15. Dan Diner is a writer and historian who lives between Germany and Israel, and who has worked on the conflict in the Middle East, the history of the twentieth century, historical memory, the holocaust and Jewish history.

16. In particular, this line of thought is developed in Detlev Claussen, *Grenzen der Aufklärung. Zur gesellschaftlichen Geschichte des modernen Antisemitismus* (Frankfurt a. M.: Fischer, 1987).

17. The Sozialistische Büro was am important German New Left organisation formed in 1969 that published the magazine *Links* and other influential publications. Participants included, among others, Oskar Negt, Elmar Altvater, Dan Diner, Joachim Hirsch and Hans-Dieter Narr.

18. Karl-Heinz Kurras was a former West Berlin police officer, who on 2 May 1967, at the demonstration against the Shah of Persia's visit to Berlin, shot and killed a student demonstrator, Benno Ohnesorg. The demonstration against the Shah and Ohnesorg's murder triggered the rise of the protest movement in the Federal Republic. The movement gained force when Kurras was exempted from all charges. In the spring of 2009 it was revealed that Kurras had in fact been working as a Stasi agent on behalf of the GDR. The German press began an effort to revise and recast the history of the student movement, suggesting that its entire operation had been organised and orchestrated by the secret services of the GDR. In this way, they hoped to downplay the meaning and scope of the protest movement, as well as the historical conflicts that it drew on, by framing the narrative as one of a simple reaction to the gunshot that killed Ohnesorg.

# Reviews

## Symbols and spirits

Erich Hörl, *Sacred Channels: The Archaic Illusion of Communication*, trans. Nils F. Schott (Amsterdam: Amsterdam University Press, 2018). 344pp., € 52,95 pb., 978 90 8964 770 2

Originally published in German in 2004, *Sacred Channels: The Archaic Illusion of Communication*, Erich Hörl's unorthodox genealogy of thinking about thinking, is now available to readers in English. Beginning with epistemological crises induced by the sciences in the nineteenth century and ending with the convergence of cybernetics and structural anthropology in the middle of the twentieth, *Sacred Channels* recounts the slow triumph of symbolic logic over intuition and representation in the human and physical sciences. In the process, Hörl braids together the formalisation of mathematics, the emergence of electromagnetic field theory, anthropological obsessions with 'primitive' thought and the coming of information theory, offering space for reflection on how intellectual paradigms mutate and exceed the bounds their authors ascribe to them. And rather than point to the limitations of digital logic for capturing the flux of life and experience – as is common in the contemporary humanities roiling in the wake of post-structuralism and world-altering computational ecologies – Hörl builds a picture of the historical contingency of formal, symbolic thought. As he teases out another era's shifting investments in reason and rationality, substance and logic, and thinking and being, he excavates unlikely resonances, reminding readers of what might be gained from greater reflection on the genesis of contemporary intellectual formations.

Hörl's book, which attends to the century of intellectual developments in Europe between 1850 and 1950, is structured into two parts. 'In the Shadow of Thinking: A History of Formalisation' traces the increasing triumph of an episteme of symbolic logic over an older model of intuition and substance. Hörl's protagonists here are the mathematicians Louis Couturat and George Boole, whose advocacy for a formal symbolic algebra untethered to arithmetical quantities or rationally apprehensible phenomena was reinforced by the contemporaneous evacuation of the sensible from electromagnetic fields. While information theory and the operationalisation of Boolean algebra lay in the future, Hörl shows that already by the late nineteenth century, thinkers were forced to contend with a 'real' beyond substance or intuition, selectively recuperating Leibniz as the progenitor of this new calculative thought. As developments in mathematics and physics undermined the dominant Kantian understanding of knowledge as a process by which a rational subject formed meaningful representations, people like Boole and Couturat abandoned 'mind' and rejected the a priori synthetic in favour of a strictly analytic knowledge.

Hörl then turns to the ways in which the human sciences grappled with the emergent crisis in thinking about thinking. As 'substance' slipped away and Aristotelean logic collapsed into the apparent contradictions of Boolean formalisms, an 'opening up' of the question of thinking inaugurated a search for the origin stories of concepts now revealed to be historically and culturally contingent. In this time of destabilisation, Europeans, Hörl argues, turned to analyse other peoples, anachronistically searching for the origins of Aristotelian categories in contemporary 'pre-rational' societies. (Here, *Sacred Channels* echoes and extends Johannes Fabian's classic critique of anthropology's tendency to frame the peoples it studies as living fossils, though Fabian and other historians of anthropology are absent from Hörl's account.) In works like Emile Durkheim's *The Elementary Forms of Religious Life* and Marcel Mauss's *Outline of a Theory of Magic*, Hörl identifies an emerging obsession with the primitive sacred, the 'archaic illusion' of the title. People grappling with the spectral qualities of the telegraph and radio became obsessed with the mysterious flows and forces appearing in ethnographies and histories of religion. Yet Hörl also identifies, particularly in Mauss, first steps on a path heading towards structural linguistics. Relational concepts like *mana* and *hau* seemed to acquire an autonomy from the realm of the sensible and from the murky historic past of society, pointing towards an abstract real which nonetheless structured social formations and towards 'an originary formalism of the human being'.

The book's second part, 'The Specter of the Primitive: A Hauntology of Communication', describes the rise of the concept of 'communication' in both anthropology of religion and information theory. Here, Lucien Lévy-Bruhl and Georges Bataille pick up where Durkheim and Mauss left off. Like his predecessors, Lévy-Bruhl went searching for the precategorical and decided he had discovered it in what he called 'primitive mentality'. In his search for laws beyond history and in his notion of participation with spectral forces, though, Hörl sees a significant step towards a more fully-fledged symbolic order. For Bataille, meanwhile, mystic experience and communication left the margins of empire and emerged in the depths of western being, where they 'could be discovered *in oneself* in silent meditation and condensed into an ontological manifesto': 'existence is *communication*'. The reinterpretation of these two theorists of the mystical as proto-structuralists, deeply entangled with an emerging computational episteme and grasping towards a nonrepresentational but immanent symbolic order, is an exemplary instance of Hörl's ability to reframe the past. The book reminds readers of the historical contingency and shifting implications of seemingly entrenched oppositions between the sensory and the abstract or the digital and the analogue. If today the affective is associated with an embodied relationality beyond discourse and logic, Hörl shows that for these thinkers, the affective *was* the abstract, a sort of communicative resonance in excess of the sensible, rationally apprehensible world.

*Sacred Channels* concludes in the mid-twentieth century with the intersection of structural anthropology and cybernetics, and with the full 'short-circuiting' of the 'pre-logical' and the 'post-logical' in the figure of Claude Lévi-Strauss. Hörl argues that Claude Shannon's articulation of a symbolic theory of information that could account for the invisible currents of communication in which society had become enmeshed finally allowed for the relinquishing of the spatio-temporal projections of the 'archaic illusion'. In this context, and over the warnings and disavowals of people like Shannon and Norbert Weiner, Lévi-Strauss attempted to formalise and algebraise human codes of language and kinship. No longer looking for an origin or a ground to thinking, he turned not to the 'primitive' but to the 'elementary', and looked beyond the content of classifications to emphasise the transcendental fact of classification itself.

*Sacred Channels* makes a convincing case that the imagined figure of 'the primitive' in the years under consideration was 'a fantastic manifestation of the lack of intelligibility of the age of communication, projected to the margins of the West.' Equally convincing is the more general point that the epistemic ramifications of mathematical formalisation, field theory and information theory emerged slowly, problematically, and in conversation with other disciplines. Hörl's project is ambitious and original, offering an intellectual history which readers are unlikely to have realised they were missing and which intervenes simultaneously into media theory, anthropology, philosophy and the history of computation. Of course, in reframing the past, some thinkers find themselves displaced. Hörl's overarching framework, pitting the intuitionist against the formalist, glosses over important differences among the various heirs of 'intuition' and 'structure', from phenomenologists and historical dialecticians to psychoanalysts. Ending in mid-century, the book leaves important subsequent developments in these conflicting paradigms in the social sciences untouched – the emergence of structural Marxism, for instance, or Pierre Bourdieu's attempts to reconcile structural, symbolic relations with a phenomenological approach to human experience.

While *Sacred Channels* stirs up more questions than one book can answer, it still resonates with other recent attempts to reappraise the influence of computation on philosophy. Orit Halpern's 2014 *Beautiful Data: A History of Vision and Reason since 1945* also situates cybernetics in a wider field of intellectual developments, directing readers not towards anthropology but towards design, architecture and pedagogies of visualisation and pattern-seeking. Where Hörl focuses on the interest in mysticism and possession that accompanied the rise of symbolic notation, Halpern draws attention to the now forgot-

ten discourse of psychosis in cybernetics. Both projects insist on a historical shift from 'reason' to 'rationality', and challenge readers to avoid conflating Enlightenment subjectivity with computational subjectivity, but Hörl demonstrates that debates about networked communication, unreason and the dissolution of classic, intuiting subjectivity began even in the nineteenth century.

*Sacred Channels* also speaks to continued interest in situating Heidegger's thinking in relation to computation. Heidegger's thought is irreducible to either an intuitionist metaphysics of substance and representation or to a pure symbolic formalism and it therefore lies outside of this story's main arc, but he resurfaces throughout the text, offering Hörl a picture of how philosophers understood their place within ongoing transformations in knowledge. The new English edition includes an appended essay which helps clarify both the inspiration Hörl draws from Heidegger's genealogy of western philosophy in light of cybernetic advances and Hörl's own investment in Heidegger's call to imagine a kind of thinking beyond the distinction between the rational and the irrational.

And what of the relations between ethnology, 'thinking', 'being', and conditions of technological communication since Lévi-Strauss? In the updated preface to the English translation, Hörl indirectly takes note of work in this area taken up since the original German publication in 2004. Presumably referencing Yuk Hui's attempts to marry the concerns of German media theory with those of the ontological turn in anthropology, Hörl optimistically gestures to the 'formation of a nonmodern decolonial counterthinking beyond the archaic illusion' represented by anthropologists like Phillipe Descola, Tim Ingold and Eduardo Viveiros de Castro. Despite a shared interest in thinkers like Heidegger and Simondon, and despite a shared desire to reconceptualise what 'ontology' has to offer after discourse, these thinkers are still rarely discussed within media philosophy. They also, crucially, engage with peoples and philosophies from outside of Europe which only ever appear in *Sacred Channels* as the belle-epoque spectres of solipsistic Europeans. While Hörl's account of obsessive projections onto 'primitive' peoples is damning, developments in western thought appear here (not least of all for Hörl himself) to emerge organically from within the western tradition as computation finally puts the intuitionist paradigm to rest.

Absent is any acknowledgement that many of the most important developments within the social sciences in the past half century have been due to increasingly effective refusals on the part of Europe's former and so-called 'primitive' subjects to play a role in the working out of western anxieties.

A full accounting of the influence of colonial exchange and fallout on European philosophy might fall beyond the scope of this book. But for a historical genealogy which traces the slippage of epistemes across the boundaries thinkers might imagine themselves to obey, and which describes key moments in an ongoing project of imperialist symbolic violence, *Sacred Channels* could have done more to contextualise these epistemic debates and point to the entangled confluence of military, cultural and epistemological encounters. As Hui has shown, scholars of media and technology might learn from contemporary anthropologists' attempts to take up the task of thinking against the modern from both within the western philosophical tradition and through engagement with entirely different intellectual traditions. This is a risky project, but, much like the project of rethinking western thought under the conditions of ecological and technological transformation, it is one that is becoming difficult to avoid.

Since *Sacred Channels*' initial publication in 2004, Hörl, like so many others, has turned his attention towards this latter task and towards the problem of what he has described elsewhere as the 'becoming-environmental of computation'. His concerns with the onticity of communication and with the possibility of a non-intuitionist sense were already present when he first wrote *Sacred Channels*, as the treatments of Bataille and Heidegger demonstrate, but the new preface's retroactive framing of the book's stakes indicates that these concerns have only solidified since:

> Even if reveries about the end of all sense have produced an entire formation of theory in media and cultural studies, it has now become questionable to what extent the concepts and conceptual strategies of this formation can still be used to work through the techno-ecological formation and to what extent this latter task requires entirely different ontological-political sets of tools that stem from a new, neither intuitive nor symbolic but, precisely, ecological-environmental image of thinking. This is what many people are working on in the most varied of ways and where one of the great challenges of thinking in our time is to be situated.

In demonstrating what might be gained from greater reflection on the origins of current frameworks for understanding computation, materiality and communicative entanglement, Hörl's history of epistemic confusion and cross-fertilisation lays valuable groundwork for this project.

Megan Wiessner

# Freedom is a constant erasure

David Marriott, *Whither Fanon? Studies in the Blackness of Being* (Stanford: Stanford University Press, 2018). 448pp., £74.00 hb., £23.99 pb., 978 0 80479 870 9 hb., 978 1 50360 572 5 pb.

Freedom is a difficult matter because sometimes we cannot separate what liberates us from what imprisons us, and sometimes, despite our conscious protestations to the contrary, we simply do not want to. This uncomfortable insight is at the heart of David Marriott's bold book, *Whither Fanon? Studies in the Blackness of Being*, which argues that the black subject (who Marriott refers to in the French as *négre*) 'unconscious[ly] consent[s]' to his or her own unfreedom, and that in the act of decolonial revolution, an emancipation that is not a humanistic re-inscription of mastery or sovereignty can never be ensured. It is not that liberation is impossible, however, only our traditional conceptions of it. Marriott argues that it is precisely because the black subject unconsciously consents to his or her own unfreedom that blackness allows us to conceive of liberation anew.

Blackness becomes *like* philosophy, insofar as 'philosophy is critical of any simple notion of liberation ... or reparation that could deliver it from the contingency that it itself is.' Blackness is another scene of philosophy, inventing 'another relationship to [the] world', which Marriott terms 'tabula rasa' after Frantz Fanon in *The*

*Wretched of the Earth.* For Marriott, the insight into and connection between blackness and the politics of invention culminating in tabula rasa was first formulated by the Martinique-born revolutionary psychiatrist but has been lost in interpretations of his work, which reduce his thinking to already-existing philosophies, whether existentialism, dialectics, phenomenology, postcolonialism or decolonial revolution. Addressing Fanon scholars like Lewis Gordon, Achille Mbembe and Sylvia Wynter, as well as the contemporary field of Afro-pessimism, Marriott's *Whither Fanon?* comprises a massive re-reading of Fanon's corpus, rehabilitating his clinical theories and advocating for the specificity and relevance of his ideas for the contemporary moment by reclaiming Fanon as the thinker of blackness and invention *par excellence.*

In arguing that blackness is akin to philosophy, *Whither Fanon?* is a welcome addition to a spate of books that take blackness as a schema within which to theorise in or from, such as Fred Moten's *In the Break: The Aesthetics of the Black Radical Tradition* (2003), Christina Sharpe's *In the Wake: On Blackness and Being* (2016) and Calvin Warren's *Ontological Terror: Blackness, Nihilism and Emancipation* (2018). *Whither Fanon?* is a dense book and, at times, difficult to follow because Marriott presupposes that the reader already has a sophisticated knowledge of Fanon's oeuvre and less than seamlessly develops his ideas in tandem with Fanon's thought. Nevertheless, the rewards of reading it are well worth the effort for the unique and provocative theoretical framework in relation to Afro-pessimism and Black Studies the book provides, especially concepts which have thus far remained undertheorised in readings of Fanon's work.

Marriott's book is divided into two main parts, which are each essentially devoted to one major theme. While I imagine Marriott would not agree with this characterisation, given his opinions on 'critique' articulated in 'The becoming-black of the world?' (see *RP* 2.02 (June 2018)), I understand Part 1, entitled 'Psychopolitics', to be an attempt, in the Kantian vein, to establish the 'proper' limits of (non-)freedom for the black subject, prompted by the question which, he asserts, drives Fanon's work: 'why do people disavow what could truly liberate them?' Advancing the Fanonian concepts of *socialthérapie*, 'real fantasy' and '*n'est pas*', Marriott concludes that freedom is impossible for the black subject *as* black.

The early Fanon of *Black Skin, White Masks,* published in French in 1952, retained an emphasis on the imaginary, arguing that while the black subject experienced him or herself alienated in the mirror as a diminished whiteness, there *existed* a submerged self that the black subject disavowed but could recognise and consent to as black. With the development of Fanon's conception of *socialthérapie*, generated between 1952 and 1958 in a series of published articles penned with François Tosquelles and Jacques Azoulay (now collected in *Alienation and Freedom*), Marriott argues that a development in Fanon's thinking on blackness occurred. For Marriott, the distinctive theoretical purchase of Fanon's *socialthérapie* in contradistinction to Fanon's mentor, Tosquelles, whose methodology attempted to alter the clinic, reintegrating both doctor and patient into a common sociality, was that it realised that such a common sociality in the space of the colony could not be used as a criterion of health for colonised subjects (who Marriott refers to in the French as *colonisé*) because of its racist dimensions. At this point Marriott turns Fanon's concept into his own, contending that because there is no space to live outside of racial phantasms governing society and the clinic, *socialthérapie* shows how the symptom functions not on an individual level, as argued by psychoanalysis, but rather 'how the symptom is *lived* as collective experience.' For the colonised it is lived as the effect of a racism which cannot be discerned as a cause transcendent to the symptom, but, as a cause-effect, it is lived as a dimension of the symptom itself. In essence, *socialthérapie* shows, in contradistinction to Freud's theorisations of group psychology, how a group can be psychically constituted at the level of the symptom by processes of racialisation. This is an extremely novel insight and in Marriot's hands *socialthérapie* becomes a limit-concept of racialisation / freedom inside of which the black subject is reflected back as a 'no-thing' or '*n'est pas*', in which his or her blackness is fundamentally non-existent, while his or her whiteness is an inescapable 'real fantasy' outside of which there is no stable existing concept of freedom. This particular interpretation of Fanon's later works leads Marriott to the conclusion that blackness is an exclusion from the ontological plane and 'without hesitation, it can be said that blackness is not consistent with the notion of conscious consent.'

In order to make this argument about blackness as '*n'est pas*' however, Marriott elides any differences between the colonised and the black subject. While Marriott remains faithful to the Fanonian text by utilising the separate terms 'colonisé' and 'négre' (presumably) to indicate two different logics of subject formation, in *Whither Fanon?* these terms become conflated to the extent that one no longer knows whether Marriott is referring to the colonised or the black subject, or whether they index the same subject (though if the latter is the case presumably it would be unnecessary to employ the phrase 'black *colonisé*' as Marriott does in Chapter 4). Moreover, he relies on the mental disorders of Algerians and Fanon's experiments on *socialthérapie* conducted on Muslim men and women to craft the ontological argument about blackness as '*n'est pas*', whereas Fanon makes a point of distinguishing between 'Arab' and 'Black' in his own work. I point this out not to nitpick or make the (false) argument that the black subject is not colonised, but to indicate that the structure of colonisation is a more encompassing category than that of blackness applying to all racialised peoples almost without exception, and to make an argument about the latter based on the former seems to take away from the specificity of what constitutes both the colonised and the black subject. In short, it appears as though Marriott employs a 'people of colour framework,' critiqued by Afro-pessimism in order to make an argument about the psychic and ontological particularity of blackness. At the very least, within the schema of blackness as '*n'est pas*' that Marriott sets out, and in a book whose subtitle is *Studies in the Blackness of Being*, it seems essential to pose the question as to just *who* counts as black here (the Arab, Muslim, *colonisé*, or all three?).

Criticisms aside, with this analysis, Marriott justifiably directs his ire toward those Fanon scholars who would dismiss Fanon's psychiatric writings in favour of his more overtly political writings. The latter are blinded by their concern with Fanon's politics and miss the point that liberation is impossible for the black and/or colonised subject precisely for the psychic reason that the latter do not desire to be liberated from their 'real fantasies,' and because the disavowal (of freedom) is a structural condition of colonisation. Nor is it possible to be liberated from 'real fantasies' as such. For Marriott, what Fanon's work shows is that there is no version of the 'real' which is not 'veiled'. Marriott leaves scholars who dispense with Fanon's psychiatric writings with no ground to stand on, demonstrating that 'psychoanalysis that is always a question of *praxis*' remains essential to Fanon's thought.

Moreover, in articulating this psychoanalytic dimension Marriott contributes, what, I believe, are important and nuanced articulations of whiteness and blackness to the field of Black Studies and Afro-pessimism. While Frank Wilderson III argues that the 'Human' world is imposed on the 'Slave', Marriott accounts explicitly for the psychic mechanism by which this imposition occurs, as 'real fantasy', and the psychic position of the 'Slave' as '*n'est pas*'.

Marriott continues to unfold his complex idea of '*n'est pas*' throughout Part 1, touching upon the topics of negrophobogenesis, guilt, desire and racial fetishism, and culminating in Chapter 7, titled 'The Condemned'. 'The Condemned' is arguably one of the most intriguing chapters in *Whither Fanon?* because Marriott unexpectedly connects Fanon's critique of negritude and decolonial revolution in *The Wretched of the Earth* to Afro-pessimism. Drawing from his analysis of *socialthérapie*, Marriott argues that that decolonial revolution, in its Senghorian guise as negritude/African nativism, is opposed by Fanon because negritude seeks redemption within the past and is consumed by 'the slavish need to will this future appearance of itself as sovereign' closing off the possibility of writing anew the present and the future outside of History. The negritude movement is still 'slavish' for Marriott and freedom is foreclosed to it, precisely because it wills itself *as* black, and he describes this 'slavish' logic of producing the future while remaining entrapped in History as the grammar of the 'future perfect' (I will have done x).

Given this 'slavish need,' and despite the fact that Afro-pessimists invariably want to claim Fanon as their own, it is negritude, according to Marriott, which has most in common with Afro-pessimism. This is not to say that Fanon has no connection to the latter, as Marriott claims he anticipates the idea of social death with his notion of '*mort á bout touchant*'. Reading Jared Sexton's 'The Social Life of Social Death' and Fred Moten's 'The Case of Blackness' together, Marriott argues that they are involved in a 'representational politics' of what 'blackness is'. Admittedly, I was not at all convinced by this point the first time I read *Whither Fanon?*, as both Sexton and Moten try very hard to describe blackness in a non-representational manner. However, Marriott's point is much subtler: both Sexton and Moten try to *describe* what blackness *is*, whether as pathology or fugitivity, respectively, when blackness *is* not, '*n'est pas*', and cannot be reduced to 'phenomenological experience'. Because both Sexton and Moten attempt to produce blackness as existing in the present, which unavoidably relies on past fictions and future projections of blackness, they fall into the same trap as negritude. In making this argument there is a certain manner in which Marriott agrees with his erstwhile student, Asad Haider, who claims, in his book *Mistaken Identity: Race and Class in the Age of Trump*, that Afro-pessimism fosters an 'ideology of identity'. Mirroring Fanon's own famously ambivalent stance toward negritude, however, Marriott favorably argues that Afro-pessimism is also an attempt to include within 'the history of blackness more diverse questions' than those offered by 'traditional identity politics'. This attempt is taken up by Fanon, who Marriott argues, exceeds Sexton and Moten by arguing against the 'ruse of a black world', a phrase by Fanon which Marriott gleefully admits is often viewed with suspicion by black thinkers. But this is precisely the task of black liberation because it involves a logic that would paradoxically produce a blackness *neither* as a '*racial* revelation' *nor* as a '*post-racial* evasion', that is, a blackness which liberates itself by no longer being black at all, at least not in the way we currently understand it: a tabula rasa.

If Part 1 of *Whither Fanon?* establishes the limits of (non-)freedom for the black subject, Part 2, entitled *Homo Négre*, is devoted to the second major idea of the book, which is an exploration of the extent to which blackness can transgress the aforementioned limits. Marriott comes to the conclusion that blackness can indeed liberate itself, but only by annihilating itself *as* black, or by 'd[ying] a racialised death', and in this moment blackness becomes philosophy. Let's be clear: by this Marriott is advocating neither a humanism, which he thinks Fanonism is unfortunately often reduced to, nor the 'fantasy of a non-racial universalism', but something altogether different. Just precisely what is meant by black invention concerns the (im)possibility of a black writing or a tabula rasa. Having once been a student of the scholar Geoffrey Bennington, it is here that we can spot Marriott's Derridean influences.

Black writing appears to be under erasure at the very moment it is written. But this can mean two things. The first meaning can already be evinced in '*n'est pas*' which is another way of saying that for Marriott blackness can never *appear,* because it becomes erased or subsumed in 'real fantasy', whiteness or the universal. The second sense of black writing as erasure can be gleaned in the last chapter of *Whither Fanon?* called 'The Abyssal', wherein Marriott undertakes an analysis of Aimé Cesaire's *Notebook of a Return to a Native Land* through the lenses of Fanon and Jean-Paul Sartre. While in an examination of Cesaire's poetry via the perspective of Sartre, blackness remains trapped in the first kind of erasure, in reading Cesaire's poetry through Fanon blackness emerges as the second kind of erasure which Marriott describes as 'corpsing' or 'an excessive collapse by which the world as sovereignly enjoyed give way to laughter and cruelty.' This denotes both an erasing of blackness (as particular) and the (white) universal such that they are both reinvented, a total blank slate of categories. This does not end up in a 'post-racialism' for Marriott because the very concept of race itself becomes annihilated. Black writing ends up being black erasure. In this sense, black writing is equivalent to a tabula rasa in its original Lockean formulation in *An Essay Concerning Human Understanding* wherein the mind enters the world as a 'blank slate'. For black writing to be truly invention, truly liberation, however, Marriott argues that this erasure has to be *constant,* an 'endless transvaluation', lest another universal be reinstalled in the former's place, even if it is a black universal. This is why he emphasises the verbal form of Cesaire's poetry and argues that blackness has to die a 'racialised death' to be incessantly born as something else, naming this grammar of invention the 'future imperfect' (I will have been doing x). And herein lies the ambitiousness of Marriott's project and its avowed connection to the philosophical. For there is a manner in which *Whither Fanon?* repeats the founding gesture of philosophy in its Platonic mode as skepticism of the given world, although it does not invest in the immortal and transcendental realm of Forms. Rather blackness is philosophy in the sense that it *almost* invests in them, but instead of doing so, instead simply repeats this founding gesture ceaselessly, writing and/as erasing itself, reinventing philosophy anew.

**Nicholas Anthony Eppert**

# The presence of the past

Chris Moffat, *India's Revolutionary Inheritance: Politics and the Promise of Bhagat Singh* (Cambridge: Cambridge University Press, 2019). 238pp., £75.00 hb., 978 1 10849 690 2

The twin defeats marked by the disappearance of the dreams of the late 1960s and the demise of the Soviet Union unanchored the Left from much of the certainty that Marxist notions of History and progress had previously provided to sustain the passion and courage of communist partisans. Yet, such defeat has also allowed the Left to re-examine its own repressed archive in which themes such as courage, shame, hope and utopian vision were as indispensable to political action as any positivist analysis of the movement of History. Recent scholarship has focused on this subterranean undercurrent in communist thought, which emphasises rupture, departure and untimeliness as essential elements of politics over the scientific certainties of Marxist orthodoxy.

Chris Moffat's Book *India's Revolutionary Inheritance* is a welcome addition to the list of works that seek to overcome the tropes of failure and defeat. The main interlocutor of the book is the legendary Indian anti-colonial fighter, Bhagat Singh, who was hanged by the colonial state at the young age of 23; a stage in life that would be more appropriate for the palatable practices of 'student politics' than for playing a foundational role in the development of a nationalism adhered to by over a billion people today. His life also presents a genealogy of Indian nationalism that sharply differs from the 'non-violence' associated with a Gandhian politics in the West.

Moffat begins with a fascinating examination of Colonial Punjab to which the protagonist belonged. The province was known in official circles as the heart of imperial rule for the heavy recruitment of military personnel into the British Indian Army, as well as for the loyalty of the province's elite to the colonial administration. The book demonstrates how, beyond the apparent calm of authoritarian rule, Punjab was also the centre of some of the most militant upheavals against colonialism. From periodic attempts to incite revolt within the military to the formation of militant groups such as the Ghadr Party, the province, as Maia Ramnath's *Haj to Utopia* (2011) describes, remained a hotbed for anti-state activities. This subterranean resistance came to the fore in perhaps the most notorious cruelty of colonial rule in India, the Amritsar Massacre in 1919, in which a battalion led by General Dyer opened fire on crowds gathered for the Spring festival of Basakhi in Punjab's Amritsar district. The killing of over 300 people was followed by a number of repressive measures aimed at humiliating and subjugating the people of the province.

The political subject in Punjab remained split between excessive loyalty and equally excessive irreverence towards power. Moffat locates this split in the social structure of Punjab's cosmopolitan urban centres, particularly Lahore. Apart from being the centre of colonial administration, the city was also home to some of the most vibrant colleges and universities, making it a distinctively young city. This network of educational institutions provided an opportunity to young people to reinvent their identities away from the burden of their familial pasts, pointing to an urban environment that facilitated departures from normative social codes.

The purpose of colonial education was part of the larger civilisational mission. In the words of Lord Thomas Macaulay, the nineteenth-century architect of Western education in India, the aim was to create a 'class of persons Indian in blood and colour, but English in taste, in opinions, in morals and in intellect'. This purported servility induced by Indian education led reformers to begin their counter-pedagogic projects in Lahore. The struggle to create a 'national education' that could inculcate a sense of pride and critical thinking in Indian students is vividly captured by Moffat, in particular through the efforts of Lajpat Rai who began a 'Tilak School of Education' to teach students the taboo subjects of politics and sociology.

Lajpat Rai is a second major interlocutor in this story, who participated in recurrent protests against colonial excesses. One such demonstration was organised against the arrival of the hated Simon Commission in Lahore, which was supposed to propose a plan for Indian representation in government but ironically had no Indian representation on it. The police reaction was unexpectedly violent, with the revered 63-year-old Lajpat Rai becoming a victim of ruthless baton charges. A month later, he succumbed to his injuries and died, leaving India stunned.

This incident triggered Bhagat Singh and his comrades in a little known underground organisation, the Hindustan Socialist Republican Army, to seek revenge for Rai's death. They orchestrated an attack on police officials in Lahore, killing a British officer (Saunders) and an Indian constable. After an unsuccessful national effort to hunt down the killers, the group offered themselves up for arrest in a spectacular manner. They intervened in the Legislative Assembly session in Delhi, lofted a bomb in an unused corner (intended to avoid casualties) and threw pamphlets that read 'It takes a Loud Voice to Make the Deaf Hear'. Bhagat Singh was arrested at the site, setting the stage for one of the most iconic court cases in colonial history.

Moffat reads this act of 'surrender' as exemplifying the Greek virtue of *Parrhesia*, where an individual is able to speak truth from a vulnerable position, irrespective of the consequences. By permitting their arrests, Bhagat Singh did not aim to defend himself but rather to question the legitimacy of colonial law. During the court proceedings, Bhagat Singh and his comrades raised anti-colonial slogans in the courtroom and were often dragged outside for their acts, rendering visible the colonial violence beyond the norms and politeness of legal discourse. The court proceedings soon became part of a national theatre as hundreds of supporters began arriving to garland the accused with flowers and to watch their spectacular defiance of the feared colonial judges.

This section of the book is indebted to Jacques Rancière's theory of dissensus, a moment that undermines the figment of consensus promoted by the ruling order. The mocking of colonial courts, the decision to undergo voluntary suffering and to engage with a wider public beyond the confines of the prison meant the accused managed to disrupt the places assigned to them by law. The case is best exemplified by the widespread support across India for these prisoners, transforming prisons from disciplining institutions into sites producing political celebrities, a legacy that continues to shape postcolonial politics in the region. Singh and his group were able to dislocate the routine workings of a court, creating a discrepancy that opened up a gap in the symbolic order and signaled new political possibilities for the future.

Singh and his comrades were hanged early in the

morning on the 23rd of March, 1931 in Lahore. Their bodies were secretly taken to the banks of the Sutlej River, where they were burnt to deny them a mass funeral procession. Their deaths only furthered the sense of incompleteness that marked their lives, inciting unexpected but spectacular afterlives for the revolutionary.

To comprehend the presence and trajectory of these afterlives, Moffat takes a position against 'Rankean concerns' of history in which the past is completely separated from the present. Such narratives render the past as a passive object open to exploration and inquiry by historians in the present. Figures such as Bhagat Singh, however, make such neat temporal separations impossible, with the present always haunted by the spectral presence of the past.

We are now familiar with critiques of linear notions of history borrowed from notions of progress cemented by enlightenment thought. In twentieth-century Marxism, revolutionary upheavals in the non-European world forced thinkers to situate political subjectivity against the flow of History, rather than in sync with it. Walter Benjamin's work on the subterranean persistence of the dreams of the past resonate with Moffat's intervention, as the past intrudes into the present to dislocate it from within, undermining the stability of the status quo in the process.

Such conceptions of non-linear time can approach politics as a contingent process rather than something that can be deduced through sociological laws. Alain Badiou, for example, considers politics to be a condition of philosophy rather than dependent on it, an assumption that runs through Moffat's work as he demonstrates the capacity of historical figures to undermine existing categories of political thought.

Yet, Moffat makes an even stronger intervention regarding the relationship between the past and the present. He argues that figures such as Bhagat Singh continue making demands on the living after their deaths. In his words:

> This invocation of shame and, indeed, contemporaneity – that we are still 'in Bhagat Singh's company' – helps to emphasise the weight of an inheritance, the seriousness of this responsibility to the dead.

This responsibility turns into a call to action in the present. More than being a figure from a finished past, Bhagat Singh continues to be invoked in the present day to escalate struggles against the status quo. Moffat also discusses Bhagat Singh's own writings, disagreeing with the tendency of historians to examine his corpus to identify his exact ideological orientation. Such works often ask whether he was a nationalist, anarchist, Narodnik or Marxist. But attempts to confine Bhagat Singh to a neat conceptual box miss the intellectual promiscuity that shaped the inter-war period in the colonial world. More importantly, they undermine the challenge posed by the interrupted life of Bhagat Singh – not only to display courage in facing the enemy but also to bravely interrogate the certainties of one's own politics. To place Singh in a teleological story of Indian nationalism or communism would be akin to sanitising his image, transforming him from someone who perpetually undermines the dominant order to someone assimilated into its structures and routines.

Moffat discusses the intense debates on appropriating the revolutionary from across the political landscape. Maoist rebels (known as Naxals) justify their armed struggle in the name of Bhagat Singh's sacrifice, while student leaders emulate him as an ideal for today's alienated youth. Even Sikh and Hindu nationalists attempt to place him within their genealogy, signifying the contested futures represented by Bhagat Singh.

Moffat uses these heterogeneous interpretations of Bhagat Singh's story to discuss the politics of monuments devoted to him. Different political groups have tried resurrecting statues of the revolutionary in order to display their public devotion to his sacrifice. At the same time, there are recurrent accusations made against this official eulogisation for undermining the sanctity of his cause. For example, the Congress government was criticised for unveiling a statue of Bhagat Singh at the Indian Parliament in 2014, with critics claiming that the revolutionary would have preferred fighting against the corruption of the contemporary government rather than being used as a tool to justify it. Through such examples, Moffat shows that monuments can be used to contain the excess that threatens the stability of the existing order. In a paradoxical way, then, monuments can end up playing a conservative role in the present, even if they aspire to pay homage to a revolutionary.

Against the fixation with monuments in India's official political culture, Moffat points out the vernacular ways in which Bhagat Singh's image continues to circulate. In particular, his discussion of street theatre, in which actors intermingle with the crowds in public spaces, is closer to the dissensual tradition where the spectre of Bhagat Singh belongs. Instead of being encapsulated in a static monument, Moffat approvingly quotes a number of activists and artists who believe that a real homage to the revolutionary would entail taking up his cause in the present.

This insistence on understanding Bhagat Singh's legacy as a work in progress places Moffat's work in conjunction with Jacques Derrida's deliberations on the subject of spectres. Derrida asserts that inheritance 'is never given, it is a task'. Throughout the book Moffat teases out this task of thinking through the multiple and often contradictory trajectories of Bhagat Singh's many afterlives. In this spirit, one can argue that Moffat himself receives the inheritance of Bhagat Singh by rethinking his place in history away from the historicism and ideological rigidity too often bestowed upon him, and posits Singh as a figure who undermines the certainties of both political actors and academics.

*India's Revolutionary Inheritance* can be read as a reflection on time in modernity. Against notions of an apolitical and homogenous time in sync with the logic of Capital, we are confronted with a world where untimeliness is central to producing political antagonisms. Thus the focus is on sudden departures and unexpected arrivals that characterise the life, death and multiple afterlives of Bhagat Singh, with each reiteration producing a rupture within the flow of time. On this point, the book is indebted to a plethora of Indian thinkers who have challenged the universalising narratives of colonial modernity. In particular, Moffat engages with the work of Dipesh Chakrabarty, one of the founders of the Subaltern Studies Collective who challenged historicism by identifying the multiple temporalities that structure postcolonial societies. Capital is unable to subsume disparate local histories, as experiences of religious and mythical pasts continue to interrupt linear time to produce a peculiar modern public space. Shruti Kapila further radicalises this position by demonstrating how the political in India was formed through contingent decisions taken in the midst of the anti-colonial struggle, with ruptural violence displacing sociological deduction as the motor of History.

This work challenges the Left to unanchor itself from a rigid understanding of historical development and political possibilities. Such a rethinking is underway in the subcontinent, where attempts to situate Bhagat Singh in the teleologies of Marxism have been replaced by rethinking him as someone whose defiance 'made communism possible in India'. In other words, the spirit of departure and sacrifice rather than fidelity to a cold 'science' of Marxism allowed for the actualisation of the idea of communism in concrete historical circumstances.

Yet Moffat at times pushes the argument against strategic and programmatic thinking to its extreme, citing the following example to demonstrate the teleological thinking that his book aims to confront:

> This sense that Bhagat Singh and his comrades did not go far enough to warrant the name 'Marxist' persists in many leftist histories of the movement ... Bipan Chandra, as we have seen, recognised that Bhagat Singh was a hero of great significance but chastised the HSRA for its failure to become more than an urban phenomenon ... P. M. S. Grewal ... [notes] Bhagat Singh's 'most striking weakness' was his failure to analyze feudal landlordism in India and, indeed, to properly comprehend the nature of gender oppression and the integral role of women in political struggle.

Moffat dismisses these interventions as misrecognitions of the challenge posed by spectral figures such as Bhagat Singh. But if pushed too far, refusal to engage with the programmatic and strategic decisions made by individuals and organisations can induce paralysis in rethinking politics in the present. In *The Actuality of Communism* Bruno Bosteels has noted that much of the Left's crisis today stems from its desire to become what Hegel called a 'Beautiful soul', a condition in which the quest for purity results in the inability to actualise itself in History.

Moffat's book at times also seems to be afflicted with such a melancholic attachment to a dead martyr with little patience to engage with critical appraisals of the revolutionary's actions and the ideologies that guided him. After all, heroism and sacrifice can equally be prevalent among fascist elements. This is why an engagement with debates on Singh's ideas and, if I dare say, even criticising aspects of his politics is important if we are to build strategic horizons adequate to the present. Otherwise, we may remain excessively attached to tragedies from the past without doing the necessary analytical labour to make the Left politically operative in today's historical conjuncture.

One of the greatest strengths of the book is the sheer passion with which the provocative thesis is presented. Take the example of the launch event for this book in Lahore that I attended in April 2019. The city where Bhagat Singh was hanged is now part of Pakistan, a country that refuses to acknowledge his legacy because of his religious denomination. The event was held in the famous Bradlaugh Hall, a meeting place for anti-colonial activists and a site frequented by Bhagat Singh himself. The decrepit colonial building was opened especially for the occasion and was filled by people eager to learn about the forgotten figure. When Moffat read an excerpt from the book, depicting a riveting account of the last moments of the revolutionary's life, there was pin drop silence in the hall. Details of his heroic embracing of death, the mystery of his missing body, and his massive funeral procession conjured up a lost past with a palpable intensity.

The narration vividly evoked images of a different Lahore and in the process opened up possibilities of what the city could be, a conversation that continues among the city's youth interested in Bhagat Singh's ideas. It is a remarkable achievement for a book on afterlives to bring to life a repressed past and play a role in shaping the trajectory of the protagonist's legacy in the city where the most dramatic moments of his life took place. Moffat's book is then not only a challenge to intellectual orthodoxies in History, but is also a political intervention in our possible futures.

**Ammar Ali Jan**

# Decolonisation and deconstruction

Abdelkebir Khatibi, *Plural Maghreb: Writings on Postcolonialism*, trans. P. Burcu Yalim (London: Bloomsbury, 2019). 197pp., £24.29 pb. 978 1 35005 395 3

Abdelkebir Khatibi's collection of essays was first published in French in 1983 as *Maghreb Pluriel*. It comprises six essays originally published between (roughly) 1970 and 1982 in various venues. The first three essays of the collection – 'Other-Thought', 'Double Critique' and 'Disoriented Orientalism' – are the best-known, and, as Françoise Lionnet has noted, have long been out of print. From this perspective, the English translation is certainly welcome, if not without its problems. It is not clear, for example, why the editors of Bloomsbury's series 'Suspensions', or perhaps the book's translator, felt the need to add the subtitle 'Writings on Postcolonialism', which does not appear in the original. Why the need to attach Khatibi to a corpus he never clearly acknowledged in his writings? For two decades after the publication of *Maghreb Pluriel*, critics have lamented that Khatibi was never included alongside the likes of Said, Fanon, Césaire and Memmi in the canon of postcolonial thought. But little justification has been offered as to why that should have been the case – does any intellectual who thinks about and hails from a formerly colonised space need to be part of postcolonial thought?

Although the six essays function as fairly discrete pieces, the common theme that runs through them is

the idea of a plural Maghreb, expressed both as a desire and as a long-existing historical reality suppressed both by hegemonic theological-nationalist and colonial/Orientalist projects. The first pages of the first essay 'Other-Thought' (*autre-pensée*) identify Khatibi's targets for his double critique (one of the core concepts he associates with the idea of decolonisation): 'Western legacy and our very theological, very charismatic, and very patriarchal heritage.' His criticism of the latter revolves around both a critique and a move beyond what he identifies as 'Third World nationalism and dogmatic Marxism', on the one hand, and a presumed unitary Arab/Islamic civilisation, on the other. His concept of *autre-pensée* (other-thought) hinges then on a transcendence of the need for origins (any origins), 'on a nonreturn to the inertia of the foundations of our being.' 'Double critique', arguably his best known essay, engages Ibn Khaldun's thought by showing his misappropriation both by Western and non-Western schools of social theory, but also by contemporary fundamentalisms. The purpose of this engagement, as Khatibi notes, is 'to rethink Maghrebi history both outside the Khaldunian system and against colonial historiography.' It is this intent to demystify pre-colonial nostalgia and colonial historiography that constitutes one of the strengths of Khatibi's theoretical engagement with colonialism. The critique of colonial historiography is given more space in his third chapter, 'Disoriented Orientalism', where he criticises the work of Jacques Berque, a respected sociologist and Arabist at the Collège de France. If Said, in his *Orientalism*, targets those scholars who exhibit an intellectual and political hostility towards the Orient (by constructing it as a space inferior to the West), Khatibi focuses on those Orientalists who sing the praises of the Orient and romanticise its various dimensions. Such romanticisation is never innocent since it is inextricably bound, in Khatibi's view, with the advancement of 'the pecuniary interests of Western technocracy.'

Khatibi's debt to Derrida and to the latter's ethics of deconstruction and alterity is obvious in both of his core concepts, double critique and other-thought. There is no surprise then that Khatibi's thought consistently promotes an anti-hegemonic (indeed non-hegemonic?) impulse towards encounters with alterity in ways that refuse to reduce the latter to sameness or to universality. However promising this may seem, this, to my mind, is also where the trouble starts with Khatibi's theoretical framework.

What distinguishes Khatibi's thought from Derridean deconstruction is the former's specific attention to colonialism as a historical experience, to decolonisation as both a process and an ongoing aspiration, and to the epistemic violence of Western thought vis-à-vis the colonial world. However, insofar as these elements are consistently subordinated to his general framework of deconstruction, Khatibi's understanding of decolonisation becomes painfully limited. As Winnifred Woodhull remarks in *Transfigurations of the Maghreb*, a 'subversive poetics' evacuates the need for 'work for change in the political field' – in Khatibi's work (and more generally in deconstruction), 'poetic language has come to be associated with an "other" politics radically divorced from social institutions and from material relations of domination.' As he re-iterates both in 'Other-Thought' and in 'Double Critique', the first two chapters of *Plural Maghreb*, Khatibi's idea of decolonisation entails a critique of what, in a different work, he calls the 'saintly trilogy' of the Arab world: 'Zionism, the Arab reaction, and imperialism'. Françoise Lionnet indicates that he condemns this trilogy 'in the name of a rigorous critique of the unhappy consciousness and of the will to power that inhabits all systematic philosophies, making them unable to accommodate irreducible otherness.' While I am sympathetic to the spirit of this statement, which captures very well the core of Khatibi's ethics of deconstruction, there is a troubling equivalence that haunts this deconstructionist project. Neither Khatibi nor Lionnet (nor, I would argue, other scholars working within deconstruction) examine the politics of placing what he calls 'Arab reaction' and imperialism on an equivalent plane, nor for that matter Zionism and 'Arab reaction'. One may agree that most (if not all) 'systematic philosophies' or cosmologies do contain (in various degrees) their own logic of exclusionary hierarchies. However, to place them all on a continuum of violence devoid of historical context and stripped of the heaviness that ties them together as violent encounters and interactions is to flatten them into an indistinguishable list of totalising philosophies.

This is where my problem with Khatibi's deconstruction lies. One may agree that there is a totalising impulse within the 'Arab reaction' (whatever that may mean to Khatibi), or put differently, that there are various gendered, racialised and socio-economic hierarchies within the Arab world (contemporary or pre-colonial), which have obviously led to a number of exclusions. But to place them all on a level of equivalence assumes that they all exist in a neutral vacuum in which each is guilty *in the same way* of its own violence. Moreover, the perversity of this assumption completely overlooks and erases the weight of structures, more specifically global structures. Are all wills to power really equivalent to each other in a global structural system of Western imperialism and white supremacy? In a 2002 article 'Interrogating Identity', Mustapha Hamil, for example, claims that in Khatibi's deconstruction, 'postcolonial reality requires a double resistance *to all the Occidents and Orients* that alienate and subjugate the postcolonial subject' (emphasis added). But do the Occident and the Orient subjugate the postcolonial subject in the same way? Does a global structure characterised by a clear domination by the Occident not matter, and not re-configure not only the relation between the various Occidents and Orients, but also that between the various Orients and postcolonial subjects? I do not want to imply that internal hierarchies and the violence they have produced are unimportant or always a minor issue alongside the looming violence of colonialism/imperialism. Indeed, in my own work I have engaged critically the national liberation project and discussed both its clear limits and the violence instantiated by the various forms of gendered, racialised and socio-economic forms of oppression that accompanied it. And while Third World nationalism has had both its uncontestable limits and shortcomings, Khatibi's deconstruction – as encapsulated by his concepts of 'other-thought' and 'double critique' – is no real alternative. Insofar as he reduces the historical process of decolonisation and national liberation to nothing but *ressentiment*, he then misses the point of both colonial difference and the specific violence of colonialism:

> Fanon's call, in its very generosity, was the reaction of the humiliated during the colonial era, which is never done with decolonising itself, and his critique of the West ... was still caught in resentment and in a simplified Hegelianism – in the Sartrean manner. And we are still asking ourselves: Which West are we talking about? Which West opposed to ourselves, in ourselves? Who is 'ourselves' in decolonisation?

To imagine that Fanon's searing description of the colonial horrors of Algeria was a sort of 'simplified Hegelianism' is not simply to misunderstand and misrepresent the specificity of colonial violence, but also to trivialise the struggles, theorisation and mobilisation of anticolonial movements and individual actors and thus to reduce them to a mere reaction to domination. Consider, for example, that Khatibi describes 'the conflict between Europe and the Arabs' as 'being age-old' and thus 'a machine of mutual incomprehension.' Again, a situation of what Fanon clearly described as systematised dehumanisation and brute violence, and which Edward Said characterised as systematic epistemic oppression, is neutralised. In a careful and nuanced engagement with both anticolonial thought and its critics, Branwen Gruffydd-Jones has examined the premises according to which anticolonial thought is seen as trapped in a teleological paradigm beholden to Enlightenment. But contrary to Khatibi (and other critics of Third World nationalism), she sees it as 'embod[ying] an autonomy and singularity which engaged with but went beyond Enlightenment traditions'. Indeed, 'to see the black radical intellectual tradition as operating wholly inside the Western canon, and then to judge its many contributors solely from that angle, is both to miss the tradition's complexity and to negate the tremendous knowledge that this tradition has postulated *about the nature of the West.*'

To follow Khatibi's logic, the historical and intellectual process of decolonisation is simply a resentful reaction to domination, whereby 'the humiliated' (as he calls them) lash back at their oppressors and are thus forever linked to them through a relation of both violent retribution and (desire for) mimicry. But Gruffydd-Jones and Anthony Bogues indicate a much more complex dynamic, one through which the colonised produce knowledge about the West and about themselves in a manner that brings to the fore the racialised logic of colonial domination, and thus prompts us to re-consider the very nature of Western societies. Indeed, the intertwined logics of racialisation, expropriation and of capital accumulation (which make colonialism a distinct form of oppression and domination) are wholly absent from Khatibi's understanding of both colonialism and decolonisation.

To Khatibi, decolonisation is: 'a third path, neither reason nor unreason as thought by the West as a whole, but a kind of double subversion that, by giving itself the power of speech and action, sets to work in an intractable difference. To be decolonised would be the other name of this other-thought, and decolonisation would be the silent completion of Western metaphysics.'

The double subversion here entails, as mentioned earlier, the subversion of both Western metaphysics and what he calls the Arab-Islamic theological-nationalist project. As Winnifred Woodhull also notes, Khatibi's idea of decolonisation (captured also by his notion of *bi-langue*) is a space open to margins (linguistic, ethnic, gendered, sexual, etc), where binaries co-exist as intractable difference without reaching unity or consensus. I concur with and applaud the spirit in which Khatibi advocates for an ontological plurality and especially for an internal critique of colonised societies that makes visible various erasures, hierarchies and forms of marginality. However, the trouble lies both with his too easy equivalence between colonial violence and internal hierarchies, and with the fact that his approach is, as remarked by several commentators, 'resolutely textualist' (see, for example, Mary Ellen Wolf's 1994 essay 'Rethinking the Radical West'). In that sense, I am in complete agreement with Winnifred Woodhull's assessment that Khatibi 'has appropriated deconstruction for third-world peoples, and for reflection on third-world cultural politics.' Ultimately, in Khatibi's oeuvre, politics and decolonisation boil down to what Lionnet calls a 'question of language'. Reading Khatibi in our contemporary of climate change, the rise of far-right, rampant neoliberal capitalism, and migracide (to name but a few issues) – when, perhaps more than ever, we need creative ways of mobilisation, intervention and action – a call for a 'return to philology' as substitute for politics seems rather out of touch with the times.

**Alina Sajed**

# Border crossings

Brigitta Kuster, *Grenze filmen. Eine kulturwissenschaftliche Analyse audiovisueller Produktionen an der Grenze Europas* (Bielefeld: Transcript Verlag, 2018). 344pp., € 29,99, 978 3 83763 981 0

'We did not cross the border, the border crossed us'. So say the migrant activists at the Mexican-US-American border. The categorisation of migration and the individual migrant does not exist apart from the formation of nations and peoples. Within the country of arrival, such categorisation of transborder movement remains a lasting description for those who do not belong and are marked as 'foreign'. Practices of migration are encoded through the patterns of perception of the (national) border. Yet, the border is not solely a matter of the state; through transnational migration the border is also constantly challenged, shifted and re-composed.

In her book *Grenze filmen* [*Filming Borders*] – unfortunately only published so far in German – Brigitta Kuster shows to what extent a political philosophy of migration may be interlaced with a study of film and cinema, in order to break free from state patterns of migration. Inspired by Gilles Deleuze and Félix Guattari, by Michel de Certeau, Donna Haraway and Jacques Derrida, *Grenze filmen* is an exuberant book that analyses a range of perspectives on migration to be found in film classics and documentaries, and is interwoven with a vast number of references to digital audio-visual material from television, the internet, DVDs, art exhibitions and mobile phone videos.

In the book's analyses of films, an affective practice and tactical narration of migration is explored, culminating with mobile phone video captured by young migrants on the open sea in their attempt to cross the windswept Mediterranean together with others. In this way, *Grenze filmen* reformulates theories of migration, along with theories of documentary filmmaking, and points to a paradigm change in our understanding of where the autonomy of migration overlaps with the audio-visual practices of its protagonists. The book is also written with a sound knowledge of various feminist and postcolonial theories of representational critique, as well as cultural studies' analyses of everyday practices.

Understanding the border as both an epistemic and a practical paradox, in de Certeau's terms, it emerges not only as a line of separation, but also, and simultaneously, as one of contact. Without contact on the border there can be no difference, and thus no migration. The pull of the border is always ambivalent. Migrants are not simply excluded foreigners, they are also actors in that they accept a certain subjectivation by the drawing of the border.

Crossing the border thereby becomes a performative and subsequently a creative act, a productivity of migration that is often not perceived by the dominant gaze of the 'West'.

The passport with its photograph belongs within a genealogy of *passing,* of letting someone pass, of a permission to pass, and of passing through: like a slave in possession of a permission slip by their owner to travel without them; or like the capacity to pass as white, in so far as white skin in itself represents a 'pass' in the sense of the racialised identification of an autonomous individual. Yet, passing is also a practice of challenging dominant forms of perception and of passing over conventions or social differentiation. Passing can become a tactic of passing for a passenger, of becoming common, evading forms of decision at the border and being waved on through. Kuster repeatedly shows that even if the passport photograph comes before migration, it is through migration that these images circulate. It is not the dominant perception that creates the images of migration, it cannot even depict migration.

This becomes particularly evident in the practice of *passing down for research*, a practice of making yourself common from a position of superiority, in order to get in close contact with those to be portrayed and researched, and to seek to put yourself in their shoes. Such practices can frequently be seen at work in 'western' knowledge production or investigative journalism, for instance in Just-In-Time image production of migrants. In her criticism of such practices of authentication, Kuster makes it clear how questions of complicity thereby pervade the movements of migration.

Taking the example of the film *I See the Stars at Noon* (2004) by Saeed Taji Farouky, Kuster asks the question of how filmmaking can work when it not simply *about* but operates *with* the practice of migration. The filmmaker follows Abdelfattah who tries to reach Europe from Morocco over the Mediterranean Sea. The project is thus not only dependent on Abdelfattah's movement, but also on the time it takes him to migrate, as it aims to follow him and document his entire journey. This is the usual narrative of a documentary film. Yet, Kuster argues, this one is different. Abdelfattah refuses to represent himself as a protagonist in the film, to speak for himself – insisting that it is not only important for the film that Saeed understands him – while all the time Saeed is trying to remain neutral behind the camera and not to involve himself as a person. The film does not only show this, but also Abdelfattah's demand that Saeed give him the remainder of the money needed for the journey. After all, the film narrative depends on Abdelfattah's illegal crossing to Europe. Both try to deal with the project of their counterpart on a tactical level. Again and again, the film reevaluates how far the complicity between film and migration goes, and, consequently, the separate roles of the author and the protagonist begin to dissolve. The path of this production is never straightforward and constantly changes, there are multiple forward time-lines and flash-backs. Then at one point, Saeed decides not to hold on to 'the story' at all costs, not to go all the way, but, rather, to stay the classic author of a film who owns all the exploitation rights. With this twist, he loses Abdelfattah as a person and a friend, according to Kuster, but wins him back as a character in his film. At the same time, however, Saeed loses the possibility for himself and for the film to connect complicitly with the narrative structure of border-crossing. He cannot evade Abdelfattah's implicit accusation that he is undertaking an abusive and exploitative use of aesthetics.

Saeed reflects upon all these power dynamics that are inscribed in the film project upon its completion. Maybe that is why *I See the Stars at Noon* is a film that so clearly articulates the relationships of migration and of clandestine border-crossing. Abdelfattah refuses to talk about his experiences of migration, and to represent them. And thus it becomes clear that migration is a dynamic social relationship, one that includes filmmaking and the filmmaker. The project of the film and of crossing the border constitute each other. Nobody migrates alone.

Kuster finds a model example of a tactical narration of border-crossing, which engages the social aspect of migration, and the social bonds that it creates, in Elia Kazan's 1963 film *America, America*. In Kazan's film, the bond of complicity between the two protagonists Stavros and Hohannes is shown as a mutual responsibility concerning the relations of exploitation and violence from which they flee. Here, social bonds are interwoven and interlocked *with* forms of complicity. It is not about merging, about becoming as one, but rather about something shared in its extreme precarity, about contact and temptation on the never linear path along and across the border. Almost at the end of their passage to the

United States, Stavros jumps into the midst of a waltzing, first-class society on the ship's deck and wildly begins a whirling dance, an ecstatic maelstrom of movement, more or less on the spot. Among other things, the film cuts between this letting-go and the first meeting of Stavros and Hohannes and his smile when he sees his friend dance in such a way. Then Hohannes jumps over board, leaving his shoes behind. The complicity is completed when Stavros enters the USA taking on his friend's phonetic name Joe Arness.

Referring to Paul Valéry and his differentiation between dance and gait, Kuster claims that dance is the opposite of moving forward here, and represents the decisive movement of border-crossing in *America, America*: not as a geographic line, but as part of a complicit, non-identitarian subjectivation, as well as one that takes place in time. In the film's parallel montage, everything becomes simultaneously present, the present condenses, and intensifies together with the past, and thus transgresses a progressive linear time. In the whirling dance the potential of the illegal crossing of the border arises, a power that grows from the screams that connects to the transatlantic space of *race* and of *blackness*, according to Kuster.

Not to affirm commonality with the first-class, to decide not to pass as a privileged subject, is part of the defining narrative of Kazan's film and of the intense movement of migration that surpasses and changes the order of space and time. Nobody migrates illegally as an autonomous legal entity. Migration breaks apart such humanist narrowness. Instead, it runs towards a boundary where everything spins and time itself gets out of joint – and you see the stars at noon. In clandestine migration, the material and embodied mode of existence is no longer isolated, but becomes one that is always more or less than one. It is precisely this 'becoming' of migration that produces mobility through affection, says Kuster, but a mobility that never has a definitive point of arrival, since the migrant never knows when, where or as who they will arrive.

What happens when the passengers get stuck in transit? What happens when that time of dancing intensifies into a standstill, and those who move do not arrive because they cannot or do not want to stay?

Sir, Alfred Mehran (Mehran Karimi Nasseri) lived in Terminal 1 of the Parisian airport Charles de Gaulle for eighteen years, from 1988 until 2006. Countless films and television programs were made about and with him. Kuster follows these image sequences and dialogues and shows how they all failed in their attempt to portray the becoming of Sir, Alfred Mehran. This becoming cannot be unfurled in a documentary manner. When he is filmed it can only be said that he performs 'well' in his role. Every film invents him as a movement-image, whose storyline entails continuing his journey, traveling on and leaving the airport. But he would rather not. Time and again, he smiles into the camera and conspires with the viewers. Despite every reflection provided by the films, the only thing they are left with in the end is to pull back up the fourth cinematographic wall and to leave Sir, Alfred Mehran as a character in a film, as a non-passing passenger in the airport.

The non-passing passenger is someone who trains themselves in becoming imperceptible, to become like every other passenger traveling in the space: like the journeying everybody. In order to see this becoming you have to develop a perception that is located in the in-between things, says Kuster. To this day, becoming imperceptible means to undermine the dominant colonial gaze. The cinema of migration renounces the colonial time and emphasises the simultaneity and the interconnectedness of Europe and Africa.

The Arabian market stands as a paradigm for the fear of losing control, as well as the temptation of the paranoid colonial viewpoint. It is only the cinema of migration that can reflect upon such places like the market, where the eurocentric world is turned upside down, such zones of commingling and simultaneity, in a manner that is independent and deficient. That is also why the cinema of migration shows the sea as a space that is not made until it is traversed, from the middle and out of its midst, and shows the practice of being-on-the-sea and its *entangled histories* – such as the history shared by Algeria and France. Up until its independence in 1962, Algeria made up eighty percent of the French territory, and as it was a part of France it was not only a member of the European Coal and Steel Community, but from 1957 onward also of the European Economic Community (EEC). In the course of the process of visa requirements and the Schengen Agreement, the late 1980s saw a new partitioning of the space between the Maghreb and Europe. And in this time the *harraga* came into being, those who burnt their passports before traveling to Europe in order not to be identified, and sent back to the countries of their passports.

*Harraga*, which is how the majority of the migrants define themselves, have posted countless mobile phone videos and video assemblages that articulate their very own history of migration. These are filmed out on the open sea, are only a few minutes long, on a windy dinghy set on a journey of less than twenty hours – if all goes well. The boat becomes a stage, one solo follows the next, many young women can be seen, *harraga*-songs are sung together and toasts raised. In this in-between space, in the midst of the sea, these mobile phone videos show celebration and improvisation. The vanishing lines of migration turn the practice of border-crossing into affective points of contact.

Indeed these flight lines of migration materialise border-crossing as an affective touch. In the middle of the sea, a cinematic dynamic comes into being that shows an affection in and as migration, something day-to-day, mundane and world-changing that is articulated over or under the dominant thresholds of perception by those who are ready to lose everything, those who left their identities behind to become everybody, passengers who pass on through. At the same time, using the newest mobile phone technology makes locating them possible in the constant whirling of the passage – both by the police as well as by a rescue boat.

Migration today is often dealt with as if it were a scandal, and even left-wing positions rarely go further than taking a reactive stance against this. *Grenze filmen* introduces a difference into this deadlock: out of a mix of philosophical perspectives and film and cultural studies approaches, Kuster draws up a precarious map of how migration over the Mediterranean Sea both destitutes and simultaneously re-constitutes Europe's borders.

**Isabell Lorey**
**Translated by Christopher Hütmannsberger**

# Reformist radicalism

Chantal Mouffe, *For a Left Populism* (London: Verso, 2018). 112pp., £10.99 hb., £9.99 pb., 978 1 78663 755 0 hb., 978 1 78663 756 7 pb.

Despite its present ubiquity, the term 'populism' remains ambiguous. Does populism describe a set of radically democratic demands, or the appeal to an exclusive society predicated on sameness? Can it be placed alongside or within the left-right spectrum that has characterised more than two centuries of political antagonism? And if so, how is 'left populism' distinct from prior articulations of mass politics?

Years before the appearance of Podemos and Syriza, Jair Bolsonaro's PSL or Steve Bannon's parasitised GOP, 'populism' was heralded by Ernesto Laclau and Chantal Mouffe as a response to a political impasse of the Left. For Laclau and Mouffe, populism describes a form of politics rather than a principle; a discursive operation whereby an otherwise heterogeneous movement marks itself apart from a common adversary, and which is, as such, highly changeable. Mouffe's latest book succinctly reiterates this position, issuing a demand for a left populism that could counter an insurgence from the contemporary right. Yet the shortcomings of Mouffe's programme are clear. Commencing from a liberal precept of individual interest and affirming the limitations of the extant nation-state, Mouffe's description of populism furnishes its roving subject with no objective standard by which to delineate left from right, let alone distinguish a revolutionary politics from a bureaucratic restatement of power. Consequently, Mouffe's description of populism appears strategically devoid of content.

As Mouffe explains, populism serves the interest of a select group under the hegemonic sign of 'the' people, marking an 'us' from a 'them' – but neither subject preexists the operation by which they are symbolised. Specific claims enter into a provisional equivalency only with reference to a common sign. Populist discourse thus establishes 'equivalential chains' of otherwise heterogeneous positions, whose meaning cannot be specified in advance. For Mouffe, this heterogeneity eludes the 'essentialist' perspective of Marxism, and the alleged incapacity of this tradition to account for demands originating elsewhere than in class. As such, Mouffe narrates, forgetting the concerted anti-communist campaigns of the Cold War era, Marxism gradually cedes purchase on the popular imaginary over the course of the twentieth century. In her account, a multiplication of demands irreducible to class produces a new politics beginning in the late 1960s with 'the second wave of feminism, the gay movement, the anti-racist struggles and issues around the environment'. This historical account tempts the identification of Mouffe's programme with so-called identity politics – somewhat ironically, considering that today's populist firebrands mobilise imprecisely against this catch-all label. Meanwhile, for many liberal commentators, populism, whether left or right, stands for a version of the very 'class essentialism' that Mouffe invokes by way of contrast.

Against this commonplace – that left and right convene upon an identical discontent – one must reinstate a properly political antagonism. Mouffe struggles on this point, despite her title's promise. In succession, she argues for a 'left populism, understood as a discursive strategy of construction of the political frontier between "the people" and "the oligarchy"', then specifies that this frontier ('people/oligarchy') should supplant that of 'left/right', for 'such a frontier is no longer adequate to articulate a collective will that contains the variety of democratic demands that exist today.' Nevertheless, she continues, this populism-to-come must be distinguished from that of the right; and so back to the language of the left we go. This self-contradictory approach reveals further problems with the empty formalism of Mouffe's account as a whole, within which populism is so generic a concept as to necessitate a meta-political doubling, without which its terms are indiscernible in reference.

Rightism, by Mouffe's own admission, has dictated the terms of populism so far, and her proposed timeline begins in the United Kingdom, with a Thatcherite revolt against a welfare state that Labour ultimately failed to protect. Here again, Mouffe's formalism invites confusion. On the one hand, she states that today's populism derives from a backlash against the neoliberal post-politics wrought by Thatcher in England, Reagan in the United States, and other leaders world over, but on the other, she asserts (correctly) that these figures were themselves originators of a populist style: 'Her project was clearly a populist one', Mouffe writes of Thatcher: '[b]y erecting a political frontier, she was able to disarticulate the key elements of the social-democratic hegemony and to establish a new hegemonic order based on popular consent.'

Stuart Hall counselled readers to learn from Thatcher's populism, which orients a constituency of absolutised individuals toward an authoritarian signifier. But Mouffe takes Hall's challenge further still, asserting that 'we should follow Thatcher's route, adopting a populist strategy, but this time with a progressive objective.' Mouffe cites Jeremy Corbyn's revivification of a moribund Labour Party, noting that Corbyn's campaign slogan, 'For the many, not the few', was used by Tony Blair as well, with 'many' and 'few' signifying differently. This says little in itself, for the right has a long history of appropriating leftist talking points; but the left must be cautious in borrowing them back. Signifiers are subject to alteration as they pass between campaigns and ideologies, with residual effects. Any programme of quotation must proceed with specificity, asking for and by whom a signal is deployed.

Mouffe's approach acknowledges that populism is empty of content and adaptable to more and less emancipatory purposes – from neoliberal agitation against bureaucracy and the subsequent rejection of that project to racist and anti-racist campaigns alike. In every case, however, it requires a formal antagonist or presumed threshold of belonging. Where do populists, both left and right, place that threshold today? Counter-intuitively, it appears that relinquishing the class emphasis of mass politics has permitted racist and scapegoating ideologies to flourish; one paradoxical effect of which is that national populisms appear to have successfully monopolised the topic of class, where it allegedly concerns the reallocation of opportunity and resources within a politically enfranchised people. Populism then appears an elite rhetorical strategy, intended to assuage a deeply felt crisis by deflecting from its factual cause – namely, the extra-discursive reality of capitalism.

Where populism concerns the rule of the signifier, it may be said to correspond to a crisis of institutional faith. In Mouffe's account, this corresponds to the rise of a global 'post-democracy', under which both parliamentary and popular power are beholden to private interest. But this imprecise periodisation implies a return to some fantasised near-past of broader representation and social cohesion. Indeed, for Mouffe, liberal democracy already expresses the range of demands that populism exerts. Throughout the book Mouffe emphasises that populism should seek to transform liberal democracy without disputing the legitimacy of this framework. Mouffe's 'radical reformism' claims to reject the 'false dilemma' of reform versus revolution – by deciding on the necessity of reform.

Mouffe outlines three modes of left politics: pure reformism, which neither disputes liberal democracy nor neoliberal hegemony; so-called radical reformism, which asserts the legitimacy of liberal democracy as well as a new hegemonic rule; and revolutionism, which seeks a rupture or break with the existing situation. Mouffe's recommendation, 'to engage with the diverse state apparatuses', endorses the middle option, avoiding questions as to the neutrality of a given apparatus in the first place.

The revolving door of populist avatars, within which left and right swap talking points, may then have as much to do with formal underdetermination as with systemic inertia. Without the political intention to transform power, power will surely transform one's politics.

Mouffe canvases for a sign of relationality that would place the individual within a political community, and in high republican style decides upon the honorific of the citizen. While Mouffe strenuously rejects the Thatcherite rewriting of the citizen as a taxpayer-consumer whose rights are essentially secured at market, she nonetheless endorses the higher-level atomisation of the nation-state. For Mouffe, radical democracy starts and remains situated at this level. Mouffe herself foresees the obvious problem, but fails to attribute it to any objective basis whatsoever: 'As the example of right populism testifies, demands for democracy can be articulated in a xenophobic vocabulary and they do not automatically have a progressive character. It is only by entering in equivalence with other democratic demands, like those of the immigrants or the feminists, that they acquire a radical democratic dimension.'

One might otherwise speak of solidarity, which Mouffe chooses to write as a provisional equivalence between demands, if not positions. With no theory of society, this suffices to account for mediation. Even Mouffe's passing evocation of intersectionality is ill-suited to her demonstrative purposes, for the non-identical antagonisms of her description fail to meet the criterion of objective simultaneity. The subject that Mouffe describes is a teeming agent of multiplicitous self-interest, not a political bloc in any traditional sense. This explains its changeability, as a formalist account of collectivity leaves the articulation of purpose largely to chance, or to power.

Moreover, the idealised autonomy of each perspective prior to a point of articulation constitutes a decision on Mouffe's part; for a summary atomisation necessarily precedes the constitution of a people from so many separate claims. Plainly, the discursive 'frontier' that allows for the formal articulation of mass politics is not so arbitrary, as it corresponds to real contradictions in the organisation of the world. To cede reality to a purely discursive play of otherwise baseless powers is to relinquish politics to the status quo under a series of different names.

On this point, Mouffe evokes a morally ambivalent group psychology in order to license the necessity that left populism address itself to the courtly delusions of the right. In her view:

> a left populist strategy cannot ignore the strong libidinal investment at work in national – or regional – forms of identification and it would be very risky to abandon this terrain to right-wing populism. This does not mean following its example in promoting closed and defensive forms of nationalism, but instead offering another outlet for those affects, mobilising them around a patriotic identification with the best and more egalitarian aspects of the national tradition.

This ominously underqualified endorsement of rightist formalism verges on pure equivocation, which, by Mouffe's admission, is a mechanism of populism too.

As noted, Mouffe's proposed populism requires a meta-political supplement from the left, and she qualifies her perspective accordingly:

> It is to avoid this political indeterminacy that I believe that it is important to speak of 'left' populism in reference to another meaning of 'left', which concerns its axiological dimension and signals the values that it defends: equality and social justice.

But if a principled leftism does not inhere in persuasion, which proceeds as a libidinal appeal rather than an argument, then so-called left populism can only realise itself as a surreptitious version of the vanguardism that Mouffe abandons to history, at best.

Faced with the practical successes of right-wing populism on a global scale, it is more pressing than ever to affirm a radical critique of society over the conciliatory solutions to crisis that Mouffe recommends. Throughout this short book, Mouffe does little more than repackage a fantasy of exclusionary stability. And while one may appreciate the impetus – to enroll as many emancipatory demands in a mass movement as possible – in order to be truly radical this cannot proceed as a simple re-description of the operations of the liberal state.

Cam Scott

# Critical universalism

Franziska Dubgen and Stefan Skupien, *Paulin Hountondji: African Philosophy as Critical Universalism* (Cham, Switzerland: Palgrave Macmillan, 2019). 192pp., €67,62 hb., 978 3 03001 994 5

During the extraordinarily intense debates on the future trajectory of modern African philosophy at the dawn of African independence, Paulin J. Hountondji, along with the likes of Kwasi Wiredu in Ghana, Henry O. Oruka in Kenya and Peter O. Bodunrin in Nigeria, played a pivotal role. This group of professional philosophers, all of whom were obviously greatly influenced by their Western educations, was called the universalists. Hountondji was born in the Republic of Benin (then known as Dahomey) in 1942 and after his secondary school education, he traveled to France where he studied philosophy at the École normale supérieure under the supervision of professors such as Jacques Derrida, Louis Althusser, Paul Ricoeur and Georges Cangulheim.

Franziska Dubgen's and Stefan Skupien's new book on Hountondji has many strengths, the most obvious of which is the coherent classification of Hountondji's diverse writings into easily identifiable conceptual categories. In France, during his decade of postgraduate studies, he famiłarised himself with deconstruction, poststructuralist thought, epistemology and phenomenology whose founder, Edmund Husserl, was the subject of his doctoral dissertation. Hountondji had wanted to continue his studies in phenomenology but decided to venture into then contested terrain of modern African thought with the boost of a UNESCO-funded fellowship to conduct research on the work of Anton-Wilhelm Amo, a Ghanaian philosopher who lectured at a number of German universities in the eighteenth century. Studying Amo undoubtedly forced Hountondji to reconsider his philosophical path and steered him permanently towards researching the discipline from an African perspective.

Hountondji conceives of philosophy more or less as a science. In this regard, he wanted to elevate the discipline above the fuzziness he believed tainted the work of those who were termed 'philosopher-kings', notably, Kwame Nkrumah, Leopold Sedar Senghor and Julius Nyerere. These so-called philosopher-kings were all embroiled in the hurly-burly of decolonisation processes that gripped Africa beginning in the 1940s. Soon after independence in the 1960s, they embarked on the arduous task of nation-building as the heads of state of their respective countries. By contrast, Hountondji sought to return philosophy to a purer, less frenetic and less politicised state and this entailed observing stricter benchmarks of professionalisation.

First, he turned to the discipline itself and found it wanting in terms of the levels of rigour he preferred. Ethnophilosophy, a discourse within the field that Hountondji all but demolished, provided him with his decisive entry into the world of established philosophical luminaries. Ethnophilosophy was pioneered by a Belgian cleric called Placide Frans Tempels (1906-1977) and a Rwandan priest, Alexis Kagame (1902-1981). In his famous book, *Bantu Philosophy* (1945), Tempels attempted to identify 'a coherent philosophical system among Bantu-speaking Africans, based on a distinct ontology which conceives of being as dynamic. This sets it apart from a Western ontology, which considers being as static'. Originally, Tempels had sought to free the African subject from the racist gaze of Eurocentric anthropology, but his exertions had, in Hountonji's view, ended up creating another mythology of the African. He faulted ethnophilosophy for harbouring 'the myth of unanimity' which denied Africans ontological mobility, agency and alterity. This supposedly polarising myth implies an essentialising homogeneity that does much to discredit Africa's incredible diversity. In addition, ideologies of authenticity are usually narrow or knee-jerk instances of nativism that are instrumentalised solely for the benefit of parochial political interests.

Kagame, for his part, just like his European counterpart, had been guilty of formulating yet another mythology by employing Aristotelian ontological categories in relation to the African subject. Hountondji believed that 'the ontological order created by Tempels' diminishes the Africans, rather than affirming them as equals, and, in the end, justifies the colonial project, as well as the missionary project'. He also criticised the scientific credentials of the discourse as unworthy of being termed philosophy. He found suspect the claim by ethnophilophers that they were presenting African systems of thought when in fact they were offering their own fictions of Africa. In addition, he accused ethnophilosophy of imposing a 'double standard: whereas Western philosophy is conscious and well-reasoned, African philosophy is unconscious and implicit'. More damagingly, Hountondji argued that the claims of ethnophilosophy can neither be validated nor disproved according to established academic criteria.

Hountondji also had unsparing words for the work of Negritudists such as Senghor and Aimé Césaire. Hountondji's antagonism towards Negritude (like the conceptual thought of Nkrumah) stemmed from his anti-essentialist outlook. Hountondji's over-riding aim was to return philosophy to standards that were unimpeachable. In this regard, the technology of writing is a vital requirement for philosophy while orality is frowned upon. Even Derrida's concept of logocentricism is not spared here as, according to Hountondji, philosophy is written by identifiable individual philosophers as opposed to being derived from the largely anonymous offerings of folk wisdom or precolonial collective thought. This stance elicited a great deal of criticism, most notably from scholars such as Olabiyi Yai and Oyekan Owomoyela. During that era, Marxist thought was the official doctrine in Benin which had rejected the capitalist mode of development after Major Mathieu Kerekou seized power in a military putsch in 1972. Hountondji, in the view of his critics, did not seem entirely convinced of the desirability of Marxism-Leninism and was thus vilified.

More specifically, Hountondji was charged with elitism; the argument was advanced that his thought had very little or no relevance to the realities of Africans. But a closer inspection of Hountondji's career demonstrates that he had always wanted to make his thought relevant and engaging. Beginning from the sixties as he pursued his studies, his central preoccupation was to discover an avenue through which an Africa-centred philosophy could be pursued as a valid and globally accepted discipline. His first teaching position in Zaire (now the Democratic Republic of Congo) gave him his initial taste of neocolonial malaise whereby public discourse and social engineering could be effectively muddled and mangled by convenient and readily available pseudo-ideologies of authenticity, as when the dictator Mobutu Sese Seko was in power.

Later, when he returned to Benin, Hountondji consistently warned against the dangers of philosophies of authenticity which tended to stifle the possibilities of free thought, unrestrained public discourse, constructive dissent and social innovation. His particular interventions during the national efforts of returning Benin to democratic rule in 1990s are noteworthy. Hountondji sought to open up the public realm for active citizens' participation, which he pointed out was of utmost necessity for the well-being of the polity. He also warned against the ills of the over-centralisation of power. Perhaps this was a way of debunking his critics' claims that he was elitist.

Another way in which he can be considered to have countered charges of elitism is through the formulation of the concept of endogenous knowledge. The concept came about through a students' seminar he organised in 1987. As usual, Hountondji had sought to provide the much-devalued and derided notion of indigenous knowledge with a scientific rationale. Although Hountondji did not publish a paper from this collective venture, the research efforts culminated in a large volume he edited for the Council for the Development of Social Science Research in Africa (CODESRIA) released in a French edition in 1994. The papers in the volume addressed traditional medicine, indigenous pharmacology and archaeology. The entire approach might be regarded as addressing the lapses of ethnophilosophy and infusing philosophy itself with greater cultural inclusivity. In theoretical terms, this late effort may also be considered Hountondji's last major contribution to the development of contemporary African philosophy.

As well as his highly influential book, *African Philosophy: Myth and Reality* (1976) that included his compelling insights on ethnophilosohy, Nkrumah's philosophy of consciencism, Amo's philosophical dilemmas and metaphilosophical questions, Hountondji also published his semi-autobiographical, *The Struggle for Meaning: Reflections on Philosophy, Culture and Democracy in Africa* (2002), which chronicles his exciting intellectual journey. In parts much less academic than his earlier book, this work is unusual in African philosophy for marrying memoir and philosophical musings in a somewhat irreverent manner. Here, he is able to respond to his numerous critics without always suppressing what is revealed to be his considerable ego. Oftentimes, he situates himself in an almost messianic crusade to save African philosophy from an ever-menacing demise or the onslaughts of pretenders who never have its best interests at heart.

Between 1990 and 1993, he served as both Minister for Education and Minister for Culture and Communication during the new democratic dispensation to which he had helped give birth. During his stint as a minister, Hountondji had planned to implement radical reforms in the education sector and also establish philosophy in a more central role in driving national development. When he sensed he was only being kept in government to furnish it with a veneer of intellectual legitimacy, he promptly returned to academia where he has continued to publish research papers and spread the gospel of African philosophy around the globe.

Dubgen and Skupien make strong arguments for receiving Hountondji as a global thinker. Hountondji refutes the condescension of racism while attempting to propel African philosophical practices towards universal goals. By reflecting on Kwasi Wiredu's formulation of conceptual decolonisation, he also supports efforts at discovering common values, concepts and orientations in different African languages in order to arrive at universal human precepts. Thus, a powerful current of transculturality becomes evident. One of the more obvious ways to acknowledge the notion of transculturality is to examine how the concept of human rights became enshrined long before its general acceptance as a global declaration. Human rights, Hountondji avers, were already in existence as rudimentary precepts and it only took the disasters of the World Wars to formalise, institutionalise and universalise them. Undoubtedly, interventions such as this lend credence to his standing as a global intellectual.

Dubgen and Skupien are granted an extensive interview by Hountondji where he is able to clarify his positions on a wide range of issues beginning with his famous critique of ethnophilosophy. The authors ask if endogenous knowledge isn't in fact 'a rehabilitation' of ethnophilosophy to which Hountondji replies: 'Not really. Rather another aspect of the same struggle against marginalization: a critique of ethno-science as a necessary complement to the critique of ethno-philosophy'. He goes on to point out that 'philosophy is first and foremost an individual exercise and by no means a collective system of thought'. For the development of a viable philosophical practice in Africa, Hountondji mentions logic, epistemology, philosophy of science, history and sociology of science, and the anthropology of knowledge in orature as key branches of the discipline including the history of Western philosophy. During the interview, he also dwells on his role in the widespread democratic agitations that dominated Benin in the early 1990s.

Through quite remarkable scholarship Dubgen and Skupien manage to piece together engraved patterns of logic, coherence and conceptual intrigue across Hountondji's eventful life and career which have been marked by bouts of furious activity. At the same time, the book's other major, related strength is that it provides a sequential context that is not always evident in the Hegelian pace and texture of Hountondji's own often inspirational and faintly apocalyptic writings.

**Sanya Osha**

# Fully automated luxury barbarism

Aaron Bastani, *Fully Automated Luxury Communism: A Manifesto* (London: Verso, 2019). 288pp., £16.99 hb., 978 1 78663 262 3

'This is not a book about the future but about a present that goes unacknowledged', Aaron Bastani writes in *Fully Automated Luxury Communism*. Bastani does not set out to describe what an ideal communist society would look like. Instead, he spends the bulk of his book making the argument that capitalism is unable to cope with a set of problems that will eventually lead to its destruction and implores us instead to create a better economic model built around the creation and distribution of abundance. What makes the book interesting is that the problems its author identifies are primarily found in capitalism's relationship to technology; and in particular, in technology's potential to eliminate the scarcity that capitalism depends upon. Bastani argues that the capacity of technology to eliminate scarcity could, under the right social arrangements, lead to shared opulence: that is, Fully Automated Luxury Communism [FALC]. He paints a picture of a future where all people could live lives equivalent to that of modern-day billionaires: 'Luxury will pervade everything as society based on waged work becomes as much a relic of history as the feudal peasant and medieval knight'.

Yet, FALC is an improbable, unhelpful and frankly undesirable blueprint for our collective future: improbable because it glosses over the ecological reality of our desperate global predicament, unhelpful because at a time when we are heading for global ecological collapse FALC advocates more climate-wrecking economic activity, and undesirable because the theory is grounded on a discredited and corrosive vision of human wellbeing.

*Fully Automated Luxury Communism* begins in his first section by identifying five global crises set to worsen under existing social conditions: global over-heating, resource scarcity, an aging non-productive population, a growing surplus of the global poor, and technology-driven unemployment. While 'green' concerns occupy two of his great crises, Bastani considers technology-driven unemployment the most determinative threat to our society. The third section of the book is dedicated to outlining some of the features that FALC ought to contain – notably, Universal Basic Services. However, the second section, which considers how technologies might undermine capitalism, occupies the bulk of the book. Here Bastani sets out to convince his readers that the current technological trajectory can eliminate poverty and deliver opulence if combined with new economic and social arrangements.

*Fully Automated Luxury Communism* is a love letter to technology. It sets out an ambitious stall about what our future could look like, making even the most ardent defenders of technophilic neoliberalism look like dour pessimists. Bastani claims that increasing automation will render much of the world's population surplus to economic requirements. He identifies the potential for limitless renewable energy to solve the climate crisis while continuing to increase production. Unfortunately, this is a non-sequitur for reasons made clear some time ago by ecological economist Nicholas Georgescu-Roegen and underscored by many recent analyses of renewable energy. Entropic limitations – not to mention resource-limits (the key components of solar technology are called '*rare* earths' for a reason) – make it unlikely that an Earth operating within ecological limits would make it possible to access to more than a small fraction of the current bonanza of energy that we experience in the flush of the fossil fuel bubble. Bastani falls into the common trap of modelling an allegedly exponentially-improving energy future on the exponential improvement (until recently) in digital technologies' capability. This widespread but ill-founded mode of modelling has, however, been comprehensively debunked; Bastani, in his enthusiasm for an energy-version of Moore's Law, ignores the Shockley-Queiser limit to the efficiency gains possible in solar-voltaic cells, a limit we are already quite close to, and he similarly ignores the Betz limit to improvements in the efficiency of wind turbines.

After outlining how scarcity in labour and clean energy will become negligible as technology-fuelled abundance is created, Bastani argues that asteroid mining could also render resource scarcity obsolete. Taken together, these three claims are perhaps the most important for Bastani's book, as between them they outline how we can supposedly eliminate the need for labour (through automation), the need for limitless clean energy (through renewables), and resource scarcity (through asteroid mining).

Bastani does a good job of making asteroid mining seem a lot more plausible than may intuitively appear to be the case, and he delves into contemporary advances in all these areas. However, despite the care that evidently went into researching this project, there are good reasons to think that Bastani has fatally overstated the potential of technology to deliver us into the near-limitless abundance that FALC depends upon. In an era of fossil-fuelled climate breakdown, in which energy will necessarily be scarce, how can it possibly make sense to blow huge quantities of our small 'energy budget' on space travel of any kind? But the empirical failure of Bastani's technophilia is most apparent in his discussion of clean energy.

Bastani believes that through harnessing renewables we can eliminate carbon emissions of energy production. However, despite growth in renewables globally, the last three years have broken records for global emissions (as well as 2016 breaking the record for temperature); in the context of a growthist economy, growing the renewables sector doesn't by itself necessarily accomplish any diminution of fossil fuels. The green economist Tim Jackson has done invaluable work in highlighting how the growth in climate-wrecking emissions is intimately tied up with growth in economic activity. His book *Prosperity Without Growth* tackles the myth that increased efficiency in the economy added to the growth of green energy makes continuing to grow the economy a feasible ecologically-compatible economic policy. Instead, he illustrates that the 'decoupling' of economic activity from emissions that neoliberals (and now FALC) have promised for so long is simply not happening at anywhere near the scale required to avert catastrophic global warming.

Bastani cites data that, 'In the UK for instance, energy consumption peaked at the turn of the millennium, and has fallen by 2 per cent every year since. This means that despite higher living standards and a larger population, Britain's energy use in 2018 is actually lower than it was

in 1970 – this in a country far from energy poor'. This paints an optimistic picture of progress meant to encourage readers that renewables are putting us on the right track to climate stability. Yet, the story of UK emissions falling by 2% a year does not include the embedded emissions present in all the products that the UK imports. Once you include embedded emissions, the UK's carbon footprint has reduced in the past twenty years by far less than 2% per annum, somewhere between 0.5% and 1% per annum at best. The reality is that the UK has simply outsourced its climate-wrecking emissions along with much of its production to overseas.

At a time when the scientific consensus is that catastrophe awaits if we do not drastically reduce carbon emissions, Bastani's naïve and hyper-optimistic political philosophy advocates creating conditions where everyone has the consumption patterns of billionaires. His position is completely dependent upon new renewable technologies advancing at a far faster rate than our climate and ecology collapses. This is irresponsible – a reckless bet, based on inadequate evidence. An ecologically wise politics requires serious reduction in consumption to go alongside heavy investment in growth in renewables and this is something that FALC does not countenance.

*Fully Automated Luxury Communism* argues that *if* automation massively increases, and *if* clean renewable technologies massively advance, and *if* asteroid mining becomes viable, *then* FALC is both possible and desirable. But these hypotheticals obscure a more likely outcome: *if* we fail to radically reduce emissions, *then* climate and ecological catastrophe certainly awaits.

Bastani demonstrates an awareness of these sorts of criticisms, but he tends to imply that a green politics of living within planetary limits is an austere and impoverished vision. For instance, he writes that, 'To the green movement of the twentieth century this is heretical. Yet it is they who, for too long, unwisely echoed the claim that "small is beautiful" and that the only way to save our planet was to retreat from modernity itself'. Consequently, Bastani makes his alternative pitch as 'advancing a red-green politics which revives ideals of progress and common plenty'. Yet, it is worth questioning whether increasing consumption patterns need form a part of this 'progress'. Would achieving the consumption patterns of billionaires really improve our wellbeing and allow us to further develop our capacities than more modest levels of consumption? Probably not. The literature in economics on the decreasing marginal utility of wealth demonstrates that, beyond a certain level, increases in wealth do not lead to increases in self-reported happiness. Given that this is the case, one has to question what exactly is motivating the 'luxury' in fully automated luxury communism.

Bastani equates luxury with wellbeing and downplays other aspects of flourishing such as community and friendship. It is these sorts of values that a deep green philosophy can make room for while simultaneously reducing consumption. Automation and luxury are not necessary to human wellbeing, and certainly not essential enough to it to risk devastating the only home we have, our planet.

There is a telling line in the book when Bastani discusses resource scarcity and writes that 'the limits of the earth would confine post-capitalism to conditions of abiding scarcity. The realm of freedom would remain out of reach'. 'Freedom' in this passage is defined in much the same way in FALC as it is in neoliberalism: through access to opulence and through the capacity to consume. Though Bastani proposes a different model of wealth distribution, the values he shares with the neoliberal paradigm may explain part of the success of his book. There is something deeply conservative about his adherence to the values of materialism and consumerism. These values have participated in driving us to the edge of climatic and ecological collapse, which can only be averted by radically and rapidly transforming society.

Bastani's book can be read symptomatically as typifying a particular wish-fulfilment-fantasy style of thinking, characteristic of our time – more science fiction than practical manifesto. But while he has correctly identified some of the problems of the present, Bastani's vision of the future is ironically outmoded. A political vision that equates wellbeing with abundance needs to be retired, if intelligent life on this planet is to have any realistic chance of outlasting the ecological emergency. We urgently need to face the brutal reality that we are not flying out to the stars but heading towards ecological collapse. The only conceivable way to stave off disaster is to be free of outdated fantasies and to strive collectively to soften our crash-landing.

**Atus Mariqueo-Russell and Rupert Read**

# Liquidated subjects

Alexi Kukuljevic, *Liquidation World: On the Art of Living Absently* (Cambridge, MA: The MIT Press, 2017). 152pp., £11.99 pb., 978 0 26253 419 2

When Gilles Deleuze described his work on the history of philosophy as an act of buggery, and showed how Kant and his likenesses could be made the fathers of monsters each would have to recognise as their own, something changed in philosophy's sense of its own orientation – dutiful exegesis quickly came to seem a way of standing in line once the age of ataraxy and anchorites had come to an end, the famed philosopher's stone a means for attracting metals precious but ultimately unproductive. But if it is to be thus concluded that philosophy must now call quits on its pursuit of the *summum bonum*, relinquish all previous claims to totality and proceed, instead, as something like an obstetrics of spirit gone to ground, then one might first ask after the kind of midwife to which the contemporary philosopher can still aspire now that all that was once so pregnant with consequence appears positively hapless and stillborn.

'It is not difficult to see that ours is a birth-time and a period of transition to a new era', announced Hegel's *Phenomenology of Spirit* in 1807. Some eighty years of revolution and retrenchment later, that long-deferred 'dawning day' was prophesied again, this time at the close of Nietzsche's *Human, All Too Human*, a book dedicated to those free spirits 'seek[ing] the philosophy of morning', even if such spirits did not in fact exist, as Nietzsche would later admit, but had instead to be invented, 'as compensation for a lack of friends.' That the daybreak divined should have given way to the neon of a new pastiche and a generation now assured of its lack of a future could still entrust itself to thinkers and sureties made for the marquee is enough to caution contemporaries against the allure of an earnestness oblivious of its opposite. In Alexi Kukuljevic's *Liquidation World: On the Art of Living Absently*, such ardent servility is replaced by a century of literary and artistic practice that took the absurd absolutely seriously. Here a set of 'absentee or dissolute subject[s]', including comedian-impersonators like Thomas Bernhard and Andy Kaufman, surrealists, symbolists, pataphysicians and conceptual artists like Jacques Vaché, Alfred Jarry, Marcel Duchamp and Marcel Broodthaers, as well as modernists like Paul Valéry and Charles Baudelaire, are presented within a series of 'theoretical portraits' that demonstrate the precise point at which the absurd becomes itself conceptual.

Yet, just as *Liquidation World* makes the last hundred years of experimental art and literature unfamiliar once again, so the reader cannot help but note how the book's singular enthusiasm for, and ambivalence towards, its artistic and philosophical forebears scrambles all traditional lines of paternity and production, sweeping away the shibboleths of a contemporary philosophy of art that still consistently lacks what it has always most plainly promised: either the philosophy or the art. For while Marx is invoked, Hegel set to work and Agamben rerouted through circuits now pixelated and patented, nothing of the rancour of the schismatic comes through and not a trace of the zealot can be discerned. As *Liquidation World* transforms doctrine into doggerel, and dogma into debasement, the reader is left to wonder what will play the part vacated by so many former authorities. Often some clue to a book's purpose can be found wherever the author invokes the terms of his or her title. Here, however, when the words 'liquidation world' appear on the book's first page, the expected copula is withheld and instead a colon is joined to this titular world's side. The expectation of easy answers is replaced by the simplest of orders: 'everything must go'.

Though the words belong to Kukuljevic, something of the discursive scene they evoke recalls the first decades of the twentieth century and returns the reader to a time when art could still scandalise and when any attempt at undermining sense, subject or some other standard of measure was understood to be inherently political – to a time, in other words, now long since past. Recalling those times when relations between art, politics and philosophy were, if not more clear, than at least more certain, may thus prove instructive.

Paris, 1929: André Breton's 'Second Manifesto of Surrealism' is published and introduces a new political, aesthetic and philosophical orthodoxy within which

Georges Bataille, author of essays with titles such as 'The Big Toe' and 'Solar Anus', becomes one of its choice, newly identified heretics. Because Bataille uses words like 'befouled, senile, rank, sordid, lewd, [and] doddering', as though they do not signify some 'unbearable state of affairs', as Breton thinks they must, that most base of materialists is indicted for a transgression Marx himself is said to have condemned in all those 'hair-philosophers, fingernail-philosophers, *toenail-philosophers*, [and] *excrement-philosophers*' that constitute the pestilence of every age. That Breton's charge would have sent someone like Bataille into hysterics is likely not lost on the author of *Liquidation World*. Indeed, the now century-old imperative that philosophy should pursue the greater glory of revolutionary politics and assume the mantle of some bespoke militancy seems to have today definitively passed over into irrelevance. Where philosophy still functions within the artistic and political nexus it inherited, it now does so as a legitimating discourse for an artworld whose straddling of the rift between penury and preposterous wealth requires that it ally itself with philosophemes whose words may have once denominated concepts but which now persist past the point beyond which philosophy's contemporary evisceration has made of each little more than a token of some nascent superstition. If *Liquidation World* is right and the work resulting from these absentee subjects' identifications with their own extinction remains essential to the tradition of artist-philosophers that Kukuljevic both analyzes and embodies, then it may be necessary to rethink this art's pitiless judgment on the state of contemporary philosophy and politics, and ask again how the most advanced philosophical consciousness might have as its condition an art that is its kin in a ruin as earnest as it is ebullient.

Some thirty years ago, Elisabeth Lenk posed a question that, departing though it does from *Liquidation World's* expressed intentions, nevertheless converges with its ends: 'The question I would like to ask today', Lenk wrote, 'is whether surrealism … was and is not precisely the practice that is appropriate to critical theory; and whether, on the other hand, critical theory was and is not precisely the theory towards which surreal practice was oriented.' No answer to this question was forthcoming, of course, but there is something in *Liquidation World's* insistence upon the cognitive import of contemporary art that recalls critical theory's own attempt at capturing a truth otherwise resistant to concept and expression alike. By pursuing this task, Kukuljevic gives back to artworks what each most wants – to be reckoned with, not as effects of knowledge, but as its agent.

It may seem surprising, however, that art's cognitive capability should emerge from what might otherwise be regarded as little more than a many-sided portrait of modern subjectivity, as though Kukuljevic had, in conformity with tradition, privileged subject and not object as the organ of artistic knowledge. But this concern is allayed when one sees what *Liquidation World* does to the subject of art. For what unites the various comedians, readymade artists, fetishists, nihilists, melancholics and dandies studied here is not only that each no longer believes in the integrity of the person – a rather inoffensive insight long since learned by heart – but also that Kukuljevic will show how the artistic subject that knows itself to be an object like any other must then look on as the artwork, returning its gaze, sees there an artist unkept by genius, a wasted something 'on the verge of being nothing more than a heap of clothes'.

In *Liquidation World* it is not the artist, but the artwork that registers what Kukuljevic calls the 'slow wheeze of art's substance' – and then draws the necessary consequences, acclimatising itself to the detritus of a culture that is still mistakenly talked about as being somehow starved of either sense or purpose, stuck somewhere between a living or a dead culture that art, politics and philosophy are given the task of enlivening. To say this, however, is to forget that it is precisely the readymade, that form of artistic production closest to the contemporary, that long ago realised that the only way art is still possible is in the form of a 'fossilised identity' at once incapable of life and unable to expire, a bone of culture much prized, much hated, and beyond either growth or decay. By sincerely presenting itself as a thing it is not, the readymade's annihilating novelty is shown to have made of the most inconspicuous of objects a force to threaten the whole of the field of art. Its knowledge of nullity and value present a paradigm for contemporary artistic subjectivity.

It is, then, not only the readymade that knows what has become of the contemporary subject; artists themselves are no less appraised of what it means to be a subject without content. Indeed, each knows far more than it is willing to let on. And for good reason – for if it is true that one's position within the social field rests on the stability of a scale meant to measure one's nearness to that which is either most base or most noble, then what is one to do with this artistic hyperconsciousness of absolute nullity? Its most base precondition, that skull, bone and mineral matter which is the true seat of consciousness, cannot be acknowledged without undermining the very priority of consciousness through which the human is said to reign preeminent. Identification with some socially sanctioned stuff like person or personality can now only ever appear as the grossest kind of imposture and imitation. It's true of course that an artist that takes the tragicomedy of contemporary subjectivity absolutely seriously cannot help but relate 'to its being as bluff'; in doing so, however, it also lends 'the void a luxurious air', endlessly disidentifying with any stable human form and experimenting, instead, with what it means to be human in the eyes of others, what it costs to achieve some value – and what profit can then be reaped from that valuation – created by others. An artist may be the prostitute of his or her idea, the collector the john, as Kukuljevic writes, but such an exchange is also the means by which the artist, all too conscious of its own nugatory identity, can then make something out of the nothing it most certainly is, forging identity as coin, as art.

This is not to say, however, that any of the familiar talk of disillusioned *zeitgeists* and misanthropic worldviews has any place here. Rather than treating its artistic subjects as the kind of period pieces to which so many artists have for so long aspired, *Liquidation World* insists that the exemplary nature of these absentee subjects consists in their having 'internalise[d] a relation to their own absence by making an object of it', detaching themselves from those tired tropes of decline and efflorescence that are today as common as they are consoling. In tracing the process through which contemporary art 'separate[es] itself from any sense-giving negativity', *Liquidation World* attends so closely to art's slag and spittle that such works finally seem capable of speaking with native fluency the foreign language of the concept, replacing that humanity that has since shown itself either unable or unwilling to give itself a law of its own, and now pronouncing, for its own purposes, and in its own name, the law that will henceforth guide its every effort: '*Art*', Kukuljevic writes, '*as the mummification of spirit*'. Few students of art, philosophy or politics would likely countenance such an idea, but once one has sworn off the saccharine pathos of all those supposedly inscrutable problems and inconstruable questions that have long left the work of cultural production, reproduction and consumption to others, it might be time to re-dedicate oneself to embalming now that a new form of midwifery might be here in the offing, one committed to 'leaving no stone unturned and no maggot lonely', as Kukuljevic writes, quoting Harold Pinter. For that, however, philosophy would have to become something rather more debauched and rigorous than it is at present. *Liquidation World* can only hope that such friends need not this time be invented.

Ryan Crawford

# Normalcy
## Letter from Kashmir
Anil Persaud

*So, how do you find Kashmir?* When confronted with that question – as one often is when visiting this beautiful place – I could only reply, *I don't know*. A third person commented *That is the only honest answer to the question*. *Who knows* and *No one knows* have been waging silent war against each other in the Valley since August 5th.

There were three deaths in the neighbourhood I was staying in. One, who must have been an older woman, was a school teacher with my host, they retired together several years ago, *She died too young*. Another was a young man of thirty who died in a car accident. The last was an older man who died of natural causes. There was much wailing in the air. Adding to it were the difficulties being faced by the bereaved trying to perform last rites. Relatives responsible for bathing the dead, for instance, could not be reached because of the ongoing communications blackout in the new Union Territory of India. The Kashmiri dead are being sent to heaven unwashed.

Kashmiris fly to Delhi and elsewhere to check their email. With them fly members of the Indian armed forces. Airlines offer special priority boarding for army men, provided they show proper ID. In the airport waiting lounge the soldier and the civilian sit separately. In-flight their elbows touch and their bags caress each other in dark overhead bins. Civilian and army men alike video and take photographs of the female flight attendants. Until they are told not to. The pilot invites *only* children into the cockpit. When the flight returns to SRX, Captain JK will not make announcements about mobile phones. Or maybe she will. Who knows?

*Today was the happiest day of my life. Mamoo's friend came and we all played badminton and Ludo. Ha ha ha ha ha ha ha ha ha ha ha ha ha ha ha.*

A thousand and one goats are marching down the hill. Winter has come a month early to the Valley. One stops to eat leaves behind a fence. A dog has a case of mistaken identity. Through villages, between cars. Past love letters to Gaza graffitied onto roadside walls and fences, doors and shutters. They march. At a brisk trot and exhibit a sense of purpose rare these days. It is as if the goats know that history is written on the ground, not in books and memos.

معمول is heartbroken today. He is running from pillar to post. He needs signatures. His papers are otherwise in order, have been so for some time now. His dissertation is bound and ready. All that is left is the permission of the head of department for him to submit. And she won't sign. Professor's Lane, where his supervisor lives, would have been unreachable had معمول been without a car. It turns out that the supervisor no longer lives on Professor's Lane. It is harder to submit a thesis than it is to submit to the will of Allah. معمول needs to work.

In the middle of a gathering someone's mobile phone rings. Eyes turn. *My husband is in Essential Services*. Among the many meanings of freedom, in the techno-state freedom is like a faucet that can be turned off and on: on for essential, off for non-essential. The overwhelming majority of Kashmiris in the arms of the state are non-essentials who provide non-essential services.

*Do I matter? Does my life count for anything?* One no longer need go to Hajj to be reminded of such profound questions. Go to Kashmir instead.

11 October 2019

www.ingramcontent.com/pod-product-compliance
Lightning Source LLC
Chambersburg PA
CBHW080230100526
44583CB00019BA/2517